CHINA'S IMPERIAL DYNASTIES

CHINA'S IMPERIAL DYNASTIES

1600 BC — AD 1912

Jonathan Fenby

METRO BOOKS

NEW YORK

CONTENTS

6
Introduction

12
The Birth of China
to 221 BC

30
The First Emperor
and the
Qin Dynasty
221–207 BC

42
The Western Han
206 BC to AD 9

62
Wang Mang
AD 9–23

66
The Eastern Han
AD 25–220

78
Period of Disunion
220–581

92
The Sui
581–618

98
Tang Dynasty:
the Founders
618–49

108
The Era of Wu
Zetian
649–705

114
The Later Tang
705–908

126
Five Dynasties and
Ten Kingdoms
907–60

Warrior statue

The Great Wall

The emperor Taizong

132
The Northern Song
960–1126

146
The Southern Song
1127–1279

154
The Yuan
1279–1368

166
The Early Ming
1368–1464

The Forbidden City

178
The Later Ming
1465–1644

194
The Early and High Qing
1644–1799

220
The Decline of the Qing
1799–1874

234
The Empire Ends
1874–1912

244
Glossary

246
Index

254
Further References

255
Picture Acknowledgements

256
Author Acknowledgements

THE DRAGON THRONE

No other system of government on earth ruled for so long over so many people as the empire of China. Even taking the last possible date for its foundation – 221 BC – it remained in place for over two millennia, during which 157 emperors sat on the Dragon Throne.

FROM VARIOUS CAPITALS, THE EMPIRE GOVERNED A DOMAIN THE SIZE OF A CONTINENT, WHICH grew to 3.7 million square miles (9.6 million sq km) at its peak and contained hundreds of millions of inhabitants. Imperial dynasties saw their realm as the centre of the world (the Middle Kingdom), enjoying superiority over all others, whatever the vicissitudes of the ruling house. Some emperors lived up to the claim, but many fell short. However, doubt about the system was not on the agenda. China's rulers drew on a national self-confidence, based on the early evolution of Chinese civilization. The nation had progressed from the prehistoric peoples of the Lower Yellow River Valley through the Bronze Age to create a culture producing a wealth of technological inventions and brilliant achievements in painting and literature, porcelain and bronze work, silk, sculpture and carving. (See Chinese Inventions, page 165.)

Monuments spoke of the majesty of empire, epitomized by the Forbidden City in Beijing, with the Tiananmen Gate from which edicts were lowered before being taken to all corners of the realm. Across the empire the homes of gentry and officials, with their carefully organized gardens and precisely disposed interiors, spoke of order and serenity – however tempestuous conditions outside their walls. Social customs constituted an art form in themselves, while Chinese writing, as well as being the earliest, was also – through calligraphy – the most artistic of scripts.

Unlike European empires, the dynasties of China ruled over a single landmass. Their fleets might roam the oceans and they might accept tribute from other Asian states, but their conquests led them only to territories adjoining the Middle Kingdom. Still, their domain was vast and diverse, taking in mountains and plains, forests, rice paddies and grain lands, great rivers and a coastline stretching from the frozen wastes of Manchuria in the north to the humid semi-tropical jungles of the southwest.

People and populations

Over the course of two millennia the empire saw an enormous rise in its population. The number of its subjects doubled from 60 million in AD 200 to 120 million in 1000, and rose more or less steadily to 500 million by 1900. Although the expanding empire

RIGHT *From the early Ming dynasty, China was ruled from inside a walled complex at the heart of Beijing, known as the Forbidden City. The elaborate palaces were flanked by symbols of imperialism, including this large dragon sculpture.*

was dominated numerically by the Han people, it was populated by 100 or more minorities. Two dynasties, the Yuan and the Qing, came from beyond the Great Wall which marked – not always very effectively – the frontier between China proper and the great northern steppes, whose nomads were a constant threat to the Sons of Heaven. As well as the nomads, traders arrived from Central Asia, seafaring merchants landed in the south and Buddhism was imported from India. Thus, the empire was usually a good deal more open to the world than is suggested by the familiar image of rulers clinging to their traditions in the Forbidden City.

There were differences within the majority population. While sharing a common written script, which most could not read, they spoke many dialects, so that people from one region were unable to understand those from another. For over 1000 years of empire, the centre of power lay in northern China and the lands of the Yangzi and beyond were regarded as barbarian territory.

Physically, the Han ranged from the tall, sturdy people of Shandong in the northeast to the smaller, more slightly built inhabitants of the south. Habits and customs varied widely. People in the eastern coastal cities were traders; those in Beijing and the earlier capital of Xi'an in the north treasured their scholastic traditions. Southerners ate delicate seafood dishes and rice; the inhabitants of Sichuan in the west and Hunan in the centre doused their fare in fiery spices.

For long periods the empire was riven by fighting between regional warlords. Some rulers were chased from their capitals by rebels, and overthrown. Factions jostled for

TIMELINE OF IMPERIAL DYNASTIES

Xia 2205–1600 BC	Western Han 206 BC–AD 9	The Five Dynasties
Shang 1600–1122 BC	Wang Mang AD 9–23	Later Liang 907–23
Zhou 1122–255 BC	Eastern Han 25–220	Later Tang 923–35
divided into:	Three Kingdoms 220–80	Later Jin 936–47
Western Zhou 1122–770 BC	Period of Disunion 265–581	Later Han 947–51
Eastern Zhou 770–255 BC	Western Jin 265–316	Later Zhou 951–60
under Eastern Zhou:	Eastern Jin 317–419	Song 960–1279
Spring and Autumn Annals 770–480 BC	Liu Song 420–79	Northern Song 960–1126
	Qi 479–501	Southern Song 1127–1279
Warring States 480–221 BC	Liang 502–57	Yuan 1279–1368
Qin 221–207 BC (First Emperor lives 259–210 BC; rules as Qin Shi Huangdi 221–210 BC)	Chen 557–89	Ming 1368–1644
	Sui 581–618	Qing 1644–1912
	Tang 618–908	

DRAGON SYMBOLISM
The mythical Chinese dragon has been a symbol of power through the ages, closely associated with the water and rain that are vital for agriculture. At the end of his reign, the First Emperor was said to have turned into a dragon.

As a result, the creature became a symbol of empire, depicted in imperial yellow with five claws on each foot. The throne was known as the Dragon Throne, and dragon motifs were carved into palaces, including in the Forbidden City in Beijing.

Stories about dragons pre-date the First Emperor by years. They include that of the carp which swam up waterways against the current as far as the top of a mountain, finally jumping the last obstacle – the Dragon Gate – before turning into a dragon as a reward for its refusal to give up its quest.

Associated with *yang* (male) properties, the dragon was described under the Han dynasty as having the trunk of a snake, the tail of a whale, the face of a camel, the claws of an eagle, the feet of a tiger, the scales of a carp, the antlers of a stag and the ears of a bull. A dragon ruled over each of the seas around China. Like their inland counterparts, when roused to anger, these creatures could unleash great storms and floods.

From earliest times the dragon symbol was associated with the imperial house. Even today dragons are revered by Chinese people, who will often refer to themselves as descendants of the dragon.

power at court, supporters of princes or dowager empresses jockeying with officials, generals, eunuchs and concubines. While the emperors in the capital enjoyed nominal sway, poor roads and forbidding terrain hampered communications; at times, the ruler commanded only a small part of the empire shown on the map. Although Confucianism was the bedrock of the imperial system, Buddhism and Taoism were widely adopted and other creeds and belief systems abounded.

For all these reasons, the traditional picture of an unchanging realm moving in stately fashion through the centuries as emperors conducted timeless rituals and peasants laboured in the same way in fields across China was fractured time and again by reality. The First Emperor sought to order everything by legislation, imposing a draconian system of control to mobilize the population in the service of the state. The model he set remained a template; it was continually tested by the movement of history, the personal vagaries of rulers and the sheer task of holding together such a huge and varied empire.

A lasting imperial tradition
Still, the system that evolved from the earliest days of empire proved remarkably resilient. The theory of the Mandate of Heaven (see page 20) handed down by the gods to the ruler meant that the underlying imperial tradition could be maintained

as dynasties came and went, taking power when the divinities smiled on them and being toppled when their behaviour angered the gods. The theory promised that the benevolent father of the people who looked after the masses in proper fashion could be sure of a long reign but, when self-interest prevailed, he and his dynasty were on the downward slope. If a ruler led armies into disastrous wars, murdered his siblings or wasted the treasury on extravagances, the Mandate would be withdrawn, and the gods' displeasure manifested by disasters and cosmic signals. Once that judgement had been delivered, a fresh ruler would take over at the head of a new ruling house, and the empire would continue.

A class of mandarin officials – many of them chosen by examination to select the best and brightest – served the throne, overseeing the administration of the realm both at the centre and in the provinces. They excelled in the classical texts which formed the parameters of their reasoning. However, this meant that, brilliant though they might be as individuals and as a class, they were creatures of the system, their book learning having little relationship with practical matters. They were major cogs in a top-down flow of authority, which began with the emperor at the summit and then involved minutely calibrated layers of rank in which, it was said, every man regarded those above him as tigers to be feared and those below him as dogs to be kicked.

> ❛ The ways of heaven are not invariable: on the good-doer it sends down all blessings, and on the evil-doer it sends down all miseries. Do you but be virtuous, be it in small things or in large, and the myriad regions will have cause for rejoicing. If you not be virtuous, be it in large things or in small, it will bring the ruin of your ancestral temple. ❜
>
> FROM THE CONFUCIAN TEXT, SHU JING (CLASSIC OF HISTORY)

To its end, imperial China remained a predominantly agricultural and rural society, male-dominated and focused on the paternally led family and its lineage. Trade and industry were ranked at the bottom of the Confucian scale. Though there were rich business families, the middle class was tiny, and depended largely on official favour. The way China operated militated against the emergence of a bourgeoisie.

Despite all the upheavals during the two millennia of imperial history, there was no dynamic to alter the system. As land clearance increased and the acreage of agricultural land and new crop strains were introduced, China generally grew just enough food to feed its people, even if most still did not have much to eat. This broad state of self-sufficiency further enhanced conservatism.

Colourful figures

Personalities surged out of history, from the commanding figure of the First Emperor to the formidable dowager empress Cixi, who dominated the court for most of the last half-century of empire. There were commanders who grabbed the throne and expansionists who sent armies deep into Central Asia. The seventh century saw the extraordinary Wu Zetian credited with abominable cruelties towards her rivals but also hailed as an early champion of the rights of women to rule. There was a string of inferior rulers, incompetent despots and wastrels, crazed murderers and dreamers. Centuries passed in which the country was torn between regional warlords and

IMPERIAL DYNASTIES AND KEY EVENTS IN WORLD HISTORY

QIN 221–207 BC
216 BC Hannibal defeats the Romans at the Battle of Cannae

HAN 206 BC–AD 220
146 BC Third Punic War – fall of Carthage
100–44 BC Julius Caesar, Rome
69–30 BC Cleopatra, Egypt
AD 33 Crucifixion of Christ
43 Romans occupy Britain
150 Pyramid of the Sun, Mexico

THREE KINGDOMS – DISUNION 220–589
Gupta empire in India
Rome splits between east and west; Christianity becomes official Roman religion
410 Visigoths sack Rome
450 Anglo-Saxons invade Britain

TANG 618–908
622 Muhammad leaves Mecca for Medina
633–42 Muslim army conquers Egypt, Mesopotamia, Palestine, North Africa
650 Koran written
742–814 Charlemagne founds Holy Roman Empire

800 Angkor temples, Cambodia
800 Borobudur temple, Java
850 Viking raids

SONG 960–1279
1000 Vikings reach Newfoundland
1066 Norman invasion of England
1095 First Christian crusade to Palestine
1215 Magna Carta signed in England
1221–42 Mongols invade Europe and India

YUAN 1279–1368
1300 Foundation of Ottoman empire
1300 Rise of Incas
1327 Aztecs found Mexico City
1347–51 Black Death in Europe

MING 1368–1644
1440–50 Incas build Cuzco and Machu Picchu
1456 Gutenberg Bible printed
1492 Columbus sails to America
1517 Martin Luther protests at Catholicism
1521 Cortés destroys Aztecs

1522 Portuguese circumnavigate the globe
1564 Shakespeare born
1588 English defeat of Spanish Armada
1607 First permanent English settlement in America at Jamestown
1616 Dutch become first Europeans to land in Australia
1620 Pilgrim Fathers land in Massachusetts
1642 English civil war breaks out

QING 1644–1912
1651 Dutch found Cape Town
1682–1725 Peter the Great
1683 Turks defeated at Vienna
1757 British presence in India established at Battle of Plassey
1776 US Declaration of Independence
1789 French Revolution
1815 Battle of Waterloo
1848 Publication of the Communist Manifesto
1853 Perry expedition to Japan
1861–5 American Civil War
1869 Suez Canal opens
1899 Boer War
1904–5 Japan defeats Russia

pretenders to the Mandate of Heaven, whose dynasties lasted for only a score of years. There were repeated invasions from the north and, at the end, incursions by the West and Japan. The strength of the empire founded in 221 BC was that it managed to continue until its own internal weaknesses caused it to implode in 1912.

That the imperial dynasties were able to survive from the dawn of history to the age of electricity and the railway makes the Chinese empire unique. Whatever their failings, the men – and one woman – who occupied the Dragon Throne were unique, too. Cast in the role of intermediaries between the divine and the mortal, they were held to personify the nation, its people and its civilization. The past was ever present, in the shape of the ancestors, and the future could only bring trouble given the accepted inevitability of the cycle of dynastic rise and fall. Even the most successful dynasties knew that the wheel of fate would bring eventual decline to rulers who were, after all, human. What mattered above all was that the mystical idea of an empire handed down from heaven, placed at the centre of the world, should live on.

THE BIRTH OF CHINA

TO 221 BC

The discovery of prehistoric human remains near Beijing shows that a form of human lived in China from the earliest times – perhaps 500,000 years ago. The remains were those of *Homo erectus* (an ancestor of modern humans, *Homo sapiens*) and were given the name 'Peking Man'. Other archaeological discoveries have placed later examples of early man across the country from the northeast to the south, from the great bend of the Yellow River to the far southwest. Neolithic cultures developed later – from about 6000 BC – in wooded river valleys in what are today Shandong, Henan and Shaanxi provinces, the historic heartland of the Chinese nation.

FARMING SPREAD SLOWLY ACROSS CHINA, REACHING THE SOUTH OF THE COUNTRY BY ABOUT 3000 BC. Farmers created a rural economy by burning down forests, tilling the soil, raising pigs and dogs, and gathering more sustenance by hunting and fishing. When they had exhausted the land, they moved on, clearing fresh ground for crops. As they evolved, they created more settled communities. They made pottery, progressing from simple techniques to the production of fine, delicate objects turned on the wheel. They fashioned tools from bones, and armed their axes and sickles with stones. They lived in mud huts or homes in holes in the ground. The major change came in the period just before 1700 BC, with the growth of a civilization that used bronze. It was led by the first of the Chinese dynasties of which there are reliable historical records, the Shang.

The story of creation

In Chinese mythology, heaven and earth were once inextricably mixed together in a universe created by Pan Ku (whose name may mean 'Coiled-up Antiquity'). This universe was compared to the yolk and white of a chicken's egg. After 18,000 years the mass divided into two parts. That which was bright and light made up heaven, the rest became earth. For another 18,000 years the two parts both grew, heaven becoming higher and earth heavier. Thus a distance of 30,000 miles (48,000 km) grew between the two worlds.

RIGHT *The Yellow River (Huang He) winds its way eastwards from the Plateau of Tibet for almost 4000 miles (6400 km) to the Yellow Sea. Often referred to as the 'cradle of Chinese civilization', it is China's second-longest river after the Yangzi, and the sixth longest in the world.*

500,000 BC Peking Man

5000–3000 BC Neolithic cultures established in different parts of China

2500 BC Houses and fortifications made of compressed earth are constructed

1800 BC Start of the Bronze Age

1600 BC Shang dynasty; development of writing on oracle bones

1122–770 BC Western Zhou dynasty

770–255 BC Eastern Zhou dynasty; Spring and Autumn Annals Period (to 480 BC)

Sixth century BC Sun Tzu and *The Art of War*

551–479 BC Life of Confucius

480–221 BC Warring States Period; rise of the dukes of Jin

450 BC Invention of the crossbow

430 BC Around this time large-scale irrigation projects are undertaken in the kingdom of Wei

403 BC Jin territory divided in three

Late 4th/early 3rd centuries BC Compilation of Taoist compendium attributed to Laozi

385 BC Rise of the state of Qin

293 BC Qin defeats alliance led by the state of Wei – 240,000 are said to have been killed

288 BC Qin ruler declares himself emperor

278–222 BC Qin campaigns overcome other states one by one

221 BC Qin Shi Huangdi declared First Emperor

On Pan Ku's death the parts of his body provided the elements of the earth. His breath became the wind and the clouds, his voice thunder, his eyes the sun and moon, his four limbs the four quarters of the earth, his fingers its mountains, his blood its rivers, his flesh the soil, his teeth metal and stones, his skin and body hair plants and trees, and his sweat the rain. The parasites in his body turned into humans.

Three sets of supreme sovereigns appeared, corresponding to heaven, earth and mankind. The celestial domain had its own 12 sovereigns, the earth 11 and humans nine. These were followed by five model rulers, or sages, who founded Chinese civilization, among them Huangdi, the Yellow Emperor. The five rulers gave mankind agriculture, calendars, fishing, fire, house construction, hunting, medicine and writing.

The legend of Kun

Much later, the myths tell, China was threatened by huge floods. One written work which collected the early stories described them in these terms: '*Everywhere the tremendous waters were wreaking destruction. Spreading afar, they embraced the mountains and rose above the hills. In a vast flow, they swelled up to heaven*'. The job of fighting the flood was given by a god to a mythical figure, Kun, who tried for nine years to contain the waters, using a magical element he stole from heaven called 'swelling mould', which continually expanded. With this he built huge dams, but the floods continued to rage. The gods had Kun executed on the sunless slopes of Feather Mountain, where his body was left to lie for three years, during which time it did not decompose.

Kun's son Yu emerged from the corpse and, aided by a dragon which flew over the land and traced places where channels should be dug, managed to divert the waters into the sea. He may also have used the 'swelling mould' to erect mountains. Kun, meanwhile, turned into a dragon, a three-legged turtle, a black fish or a yellow bear according to various versions of the story, and may have been restored to human life by a shaman.

Yu worked so hard at his labours that he wore the nails off his fingers and became lame. While digging a way through a mountain, he was turned into a bear; frightened, his pregnant wife ran away, but was turned to stone. '*Give me my son*', Yu shouted. The stone split open and the baby emerged.

In the end, Yu succeeded in diverting the floods and made the land safe by getting rid of snakes and dragons. The divinities rewarded his efforts by naming him as the first king of China, at the head of the Xia dynasty. In that role he ordered his officials to mark out the world by pacing across it; they concluded that the planet was square with sides measuring 77,800 miles (125,000 km).

A great warrior, the king established supremacy over 10,000 states and made extensive travels to holy places and to visit the Winged People, the Black Feet People and the Naked People, taking off his clothes to accord with the custom of the last group. His position in mythology is secure both as the head of the first dynasty, which remains in the realms of legend, and as the man who made China inhabitable: as a noble was reported to have remarked in 541 BC, '*Were it not for Yu, we would be fish!*'

EARLY RULING HOUSES

Xia	2200–1600 BC
Shang	1600–1122 BC
Western Zhou	1122–770 BC
Eastern Zhou (overlapping with Spring and Autumn Annals Period 770–480 BC)	770–255 BC
Warring States Period	480–221 BC

BELOW *Drummers perform an official memorial ceremony to honour the legendary Yellow Emperor, Huangdi, the founder of Chinese civilization who is said to have reigned from 2697 to 2598 BC.*

The Shang

The legendary Xia dynasty was reputed to have been entrusted with its mandate to rule by the gods after Yu had conquered the huge floods. But its last ruler's decadence was said to have lost him divine favour, and the Shang took power early in the 17th century BC. This early dynasty moved China into the long trajectory that would lead to the crowning of the First Emperor in 221 BC and subsequently to the

succession of imperial houses that would span the years until 1912. In all, the Shang counted 30 kings governing over seven centuries.

Their lands in the eastern valley of the Yellow River in the north of the country were the cradle of Chinese civilization. The river would become known as 'China's Sorrow', for the recurrent flooding caused by the heavy deposits of loess soil that washed down from its upper reaches and raised the level of its bed. But from the earliest times it offered the great advantages of ecological diversity, access to the wide north China plain and a position at the crossroads between the different parts of the country.

Manufacture of bronze objects, which probably began before the Shang came to power, was developed to become a hallmark of their era. (See Bronze-working in China, right.) Bronze vessels became a sign of rank. There were constant power struggles under the Shang, with different groups taking and losing control in recurring outbreaks of war. If succession was peaceful, the throne passed to the younger brother of the dead ruler in the early period of the dynasty, though father–son succession became common at its end. The capital moved many times. In Shang settlements, which were often walled, archaeologists have found the remains of workshops, bronze furnaces, royal tombs, tortoise shells and 'oracle bones' that were used for divination. At one site, a small citadel with walls of compacted earth was unearthed. Some funerary pits discovered in one capital contained the decapitated bodies of human sacrificial victims, together with dogs and five harnessed chariots complete with drivers.

The Shang reigned over a society that was both urban and rural, its main preoccupations being farming, hunting and warfare. Power lay in the hands of an élite class of aristocratic warriors. Dominating this social pyramid was the king in his palace at the centre of the capital. Ten lineages were associated with the royal family, as were 200 élite clans. The authority the monarchs exerted over their domain was never absolute; smaller states existed within the kingdom. The Shang have been described by the historian Jacques Gernet as living in 'a world of luxury and violence' as chiefs of politics, war, religion and administration. They and their people worshipped 'the Lord on High', who presided over the gods of the sun, moon, wind, rain and other elements, as well as over humans and their world. There were lavish ritual ceremonies for the gods and for ancestors, with sacrifices followed by banquets that might on occasion turn into orgies.

ABOVE *An inscribed oracle bone dating from the Shang dynasty, c.14th–13th century BC. Such inscriptions were used mainly for divination purposes and to record significant events.*

Ancestral spirits

The spirits of the ancestors were held to have great powers and were consulted by means of questions written by scribes on animal bones or tortoise shells. A priest applied a hot poker to these until they cracked. The form of the cracks was interpreted to draw the message from the spirit world. *'Will the king win a victory?'*,

BRONZE-WORKING IN CHINA The development

of the bronze industry and bronze art in China, which first flourished under the Shang, came at a time when society began to be more settled, providing the conditions needed to mine the copper and tin that went into the metal as well as to smelt it and design objects made from bronze. The oldest bronze artefacts discovered so far date back to 1800 BC.

Bronze-working meant that the early Chinese had stronger weapons and farming tools than before; but bronze was also used extensively to make drinking cups and containers for the food that was an important element in ceremonies at which the ruler, his family and the nobility venerated and consulted their ancestors.

Bronze vessels were often ornately decorated using ritualistic designs, including frequent depictions of animal faces and heads, with two figures shown in profile facing one another. Nine special vessels made up the Auspicious Bronzes of the State, which were captured by the Zhou when they succeeded the Shang. Another bronze vessel found in 1976 has an inscription stating that it was commissioned a week after the change of dynasties. Many of the bronzes found from the Shang era were for drinking wine, but the Zhou, who spread stories of the dissolute behaviour of their predecessors, made more bronze boxes to contain offerings of food. As time went on, rich members of the Zhou élite used bronze artefacts in their homes rather than for ancestor worship, ordering finely crafted objects inlaid with jewels and precious stones.

The burial of bronze treasures with their owners ensured their preservation, and many examples have been unearthed by modern archaeologists – for instance, the find of more than 200 pieces in the tomb of the wife of a Shang king. The museum of Chinese history and culture in Shanghai has a particularly fine collection, and the building which houses it is designed in the shape of a great bronze pot.

This Shang dynasty bronze face mask was one of over 100 such objects found in 1986 in royal burial pits at Sanxingdui, a village in Sichuan in southwest China.

the written question might read. '*Yes*', would come the reply. So the king could go to war. The work of these scribes constituted the earliest forms of writing. (See Chinese Writing, page 18.)

The oracle bones were preserved as a type of archive for the dynasty. Other court scholars developed astronomy, noting the existence of Mars and comets. So, from the earliest days, the Chinese dynastic system combined warfare, ancestor worship, the claim to be in touch with other-worldly powers, the compilation of written records and the nurturing of scholarship among an élite gathered at court.

CHINESE WRITING

'Out of the river crept the half-divine tortoise with mysterious writing on its back'. This was the legendary account of the origin of Chinese writing. How writing really originated is not known but, by the Shang dynasty, the characters that would become Chinese script had developed on oracle bones with which priests consulted the gods. Inscriptions on bronze objects from the same era show the evolution of the characters. Bamboo, wood and silk were also used.

By the 11th century BC, Chinese characters had become stylized, containing abstract figures and combinations of characters, and the script can thus be counted as a written language. Some 4500 Shang signs have been distinguished; they were often based on pictograms but other elements went into their formation. Since they were not composed of letters with distinct sounds, a link was made between these characters and the spoken words they depicted, marrying semantic and phonetic aspects. Characters were generally arranged in vertical columns running from right to left.

Under the Zhou dynasty, which followed the Shang, writing evolved into what was known as the Great Seal style which is found on bronze vessels and objects. The decline in the authority of the Zhou and the ensuing disunion meant that writing developed in different ways in different regions.

It was the First Emperor who imposed the Small Seal script which formed the basis for written Chinese until the introduction of simplified characters under the Communist Republic.

As the empire grew, so did the written language by which it functioned and in which its central texts were handed down. By the early part of the first millennium AD, there were 10,000 characters. By 1200, this had more than doubled and, in the 18th century, Chinese had almost 50,000 characters. Over the centuries, some characters changed their appearance; others became redundant or were neglected. But the line back to the oracle bones – or even earlier – was clear, giving the Chinese a permanent link with the distant past.

The four-stage development from symbol to script of two words (far left, 'hand'; fifth from left, 'mountain').

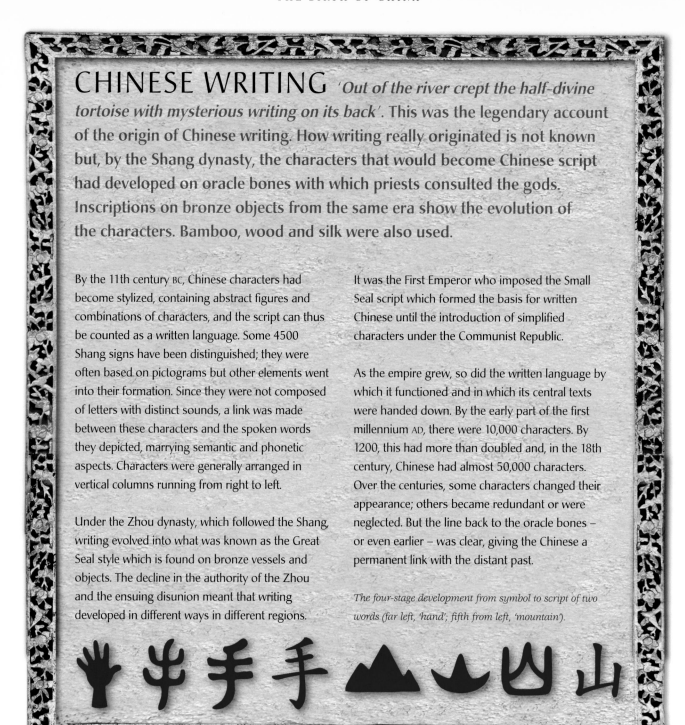

Foreign contacts

As their main attacking force, Shang armies used chariots bearing archers wielding powerful bows, and soldiers armed with bronze weapons. Many wars of the Shang era were waged against nomadic raiders from the northern steppes – these disputes would become a constant theme throughout imperial history. Other conflicts involved Chinese groups to the south and east of their domain, particularly the people of the Huai River Valley which marks the frontier between north and south of the country.

Despite the recurrent warfare, the Shang kingdom became the centre of a network of growing links between the steppes, the vast expanse of Central Asia to the west and the Yangzi Valley to the south. Imperial China is often seen as a closed realm, largely as a result of the rejection of the West by the Qing dynasty in the late 18th and 19th centuries. But from the earliest days the dynasties were open to influences from far away, and spread their own influence as widely. Relics found in the Yellow River Valley suggest that the Shang people traded with Mesopotamia and possibly with Greece, as well as with Southeast Asia. Pottery from China of this time has been found in northern India.

The Shang grew steadily weaker, however, as they lost control of smaller states within their realm and had to fight difficult wars against tribes from the north. A vassal people, the Zhou, who lived in the valley of the Wei River to the west, grew steadily in power; such was the king's wariness of them that, at one point, he held the visiting Zhou chief prisoner for three years. When the Shang were distracted by a campaign in the east in around 1040–1030 BC, the Zhou launched a major attack.

ABOVE A Chinese archaeologist uncovers the remains of war chariots and horses in burial pits at Yin (or Anyang), the last capital of the Shang dynasty, in today's Henan province.

The offensive took the Shang capital of Anyang, where the heir to the throne was captured. But the Zhou then fell out among themselves, and the Shang fought back, enlisting the support of people to the south and east. The Zhou king sorted out the internal squabbles by executing his quarrelling brothers and murdering the heir-prisoner. He then resumed the attack, defeating the Shang. Their last king was said to have committed suicide by leaping into a fire. His head was cut off and impaled on a pole. Revolts continued into the new millennium, but the Zhou were established as the new rulers of the Lower Yellow River region, starting the process of China's universalist tradition that would underpin the empires to come.

The Mandate of Heaven

To justify their seizure of the throne, the Zhou evolved the doctrine of the Mandate of Heaven, by which a ruler held power until his conduct alienated the gods. The Mandate of Heaven provided a means of underpinning the imperial system through changing dynasties over more than two millennia. It held that heaven sanctioned the temporal authority of rulers so long as they looked after the welfare of their people and governed in a wise, benevolent and caring manner.

> From ancient times, the virtuous kings certainly had an upright wife as a mate. If their consorts were upright, then they flourished; if they were not upright, then there was chaos.

HAN-ERA HISTORIAN LIU XIANG ON THE EARLY RULERS OF CHINA, 79–78 BC

If they failed to do this, the Mandate would be withdrawn. Heaven showed its displeasure by bringing about natural disasters, eclipses, comets and other celestial signs; its dissatisfaction could also be manifested in the failure of the ruler to produce an heir, and in discord, strife and, eventually, military defeat. Another dynasty would then ascend the throne, declaring that it would carry out heaven's wishes.

The doctrine had two great advantages. It explained why things on earth could go wrong despite the omniscient divine power; this was the fault of rulers who fell short of the Mandate. It also provided for changes of regime without any questioning of the fundamental basis of belief. The ultimate power of the divine was thus not brought into jeopardy, as men were blamed for their own failings.

In the case of the last Shang ruler, the Zhou declared him guilty of 'vicious acts', including roasting dissenters on a rack or having their bodies cut into strips of dried meat. He was also alleged to have drunk too much, held orgies, enjoyed songs with erotic lyrics and generally to have neglected his duties. At the same time, he was infatuated with his consort and allowed her to dictate government policy – the influence of queens and empresses on their husbands was held by early historians to be extremely important.

The Han-era historian, Sima Qian (see page 50) recounted that the Zhou king initially declined to attack the Shang because he did not have the Mandate. But he later learned that the Shang king had ordered that a critic's chest should be cut open so that he could examine the man's heart while it was still beating. The Zhou took the episode as proof that the Shang had lost the Mandate, so they launched their

TAOISM VERSUS CONFUCIANISM

The creed of Taoism (or Daoism) exalted the individual and nature in mystical contrast to the social concerns of Confucianism. Generally dated from the later Zhou era, Taoism grew from much older roots, bringing together ancient beliefs about the relationship between man and the world around him and the universe beyond that.

Though its founding figure, Laozi, was recognized as a divinity during the second century AD, some historians believe he may never have existed at all. Its other major progenitor, Zhuangzi, was a contemporary of the great Confucian, Mencius. (See Confucius and Confucianism, pages 28–9.)

Taoism is an extremely wide-ranging system of beliefs that cover the fields of alchemy, magic and divination and is virtually impossible to sum up, particularly since some of its basic teachings are both highly compact and highly ambiguous. But the kernel lies in man's relationship with nature, which is held to be the arbiter of mankind and human society. Man is seen as a microcosm of the universe. His aim, therefore, should be to understand nature and to achieve harmony with the Tao – the way of nature – and the flow of the universe.

Believers have to accept that the universe is subject to constant change as the sun, moon and earth all revolve constantly. Man cannot alter this. He is essentially passive. But he should also embrace spontaneity and reject external rules as well as human wisdom and knowledge.

This is far from the social order and stability sought by the Confucians, and leads to what was often regarded as the subversive aspect of Taoism. In the golden olden days, the creed taught, men had not been subject to a government since they lived in accord with the Tao. So, in the ideal society, state administration was not required. Right and wrong had no meaning; men should not care about possessions or see the need for organization.

The contrast between Confucianism and Taoism runs through Chinese imperial history, with some emperors and their consorts seeing the appeal of the way of the Tao. It may also be apparent again in the 21st century as both belief systems enjoy a revival. Confucians regarded Taoists as irresponsible other-worldly figures who sought to return to an age in which no rules were required. The Taoists saw the Confucians as oppressive bureaucrats out to regulate mankind. Despite the stark difference, each represented a strand that resonated in the Chinese mind – on the one hand, the need to achieve order and harmony to run the state and ensure national unity, and on the other, the harking back to an idealized epoch when life was simpler and the secrets of the universe could be attained by mortals.

A Song dynasty bronze figure from c.AD 960–1280 represents Laozi riding a water buffalo. Laozi is thought to have formulated the teachings in Dao de Jing (The Book of the Way and Its Virtue), *a philosophical treatise that forms the basis of Taoism.*

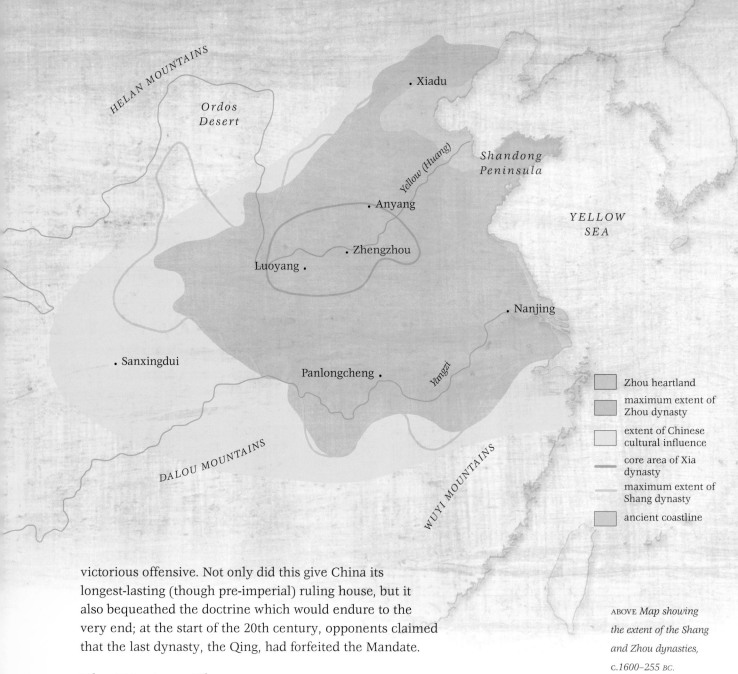

HELAN MOUNTAINS

Ordos
Desert

. Xiadu

Yellow (Huang)

*Shandong
Peninsula*

. Anyang

YELLOW
SEA

. Zhengzhou

Luoyang .

. Nanjing

. Sanxingdui

Yangzi

Panlongcheng .

DALOU MOUNTAINS

WUYI MOUNTAINS

Zhou heartland

maximum extent of
Zhou dynasty

extent of Chinese
cultural influence

core area of Xia
dynasty

maximum extent of
Shang dynasty

ancient coastline

victorious offensive. Not only did this give China its
longest-lasting (though pre-imperial) ruling house, but it
also bequeathed the doctrine which would endure to the
very end; at the start of the 20th century, opponents claimed
that the last dynasty, the Qing, had forfeited the Mandate.

ABOVE *Map showing
the extent of the Shang
and Zhou dynasties,
c.1600–255 BC.*

The Western Zhou

Despite the violent means by which the change of dynasty took place, the new Zhou
rulers represented continuity in many ways as they governed from their capital close
to present-day Xi'an. Their reign was known as the Western Zhou period, which
lasted from 1040 BC to around 770 BC. They adopted the Shang way of life and
administrative methods, as well as their writing. Like the Shang, they ruled over

❛When the prince regards his ministers as his hands and feet, his ministers
regard their prince as their belly and heart; when he regards them as his dogs
and horses, they regard him as any other man; when he regards them as the
ground or as grass, they regard him as a robber and an enemy.❜

MENCIUS

an array of less powerful kingdoms rather than a single, unified realm. They also developed something like a feudal system.

All land belonged initially to the throne, but it was then handed out to royal relatives and successful generals. Those who received such gifts became vassals of the monarch – they might further distribute land to their subordinates, who were their vassals in turn. Land was handed down from father to son. Officials were also given land instead of wages. Over time, this created a system in which the great lords in their fiefdoms enjoyed virtual autonomy, and the Zhou kings came to depend on personal relationships for their authority.

Kinship lay at the heart of the system. Marriages between the rulers and the children of powerful vassals were used to knit the realm together. A strict hierarchy extended from the king through princes and great lords, who lived at court, to provincial barons and the local gentry and then to the peasants, who provided food and the manpower for war.

Life under the Zhou

Agriculture grew in importance during the Zhou period, which saw the start of China's great hydraulic engineering projects with the construction of a huge reservoir in what is today Anhui province. But power also lay in the towns, where the élite lived and where bronze was worked. These towns were small in size: those that have been excavated had perimeters of 800 metres (2600 ft) girded by thick, high ramparts. The soldiers kept by the élite in the towns provided protection for the surrounding countryside.

Much of the northern plains country was still covered with woods and swamps that were home to many wild animals and fruit trees. Farmers worked the soil with stone hoes and wooden spades, growing sorghum millet and hemp with edible seeds. Women were occupied with weaving, raising silk worms, cooking and making wine, while men tilled the fields, and hunted and fished. This traditional division of labour set up a dichotomy between indoor and outdoor activity – life in the light and in the shade – which led to the distinction between the feminine *yin* and the masculine *yang* life forces.

Like their predecessors, the Zhou worshipped ancestors and had elaborate rituals. But they did not practise human sacrifice and they introduced the universalist cult of the supremacy of heaven, in which the sun and stars were venerated. Perfecting the bronze culture, their workmen crafted some of the finest objects in Chinese history, including bells, altar tables and ornaments. The production of lacquer work and manuscripts made of silk was also encouraged. Successful warriors were rewarded with gifts of large quantities of bronze. Among treasures found in the capital of a leading noble, the 'Double Ears' Duke Wen of Jin, was a celebrated buffalo-shaped

ABOVE *Under the Zhou, the technique of lacquer work was developed for use on ritual objects. This wooden bowl, dating from the third century* BC, *is coated in red and black lacquer and decorated with stylized birds and animals.*

bronze vessel made by a single stamp pressed two dozen times on the moulding to show the face of the animal, with two dragons above it and ribbons on the side.

The population grew and land was cleared for agriculture. The Zhou encouraged the development of courtly warfare consisting of tournaments to decide the outcome rather than full-scale battles. They employed Shang people to work on their towns, including the capital, but divided their communities into segregated sections for their own people and for the Shang. Our knowledge of the period has been enhanced by several books that have survived, including the remarkable collection known as *The Book of Songs*, which chronicles the lives of ordinary people as well as the lordly élite.

The Eastern Zhou

After 800 BC the Zhou came under increasing pressure from autonomy-minded nobles in western China and from incursions by nomadic tribes. This led to the capital being moved eastwards to the ancient city of Luoyang in present-day Henan province. From about that time, the dynasty became known as the Eastern Zhou.

> We will all assist the royal house, and do no harm to one another. If any one transgresses this covenant, may the intelligent spirits destroy him, so that he shall lose his people and not be able to possess his state, and, to the remotest posterity, let him have no descendants, old or young.
>
> COVENANT OF ZHOU STATES, 632 BC

The territory over which it claimed sovereignty blessed by heaven expanded. Outposts were established to the south, including one in Nanjing. New cities were founded, controlling the surrounding countryside but also forming a counterbalance to Luoyang that could not have been welcome to the rulers politically, but which they were powerless to prevent. The Eastern Zhou survived for more than 500 years, and the leaders of the great fiefdoms signed solemn covenants to help the royal house and not fight among themselves. Despite this, the move from the western capital saw the authority of the throne wane as the rise of feudal states and their jockeying for power became a feature of the last centuries of pre-imperial China.

Each of these states was self-governing, with its own administrative system, culture and legal apparatus. The diversity encouraged internal changes, including greater social mobility, the buying and selling of land and the growth of cities. Their armies had no time for courtly warfare or tournaments. The Zhou became figurehead sovereigns, their authority confined to the area around their capital at Luoyang, their supposed religious pre-eminence counting for less and less. In what was known as the Spring and Autumn Annals period of the dynasty, they were obliged to ally themselves with the powerful state of Jin and recognize its duke as Lord Protector (or Hegemon). The rulers of the rising states asserted their power by calling themselves kings.

Warring states

The resulting division developed into the Period of the Warring States, which began around 480 BC and which would see the major regional lords, who proclaimed themselves kings, struggling for supremacy. By the third century BC, seven major entities had emerged in northern China round the Yellow River. Collectively, they

were known as the 'central states', and the singular form of this term was later used as the name for China as a whole: the Middle Kingdom. In 403 BC, the Jin state was partitioned into three, the Han, Zhao and Wei, which then took control of the dynasty's territory – the Zhou king remained on the throne, but powerless. In the old Zhou heartland of Shanxi, the ambitious Qin kings ruled from their capital Chang'an (near modern Xi'an). To the south, the kingdom of Chu emerged as a major force.

Despite the divisions and warfare, the era saw the further development of agriculture and irrigation as well as the spread of ironworking. Tax revenue rose. Weapons

ABOVE *A stone carving (c.200 BC–AD 200) depicts a Chinese warrior shooting an arrow to the rear as he rides away on a galloping horse, a tactic that has become known as a 'Parthian shot'.*

SUN TZU AND THE ART OF WAR

A general from the sixth century BC, Sun Wu, became China's most celebrated military strategist and theoretician thanks to his book, *The Art of War*, and was given the accolade of Sun Tzu (Master Sun). He stressed the importance of moral and intellectual qualities when waging war. *'Weapons'*, he wrote, *'are ominous tools to be used only when there is no alternative'*.

Sun was a Confucian disciple (see pages 28–9) who, like the sage, venerated reason. A supposed conversation between the two had him asking the Master what kind of man he would take with him into battle. *'The man who was ready to beard a tiger or rush a river without caring whether he lived or died – that sort of man I should not take'*, Confucius replied. *'I should certainly take someone who approached difficulties with due caution and who preferred to succeed by strategy'*.

In keeping with such an approach, Sun advocated the use of political manoeuvres to weaken the enemy in advance, while spies collected information and fifth-column agents sowed discord in the opposing ranks. The enemy's weakness should be noted and acted upon. Deception was important, as was an understanding of the opponent's thinking. In such ways the enemy might be defeated without soldiers having to come to blows. Only when that proved impossible should the army be mobilized.

When it did move, its aims should be to win quickly and with as few casualties and as little material damage as possible. Enemy casualties should also be minimized, to help in the restoration of peace. A good general would have created the conditions for a speedy outcome by the way in which he weakened the foe in advance. Indeed, one of his prime responsibilities was to have ensured victory before committing his troops. He should be adaptable, perhaps yielding up a position in order to gain a stronger one, and always taking account of the terrain and the weather.

Like other figures of his time who have achieved legendary status, we know little of Sun. Tradition has it that, like Confucius, he was a member of the *shi* class of landless aristocrats and was recruited as a commander by the king of the state of Wu. After helping Wu to defeat the kingdom of Chu, Sun gave up warfare and retired to write his classic text.

'There are no fixed forms or inflexible rules in military tactics. Only those who are able to vary their tactics according to the changing manoeuvre of the enemy and win victories have really miraculous skills'.

'Skilful military leaders conquer the enemy without fighting battles, capture cities without attacking them and overcome states without protracted warfare'.

SUN TZU, THE ART OF WAR, 61, 33

Though doubts have been raised about whether *The Art of War* was really his work or, like the *Analects* of Confucius, was put together subsequently and attributed to him, archaeological discoveries suggest the existence of ancient texts, and a writer of around 300 BC told of Sun's ideas being incorporated into martial techniques. There is no doubting his influence on Chinese strategists down the years. In the 20th century, he found a dedicated adept in the person of Mao Zedong (Mao Tse-tung), whose combination of politics, subversion and feints in winning power came straight out of Sun's teachings. More recently, he has been held up as a guru for business people and a man whose ideas have been applied by the People's Republic in its economic policies.

became more lethal and included crossbows and dagger-axes up to 5.5 metres (18 ft) long. Philosophers and scholars established themselves at court or travelled from kingdom to kingdom expounding ideas on how society should be organized – among them was Confucius, who had little success at the time but whose ideas would later form the foundation for China's main belief system for millennia to come. (See Confucius and Confucianism, pages 28–9.) The unsettled times also gave rise to strategists led by Sun Tzu, whose work, *The Art of War*, would influence military thinking up to the present day. (See Sun Tzu and the Art of War, left.)

Rise of the Qin

By the third century BC, the Qin stood out among the warring states for their military skill, fierce discipline, administrative systems and economic development. Their state was based on the strict application of harsh laws, with fear at the root of their governance; as one theoretician of the Qin state explained, *'Fire appears severe, wherefore men rarely get burned; water appears tender, wherefore men often get drowned'.*

The constant danger posed by the other major states was held to require militarization and the imposition of centralized direction, which swept aside old values of merit and virtue. As another Qin thinker put it, *'To govern with generous or lenient regulations a people in imminent danger is the same as driving wild horses without reins ... this is a calamity of ignorance'.*

ABOVE *The crossbow trigger mechanism was invented in China in about the fifth century BC. The inlaid decoration of this example from the Eastern Zhou dynasty suggests that it was part of a prestige crossbow reserved for ceremonial purposes rather than for practical use.*

The Qin military machine, allying cavalry with heavily armed infantry, appeared invincible, and was complemented by espionage, subversion and assassinations. In keeping with their iron control over the growing population, the kings ordered large-scale transfers of people to colonize conquered lands. Their appetite for conquest was insatiable, showing what historian Jacques Gernet has called 'an almost demoniacal spirit'. A visitor to their court wrote that they treated their people *'harshly, terrorize[d] them with authority, embitter[ed] them with hardship, coax[ed] them with rewards and cow[ed] them with punishments'.*

The Qin defeated the Han kingdom and won over smaller states by force of arms or by diplomacy or bribery. They decisively defeated the Wei, who were forced to cede a large portion of their territory. Their conquests of Sichuan in the fourth century BC gave them a springboard from which to attack territory that the Chu had acquired in central China. They turned the region into a military base, integrating it into their domain and suppressing a rebellion at the turn of the century. After that they advanced eastwards, forcing the Chu to retreat. Pursuing them, the Qin fought fierce battles for a period of two years before conquering the final Chu stronghold in the Huai River region in 223 BC. Two years later, they defeated the last remaining kingdom, the Qi, and their king took supreme power as the first emperor of China.

CONFUCIUS AND CONFUCIANISM 'Master Kung', an

official and wandering scholar of the Spring and Autumn Period of the Zhou dynasty, subsequently became the greatest influence on Chinese thought and behaviour, under the name of Confucius. He had little success during his lifetime, generally dated from 551 to 479 BC; but his teachings would be adopted by the empire as the equivalent of a lay religion, and today his name is used by the Communist regime as the title for Chinese cultural institutes around the world.

The future sage was born in the state of Lu in northeastern China (today's Shandong province) to a former soldier and a much younger mother. They were members of the class known as the *shi*, consisting of members of noble families who had lost their lands during the warfare of the period. Tradition has it that Confucius's father died when he was three and that he was brought up in relative poverty. During his youth he worked as a shepherd, clerk and book-keeper before becoming a teacher and entering state service, in which he rose to a senior post in the administration of justice. But he disapproved of his ruler's behaviour, so resigned and set out to travel across the kingdoms and states that operated in near autonomy under the nominal oversight of the Zhou, expounding his ideas of good government as he went.

'If some ruler would employ me, in a month I should have my system working', he declared. *'In three years, everything would be running smoothly'.*

But his confidence was not shared by others, and he faced competing philosophies such as that of an eccentric teacher, Mo Tzu, who also moved about from court to court attacking Confucianism and preaching the equality of human beings. Neither of the thinkers made much impact on kings and dukes, who were more concerned with temporal power; Confucius eventually returned home to teach a group of local students, and died at the age of 72.

The superior man

The works attributed to the sage from Shandong, notably the compilation of sayings in the *Analects*, were not the direct work of Confucius, but were put together long after his death by disciples of disciples. In other cases, writing said to be by him is a version of earlier works. Accounts of his life in the *Analects* exaggerate his importance at the time and the number of followers he attracted. Naturally enough, he is presented as the embodiment of reason, a man who was simple and unassuming when in his native village but who, when advising the ruler *'speaks readily, though always choosing his words with due caution'*.

But the apocryphal nature of many of the teachings attributed to Master Kung and the legends that grew up around him do not lessen the importance of Confucius for China. Indeed, the teachings as set down after his death include the acknowledgement *'I am a transmitter, not an originator'*.

Confucius was concerned above all with the achievement of social order and man's place in it. At a time when China was divided into feuding states, he preached the idea of harmony, which was to be maintained by obligations between human beings based on tradition, morality and mutual respect. In place of superstition, he exalted the importance of reason and of reasonable behaviour. Rulers should face the truth. Men should do to others as they would have others do to them. His 'superior man' became the template for wise rulers, scholars and millions of others, even if the stratified, self-contained nature of Confucianism meant that it could easily be perverted into an apologia for despotism and the rejection of new thinking.

'The superior man understands what is right; the inferior man understands what will sell. The superior man loves his soul; the inferior man loves his property … The superior man goes through life without any one preconceived course of action or any taboo; he merely decides for the moment what the right thing is to do'.

CONFUCIUS, *ANALECTS*, CHAPTER 8

While Confucianism emphasized the importance of accepting responsibilities, acting benevolently towards others and showing compassion, its stress on men knowing their proper status reflected a deep conservatism, which would be blamed for China's failure to modernize. If those in charge behaved well, those below were required to show obedience and not question the system that governed their lives. The superior men promised benevolence and protection; inferiors had only to serve.

The philosophy treasured rituals and ceremonials as the manifestation of the verities handed down from heaven. In this and in its embrace of tradition and praise for piety towards the ancestors, it easily became an excuse for immobilism and the glorification of the emperor. It had no time for diverse groups in society, certainly not for merchants, trade or property. Nor did it offer remedies when rulers behaved badly.

Mencius and other followers

The Confucian tradition was adopted in the fourth century BC by another revered teacher, Master Meng, or Mencius, who proclaimed that *'since man came into this world, there has never been one greater than Confucius'*. Supposedly taught by Confucius's grandson, he was another itinerant scholar who insisted that *'human nature is disposed towards goodness, just as water tends to flow downwards. All men have a mind which cannot bear to see the sufferings of others'*.

This brought him into conflict with another eminent Confucian, Xun Zi, who thought that

human nature was inherently evil and that *'goodness is the result of conscious activity'*. The great task for the superior man was, therefore, to evolve towards goodness through learning and proper conduct; for Xun *'the sage is the man who has cultivated himself'* – the model for scholar-officials who served the dynasties through the centuries. Such disputes aside, Mencius added an important element to the Confucian creed by arguing that, when rulers behaved badly, revolt could be justified. This provided what the historian John Harrison has termed the 'escape valve' of Confucianism and the theory of the Mandate of Heaven.

Harmonious society

Though it faced periodic rejection by rulers who preferred Buddhism or resented the authority of the scholarly élite, the appeal of Confucianism to the dynasties which ruled China and to the official and gentry classes that supported them was obvious. Two-and-a-half millennia after the life of the sage (and four decades after Red Guards sacked the sage's ancestral home in Shandong) the 'harmonious society' proclaimed as his target by China's president, Hu Jintao, lays out Confucian themes for the early 21st century.

'When asked about the good man, the Master answered, "He moves others. What you do not like about yourself, do not do to others. The good man, wishing himself to stand helps others to stand, wishing himself to arrive helps others to arrive; the ability to recognize the parallel to one's own case may be called the secret to goodness".'
CONFUCIUS, ANALECTS

A statue of Confucius, the father of an ideology that would become official Chinese doctrine long after his death.

THE FIRST EMPEROR AND THE QIN DYNASTY

221–207 BC

The man who unified China as its first true emperor, Qin Shi Huangdi, is depicted in portraits made well after his death as a dominating figure, a full-faced, bearded man with intensely staring eyes and thick eyebrows. A true totalitarian characterized by a fearful efficiency and determination, he established his power nationally with a series of victories that ended the tumult of the Period of the Warring States. He would be vilified by subsequent dynasties for his tyrannical ways, but he remained the lodestone for imperial rule, a man who epitomized China and the power needed to rule it.

OFFICIALLY, SHI HUANGDI WAS THE SON OF KING ZHUANGXIANG OF QIN, WHICH LAY ON THE western edge of a belt of kingdoms in central eastern China. The early Chinese historian Sima Qian (see The Historian Sima Qian, page 50) tells a different story, according to which his mother was a concubine of a rich merchant, Lü Buwei, in a neighbouring kingdom; his father may have been either the merchant or Prince Zi Chu, a son of Zhuangxiang, who had been sent there as a hostage and had taken up with the concubine. Sima was writing under the subsequent Han dynasty, and this may simply have been anti-Qin propaganda, but the tale is symptomatic of a period during which sexual intrigues played a considerable role in court affairs.

After Zi Chu's death in 247 BC, his son (the future Shi Huangdi) assumed the throne the following year, aged 13, under the name of Zheng. At this time the merchant moved to the Qin domain to become prime minister and took the title Duke Wenxinn. (See Lü Buwei's Quest for the Son of Heaven, page 38.) He resumed his relationship with the concubine who may have been Zheng's mother. Their affair became a court scandal, and the prime minister tried to divert attention by setting up the queen mother with one of his servants, Lao Ai, who is noted in Chinese histories

RIGHT The First Emperor, Shi Huangdi, earned a reputation for brutality and political intolerance. However, his legacy was the creation of a strong administration and a unified realm, the Qin (pronounced 'Chin'), which would give the nation its name.

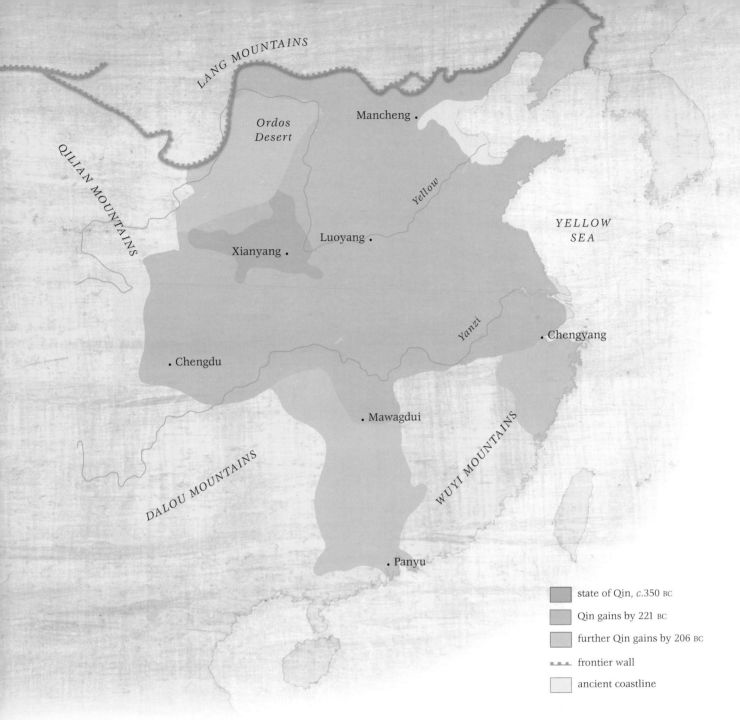

LANG MOUNTAINS

QILIAN MOUNTAINS

Ordos
Desert

Mancheng .

Yellow

Luoyang .

Xianyang .

YELLOW
SEA

Yanzi

. Chengyang

. Chengdu

. Mawagdui

WUYI MOUNTAINS

DALOU MOUNTAINS

. Panyu

state of Qin, *c.*350 BC

Qin gains by 221 BC

further Qin gains by 206 BC

frontier wall

ancient coastline

as having 'a large penis'. Forced into hiding, she had two children by the servant.
Zheng came to hear of the children and, fearing that Lao Ai was planning to usurp
the throne on behalf of one of them, had his mother banished. The children were
killed. Lao Ai and three generations of his family were executed.

Jealous of Lü Buwei's continuing popularity at court, Zheng ordered him to be
banished to the wilds of Sichuan in the west. To the people of central China, that
would have been a fate worse than death, so Lü drank poison. He was described by
Sima Qian as a 'man of notoriety' and was certainly a social climber, determined to
make himself even richer than when he first came into contact with the Qin. But he
also left behind a political testament that would enshrine the idea of a strong Son of
Heaven to bring order to China and the world.

ABOVE *Map of Qin
territories. In c.350 BC
the Qin kingdom was
limited to an area around
Chang'an in the
northwest; by the time
of the First Emperor's
death in 206 BC, the
Qin controlled all
of the central region
and a large section of
south-central China.*

A unified China

When he reached the age of 22 in 237 BC, Zheng took power into his own hands. As the Qin king, he set out to master the other six main kingdoms of central, northern and eastern China, most of which were bigger and stronger than his realm. But one by one he got the better of them. The Han kingdom conceded in 230 BC, Zhao in 228 BC, Wei in 225 BC, Chu in 223 BC, Yan in 222 BC and, finally, Qi in 221 BC.

There were several reasons for this success. The first was a strong army – an essential attribute in an age of constant military conflict. The way in which the Qin forces slaughtered prisoners and destroyed enemies *'like a silkworm eating a mulberry leaf'*, as an early chronicle put it, had the desired psychological effect of inducing enemies to give way. But there was more to it than sheer force and ruthlessness. The future First Emperor was skilled in diplomacy and adept at exploiting divisions among his adversaries. Crucially, he also forged a strong state, drawing on two major influences.

One was a shadowy figure from the previous century, Lord Shang. Unable to find a suitable post in his native state of Wei, he moved west to the more remote and poorer kingdom of Qin. There, under an ancestor of the First Emperor, Shang overhauled the system of government, building a strong centralized state underpinned by a harsh doctrine based on laws and punishment, known as legalism. (See Lord Shang's Legalism, page 37.) The rituals of Confucianism were discarded, and life was regulated by strict rules with prescribed rewards and punishments. For example, a person who reported a crime would receive the recompense given for killing an enemy in battle, while anybody who failed to inform the authorities of a misdemeanour would be chopped in half at the waist. A population register was drawn up, and inhabitants were divided into groups whose members would be collectively responsible if one among them committed a crime.

221 BC Qin Shi Huangdi becomes First Emperor. An estimated one million men work on the capital near Xianyang and begin construction of some 4700 miles (7500 km) of roads

214 BC Work begins on the Great Wall

213 BC The emperor decrees the burning of most books in an attempt to impose orthodox thought

210 BC Death of First Emperor; he is buried in a vast necropolis outside the capital with the Terracotta Army to guard him in the afterlife

210 BC Ershi Huangdi succeeds to the throne

207–206 BC Ershi is overthrown by the powerful eunuch-official, Zhao Gao, who puts a new emperor on the throne

206 BC The new ruler's reign lasts for 46 days. A rebel general has all the Qin family killed. Civil warfare breaks out

Murder attempts

More positively, Shang's policies included the promotion of farming and the allocation of land to those who had given military service. Promotion was by merit rather than birth. This, together with the imposition of central rule, alienated the aristocracy and, when the king who had backed him died, Shang could not survive. Sentenced to death for rebellion, he tried to go into hiding but was apparently refused refuge in a hotel under his own law forbidding the granting of lodgings to unregistered guests. He was caught in 338 BC and torn apart between chariots, but his ideas would live on to be taken up by the future first Qin emperor.

ASSASSINATION ATTEMPT *'When the Map is Unrolled, the Dagger is Revealed'*. This Chinese saying has its origins in an attempt to kill the future First Emperor by an assassin dispatched by the king of the rival state of Yan, which Zheng was poised to attack.

The killer, Jing Ke, was himself a native of another of the warring states, the kingdom of Wei. He gained admission to the Qin court by claiming he had a map that could be used in the campaign against Yan. Concealed inside was a dagger. As the map was unrolled, the would-be assassin grabbed the knife, but the monarch dived out of the way just in time. Jing then threw the weapon, but it hit a pillar. In the end, the assassin was stabbed to death with eight thrusts by the future emperor. This story was brought to the cinema screen in a dramatic film by Chinese director Chen Kaige in 1998.

The second important influence on the First Emperor was Li Si, a man who rose from humble origins in the kingdom of Chu to the south, studied under a Confucian philosopher and then moved to Qin, where he arrived in 247 BC in time for the coronation of the new king. Li introduced to Qin policy the 'carrot' to accompany the 'stick' of legalism. This enabled the state to mobilize its population more effectively than its neighbours could and, through propaganda, to convince its people that they were working for the greater good. Immigrants from other kingdoms were attracted by offers of land and exemption from military service. As the Qin domain expanded, the authority of the ruling groups in the newly acquired territories was undermined by the removal of inhabitants to new areas. There they were given farms and were required to pay taxes to the new masters and to do military service for the central government rather than for their local lords.

While Zheng expanded his domains, there were at least four attempts on his life. The most famous was by a native of the kingdom of Wei, Jing Ke, who was sent by the ruler of Yan, a region to the northwest, stretching from what was later Manchuria to present-day Beijing. (See Assassination Attempt, above.)

A strong state

Having completed his conquests, Zheng proclaimed himself emperor in 221 BC, adopting the reign name of Shi Huangdi – First August Emperor – and proclaiming that *'all six corners of the earth belong to the August Emperor'*. The defeated kings and their families were obliged to move to his capital of Xianyang, near present-day Xi'an. As the father of more than 20 children, he was convinced that his dynasty would rule for *'endless generations'*.

The policies he pursued and his relentless application of the legalist philosophy have led to the First Emperor being seen simply as a terrible despot who buried scholars alive, burned books and imposed a draconian militarized regime. Others, such as China's Communist leader Mao Zedong (Mao Tse-tung; 1893–1976), looked back to him as a model figure who sowed the seeds for China's greatness. The truth, as so often, lies somewhere in between, and it should be remembered that personal liberty had never been a feature of previous kingdoms. The First Emperor was simply more efficient than his predecessors and peers at running a dictatorship.

QIN DYNASTY EMPERORS

Qin Shi Huangdi	221–210 BC
Ershi Huangdi	210–207/206 BC

The repressive nature of the regime is not in doubt, nor is the importance of the army. Forced labour was used on a mass scale to expand agriculture, but this increased the supply of food. Other measures to strengthen the state brought material progress. Transport and infrastructure were developed: 5000 miles (8000 km) of roads, three lanes wide, were constructed, lined with trees for shade. The middle lane was reserved for imperial vehicles, and a standard width was set for cart and carriage axles so that they would all fit into the ruts on the highways. Major building projects included the first stretch of the Great Wall. (See The Great Wall of China, pages 60–1.) Centralization brought standardized weights and measures and a common, simplified writing system, all of which helped to drive economic progress.

The emperor's subjects were instructed to engage in productive occupations such as farming, construction or handicrafts rather than wasting their efforts on commerce or intellectual pursuits. A particularly striking form of propaganda was undertaken by carving Qin's edicts on mountain rock faces. The walls of cities were torn down to deprive them of their separate identities. The population was

BELOW *This painted horse-drawn chariot – one of two found in the First Emperor's underground mausoleum outside present-day Xi'an – is the largest bronze artefact uncovered anywhere in the world.*

classified into 20 grades. People were ordered to hand over their weapons, which were then melted down and used to cast huge bells and figures that would stand in the courtyard of the imperial palace.

On Li Si's advice, a system of magistrates reporting directly to the throne was instituted, replacing the old policy by which regional power was devolved to members of the ruling family and victorious warriors. These officials were sent from other parts of the empire and therefore had no local links, starting a bureaucratic practice that would last to the end of the empire in AD 1912. Thus the Qin empire was split into 36 commanderies, sub-divided into counties, all ruled by non-hereditary magistrates.

The new empire looked north and south – north to defend itself against the nomads of the steppes and south for further expansion. A veteran general, Meng Tian (who had fought the Han, Zhao and Chu), was entrusted with the task of defending the northern borders, reportedly employing 300,000 labourers to build fortifications. Moving through the former Chu domains to the south, in present-day Hunan, the empire annexed the kingdom of Nanyue in today's Guangdong province, which was viewed by the northerners as dangerous, disease-ridden barbarian territory. Little is known of the Qin presence there, but it is a fair bet that the empire's control was tenuous and that its settled southern border lay on the edge of the former Chu lands in what are now Hunan, Jiangxi and Zhejiang provinces.

Immortality, madness and the afterlife

As he grew older, the emperor became increasingly obsessed with the search for immortality. A magician from the coast told him that if he kept away from other people he might find the elixir of everlasting life. The story, as written during a later dynasty, has Qin constructing 270 palaces, with harems of beautiful women. These buildings were linked by walls and roads covered with roofs. In that way, he would not have to show himself in public. The magician subsequently fled, accusing the emperor of cruelty and violence and apparently expressing doubt that anyone could, in fact, live forever. Qin was furious and ordered an investigation of the scholars with whom the wizard had consorted. As a result, 460 of them were killed; the term used subsequently to describe their fate has been interpreted to signify that they were buried alive, although it may simply have meant that they were executed. When his son objected, the dynast sent him away to join General Meng Tian in the north.

This alleged episode has heightened the First Emperor's reputation for evil (although it was used during the Cultural Revolution of 1966– 76 as evidence that he was a progressive figure who had struck at the élite establishment in the same way as Mao was trying to purge the Communist Party at the time). Recent scholars have cast

LORD SHANG'S LEGALISM

Lord Shang, an adviser to the Qin kings around 300 BC, laid down the doctrine that became known as legalism and would be adopted by the First Emperor as the basis for his rule. Its core lay in the recognition of the law as the central element in government. Lord Shang, who lived from about 390 to 338 BC, saw a strict system of punishment and reward as the only way to control the population.

'If you govern the people by punishment, the people will fear', his doctrine held. *'Being fearful, they will not commit villainies'*. He proposed a system of standards from which unbiased judgements could be drawn: *'The ancient kings understood that no reliance should be placed on individual opinions or biased approval, so they set up models and made the distinction clear'*.

Writing on bamboo strips found in the tomb of a Qin magistrate in Hubei province contains details of the punishments that were used to keep the people in fear.

The death penalty usually took the form of public beheading. Below this came mutilation of the feet or nose, imprisonment, banishment and hard labour, known as 'wall building' (*chengdan*).

Shang's harsh doctrine would be superseded by the more humane Confucianism (see Confucius and Confucianism, pages 28–9), but the idea of a system of punishments based on a central set of principles to control the population remained a potent theme in Chinese imperial history.

considerable doubt on the story, seeing it as a dramatic fiction conjured up to sully his name. As always, however, the nature of Qin's rule perhaps lends spurious veracity to the tale of the ruthless ruler descending into paranoia.

Having achieved so much, he certainly appears to have thought he could cheat death. Two more assassination attempts led him in 210 BC to send a servant, Xu Shi, on a mission to find the legendary islands of Penglai, purported to be the home of the immortal spirits, so that he could share in their secret. Xu Shi was never heard from again – reports came back that he had been swallowed by a giant whale. Around 212 BC Qin made a trip to a holy mountain in eastern China to plead with the gods for immortality. Advisers told him he would prolong his life if he took mercury tablets; the effect appears to have been to heighten his paranoia and rages. He then had a dream which led him to go to the coast to hunt for a mythical fish whose death could help him to remain alive. On his way back to the capital he fell into a high fever and, his condition weakened by the mercury pills that were supposed to prolong life, died in 210 BC.

Dynasty's end

As the First Emperor lay dying, his chief minister, Li Si, and the head eunuch, Zhao Gao, who controlled the dispatch of imperial messages, formulated a plan to seize power. Qin had written instructions that his first-born son, Fu Su, was to succeed him, despite having sent him off to the north for disagreeing with him over his repressive ways. Instead, Li and Zhao plotted the rise of the younger, controllable second son, the dissolute Hu Hai. To achieve their goal, they kept Qin's death secret – the foul

LEFT *The Qin empire established an administrative system that would survive for 1000 years. This sancai-glazed pottery figure, with its characteristic three-colour glaze of cream, green and amber, is of an official from the Tang era.*

LÜ BUWEI'S QUEST FOR THE SON OF HEAVEN

The *Annals of Lü Buwei* (*Lüshi Chunqiu*), compiled by a large team of scholars around 240 BC, set out the philosophical basis on which the Chinese empire would rest for more than two millennia. It was drawn up for the prime minister of the realm of Qin, who gave it its name. Dealing with philosophy, customs and political theory, it was so concisely written that Lü offered a large prize of gold to anyone who could add or subtract a single character from the text.

The main theme of the work is the idea of governing through wise officials in an attempt to recreate a 'golden age' of sage kings and a united, peaceful world. The contemporary world was seen as a bad time in which *'the position of the Son of Heaven has been abolished and the worthies have been cast down'*. The answer was held to be a strong leader who would pacify the world, assuming the Mandate of Heaven. (See page 20.)

'No disorder is worse than lacking a Son of Heaven, for, when there is no Son of Heaven, there is no end to the strong conquering the weak, the many tyrannizing the few and armies destroying people', the text argues, adding that the leader would maintain power through balancing the cosmic order. This would be achieved by choosing the correct colour and element symbol for the dynasty, according to the cosmic cycle purported to have been employed by the Sage Kings of Antiquity.

Its precepts were just what the Qin ruler enacted a few years later when his armies moved beyond their kingdom to defeat the other main realms, and subsequently established the first real dynasty under the Son of Heaven. The irony was that, by then, Lü had fallen from his master's favour and had poisoned himself.

smell emanating from the cart in which the corpse was brought back to Xi'an was attributed to rotten fish. Li and Zhao forged a letter said to come from the late ruler, accusing Fu of disloyalty and telling him to commit suicide, which he promptly did. General Meng Tian also received the same order, but refused to obey and later died in prison. Another forgery proclaimed Hu Hai as the late ruler's preferred successor.

Qin was buried in the vast mausoleum he had constructed for himself outside his capital, surrounded by valuables and guarded by serried ranks of terracotta warriors. (See The Terracotta Army, pages 40–1.) Hu Hai became the August Emperor of the Second Generation (Ershi Huangdi), but real power lay with Li and Zhao.

The Second Emperor fell increasingly under the influence of the eunuch. He tightened the laws even further, and is alleged to have had several siblings killed. Li Si was also executed, cut in half at the waist after being mutilated. Factionalism spread through the court, and dynastic decline set in within a couple of years of the founder's death. The system the First Emperor had instituted needed an extremely strong figure at the helm, which Ershi was not. Its policies had stirred up deep and widespread alienation. Peasants suffered from high taxation, military conscription and forced labour. Noble families were angry at the loss of their privileges and power, and the regime had few friends. In 207 BC a general from one of these families raised an army in revolt. Other uprisings followed.

After the execution of Li Si, Zhao became chief minister. In 207 BC the eunuch tested his authority by parading a deer at court, saying it was a horse. Most of those present agreed with him out of fear. But the emperor believed himself to be suffering from delusion and went into retreat at an isolated palace. The chief minister sent in troops disguised as bandit rebels. In the affray that followed, Ershi was killed – the accepted account is that he killed himself.

In his place, Zhao installed a grandson of the First Emperor on the throne. Significantly, in view of the rising tide of revolts, he was given the title of king, not emperor. He showed no gratitude to the eunuch for the poisoned chalice he had been handed. A few days after his coronation, he pretended to be ill. When the chief minister visited him, the young king either stabbed him to death himself or had him killed by one of his attendants. Six weeks later, a rebel army surrounded Xianyang and the king had to surrender. His life was spared, but not for long. Another rebel general took him prisoner and either forced him and his relatives to commit suicide or had them beheaded. The capital was burned down.

BELOW *The mountainous islands of Penglai were believed by ancient Chinese magicians to be the home of spirits who held the secret of immortality. A real island named Penglai, pictured here, lies in the East China Sea in Shandong province.*

So it was that the Qin came to an end after seven centuries of rule as kings and just 14 years as emperors. A subsequent Confucian writer would judge that the empire fell *'because it failed to display humanity and righteousness, or to realize that there is a difference between the power to attack and the power to consolidate'*. A simpler reason may be that the First Emperor simply tried to do too much too fast. In a few years his realm went from being a kingdom on the edge of what the Chinese regarded as the rest of the world to an empire encompassing eight kingdoms. For all the machinery of state power, it was always under strain, unable to relax or lift its oppression. For all that, it bequeathed vital principles for succeeding dynasties, notably those of unity, centralization and a bureaucratic structure independent of feudal lords. The idea of the Chinese empire had been implanted and would, with some major interruptions, last for 2100 years.

THE TERRACOTTA ARMY

Having established his dynasty and his own position as the First Emperor of a united China, Shi Huangdi needed an appropriate retinue to accompany him into the afterlife. A vast necropolis was built near the Qin capital Chang'an (near modern Xi'an). Work began long before the emperor's death and involved the mobilization of hundreds of thousands of workers.

On his death, the ruler himself was entombed in a 350-square-metre (3800-sq-ft) pyramid surrounded by ancillary buildings that replicated the centre of imperial administration. The workers who completed the project are believed to have been shut up inside the tomb when it was finished in order that the secret it held should not be revealed.

In 1974, a farmer drilling for water broke into a vast underground chamber which was found to contain serried ranks of figures representing soldiers in terracotta – an 8000-strong, life-sized bodyguard. The figures had been made in local workshops on assembly-line principles, with different parts mass-manufactured and then put together; but each individual soldier was given different features. They were then placed in a great wooden barn in military formations that reflected their real-life ranks and specializations.

Evidence of grave robbers

Originally, the soldiers carried authentic weapons, but these were stolen by tomb raiders. According to the Han-era historian, Sima Qian (see The Historian Sima Qian, page 50), a general, Xiang Yu, pillaged the tomb complex during the instability that followed the ruler's death, setting off a fire which burned down the wooden structure housing the terracotta troops. The blaze, he added, went on for three months. But the figures survived, though some were damaged and most lost their original colouring.

The warriors represent only a small part of the elaborate preparations to ensure that the First Emperor of China could continue to operate in the netherworld. Some other tombs have been excavated, revealing further treasures. But the emperor's own final resting place has not been disturbed; tradition holds that it is covered with booby traps. On the floor of the innermost room, there is said to be a map of China, with mercury representing the rivers and seas. An investigation with remote sensors has shown that the main pyramid contains a construction that is 30 metres (90 ft) tall, with four walls, each of which has nine steps. These, it is thought, were for the First Emperor to start his ascent to heaven from earthly life.

Around 2 million people visit the famous 'terracotta warriors' each year. Concerns have been raised in recent times about the effect on the figures of exposure to the air and of industrial pollution, but officials insist there is no danger of deterioration.

RIGHT *Standing in battle formation, 11 columns of life-sized terracotta foot soldiers guard the tomb of the First Emperor. The figures, each with a distinctive face, are thought to have been modelled on real soldiers.*

THE WESTERN HAN

206 BC—AD 9

The Han was the longest-lived imperial dynasty. As heir to the founding house of Qin, it developed the nature of rule over four centuries. Its 24 emperors re-unified China after the divisions caused by the toppling of the Qin, enlisted the support of the scholar class and embedded the template for empire on Confucian principles before crashing to disaster.

THE DYNASTY IS DIVIDED INTO TWO DISTINCT PERIODS – THE WESTERN HAN AND THE EASTERN HAN, their names stemming from the geographical location of their capitals – interrupted by a brief inter-regnum.

The Han dynasty was founded by a sharp, impressive-looking peasant, Liu Bang, who raised an army of 3000 men to fight the oppression of the later Qin. He would go down as a major figure in China's collective consciousness. This was a period in time when history seemed to have been turned on its head. No sooner had the Qin empire put an end to the chaos of the Warring States era than China once more descended into mayhem. In the end, Liu would win the throne after battles, intrigues and feuds between the house of Han and that of Chu, led by the tall and striking Xiang Yu. First, brutal wars had to be fought, for which it is necessary to return to the last days of the first dynasty.

Attacks on the Qin

As revolts against the Qin spread, Liu Bang and his army linked up with other rebel groups in 208 BC. Smaller kingdoms, such as Yan and Qi, declared their independence. The crucial moment came in a confrontation at the city of Julu in the heart of the north-western kingdom of Zhao, which lay on a key artery connecting the Qin heartland in Shaanxi with the plains of central and eastern China.

Another king, of Chu, sent his best general, Song Yi, to the campaign; he was not up to the task and was murdered by Xiang Yu, who declared himself the overall commander of the entire anti-Qin forces in 207 BC. At the same time, the Chu monarch sent Liu Bang through the difficult mountain passes into Shaanxi to attack the Qin stronghold. Riven by internal feuds, the failing imperial household was in no state to respond. The emperor surrendered to Liu in the tenth month of 206 BC, and

RIGHT *Gaodi, the founder of the Han dynasty, from an 18th-century album of portraits depicting Chinese emperors. A peasant by birth, Liu Bang emerged to take control of China after a period of civil war following the death of the First Emperor.*

his life was spared. But within two months of Liu's victory, Xiang Yu arrived at the Qin capital and had the surviving members of the imperial house exterminated, the royal palace burned to the ground and the monuments to the first Qin emperor vandalized. In a bid to satisfy the local leaders, he divided China into small kingdoms. What he was suggesting was a return to 18 kingdoms of ancient times, with his own serving as a hegemonic overseer. He ordered the assassination of the king of Chu and took the title 'Protector of the Western Chu'. Liu Bang was made king of Han.

Liu was not going to be bought off, however. He could raise support among those who objected to Xiang's execution of the Chu king. He also had grounds to complain that Xiang had denied him his right to the sacred Qin heartland in the passes of Shaanxi to which – as the first general to have entered them – he was entitled. So, in 206 BC, Liu set out to destroy Xiang and make himself ruler of China.

His campaign went well at first as he took mountain passes into Shaanxi and used the pretext of avenging the Chu king's death to attack Xiang's capital, Pengcheng. But he suffered a crushing defeat outside the city and was only able to escape thanks to a storm. Still, he held on and mustered superior forces. After three years of cat-and-mouse battles and tactical retreats on both sides, the final showdown came. With few followers left, Xiang was finally beaten and committed suicide in 202 BC.

> If any of the princes or governors discovers a man of talent and virtue in his jurisdiction, he should personally invite him to serve the government ... An official who knows a virtuous man within his jurisdiction and choose not to report it shall lose his position.
>
> EMPEROR GAODI, 195 BC

The new emperor

Liu was enthroned as the first Han emperor, under the reign name of Gaodi. He was still a peasant at heart, speaking in a rough accent and using countryside expressions. On one occasion he showed his disdain for a group of scholars by urinating in a hat belonging to one of them. His humble roots provided a dynamism and established a tradition of popular culture that lent vitality to the arts and, behind the façade of rituals and rotes, to court life.

The new ruler was perceptive and appears to have chosen his subordinates well. He had shown his charisma early on during his peasant days in winning his bride. At the time he was so poor that he could not afford to buy a place at table for a village banquet. A fortune-teller who predicted people's future from their facial appearance took one look at Liu's face – shown in subsequent portraits as well rounded with a broad forehead and deep, piercing eyes – and gave him his daughter in marriage.

Liu understood the importance of the past, inaugurating rituals that harked back to the ancient Zhou rulers, who had first proclaimed themselves Sons of Heaven. He also grasped the limits of the harsh Qin legalistic system and introduced what came to be known as Han Confucianism. This rested on the idea that successful rule depended on consent. As the saying went, '*An empire can be conquered on horseback, but cannot be governed from a horse*'. The old laws were not abolished as fully as the new ruler initially promised – they were too useful in ensuring law and

order and keeping the regime together. But the philosophy underlying the empire and some of its practices shifted significantly; fines were substituted for some physical punishments, and the most gruesome forms of execution were abolished. In the words of the historian Sima Qian (see The Historian Sima Qian, page 50), the Han 'lopped off the harsh corners of the Qin code and retreated to an easy roundness, whittled away the embellishments, and achieved simplicity'.

To ensure the continuation of the Han after the short-lived experience of the Qin, Gaodi proclaimed that no-one outside his family could inherit the throne. He sent his sons and commanders, who had won the battles of the previous three years, to rule

'The Way brings forth law. Law is the mark that indicates success and failure, and distinguishes the crooked from the straight. Therefore, one who holds fast to the Way can produce laws but does not dare to transgress them.'

FROM *THE CLASSIC OF LAW* DISCOVERED IN A SECOND-CENTURY-BC TOMB

ABOVE *Detail of a
12th-century painting
showing the first emperor
of the Han dynasty,
Gaodi, with his
entourage in the
mountains. The Han
dynasty lasted for over
400 years and is
regarded as one of the
golden periods in
Chinese history.*

regions that stretched over two-thirds of China, hoping to establish a loyal group of powerful subordinates. Only the third of the imperial territory around the capital of Chang'an remained under his direct rule. (See Chang'an – Capital of the Western Han, page 59.) This meant dividing China into many different fiefdoms, leading to the re-awakening of regional power that the Qin had sought to suppress. The idea was that by creating many different kingships for his sons and local barons, the emperor could count on them to defend China against foreign powers. But if he sought security in this manner, he was disappointed. His life was threatened on a number of occasions – in 199 BC, for example, he narrowly avoided being assassinated by a minister from the kingdom of Zhao.

Northern raiders

Perhaps his greatest challenge came in the shape of the Xiongnu (sometimes referred to as Huns), a confederation of semi-nomadic people from the steppes in what is now Mongolia. The imperial assumption had been that, while they represented a threat, these northerners could be kept at bay by an array of well-chosen kings to control the land bordering their steppes. This assumption was sundered after one of these Chinese kings surrendered.

Thus began a long period when, despite repeated attempts by the empire to confront the threat either with force or by means of treaties, it was at the mercy of raids from the north. Han attempts to confront the nomad cavalry in battle often failed, as Gaodi found out in 201 BC when he nearly paid with his life in one clash. Soon after that, his government adopted the tribute method of keeping the *'barbarians from the gates'*.

The system of *heqin* (harmonious kinship), in which a Han princess was married off to a Xiongnu chief every time a new *shanyu* (khan) came to the throne, was established; in the winter of 198 BC, Gaodi's minister Liu Jing escorted the first of many of these princesses to the far north with the required gifts of silk, wine, rice and other luxuries.

Restoring order

Within his domains, Gaodi concentrated on rebuilding the empire and its economy after the damage done by the wars following the fall of the Qin. Life generally improved, particularly for the élite. (See Food for the Afterlife, page 49.) He himself lived simply and set an example. While complicated rituals evoking the past were celebrated, ostentation was discouraged – merchants, who ranked at the bottom of the Confucian social scale, were forbidden to wear silks or to ride in carriages. The ambitious infrastructure projects of the First Emperor were not repeated. As a man from the countryside, Gaodi looked to rural gentlemen farmers – the gentry – to supply administrators and to support the empire at the grass roots.

In 195 BC the ruler showed that he was still a man of action by participating in a minor frontier war. He was hit by a stray arrow, and died. He had instructed that the throne should pass not to his eldest son, who had been born to his first wife, the daughter of the fortune-teller, but to Ruyi, a son by his second wife. That decision set off a power struggle within the new dynasty, and the emergence of the first of a series of powerful women who defied the low status usually accorded to their gender to rule as regents and dowagers.

Empress Lü and the struggle for power

Less than a year after Gaodi's death his first wife, Empress Lü, made her bid for power. It was violent and effective. Firstly, she hushed up news of the death of her husband to give herself time to prepare. His chosen heir, Ruyi, was poisoned, and Ruyi's mother is said to have had her arms and legs chopped off and been blinded before being thrown into a pigsty to die. Lü called in her own son to witness the plight of her rival, terrifying him into submission to her wishes thereafter. She then had Gaodi's succession command altered in favour of her son, who duly ascended the throne as Emperor Huidi in 195 BC at the age of 15.

> ❛ Only to teach men and not to teach women – is that not ignoring the essential relation between them? According to the Rites, it is the rule to begin to teach children to read at the age of eight years, and, by the age of 15, they ought to be ready for cultural training. Why should it not be that girls' education as well as boys' be according to this principle? ❜
>
> WOMAN SCHOLAR BAN ZHAO, FIRST CENTURY AD

The horrific scenes his mother had shown him evidently worked because, after he reached maturity at the age of 19, the already docile young emperor remained under her thumb. During his reign, the presence of the dynasty was asserted throughout the empire by the erection of shrines to the first Han ruler. Huge fortifications were also put up around Chang'an. The work took five years and was carried out by gangs of up to 150,000 people. Huidi died in 188 BC, aged 23. No foul play was suspected.

Dominating the court, the dowager empress Lü arranged for an infant, Shaodi Kong, to be installed on the throne; when he died, she followed him with another child,

ABOVE *The early years of the Han dynasty were considered to be a 'golden age', in which the arts flourished. Craftsmen made jade jewellery and carvings, and the élite wore fine clothes with gold ornamentation, such as this gilded belt hook.*

Shaodi Hong. In this way she was able to act as regent for eight years. She urged the Chinese to *'recuperate and multiply'* after the warfare they had suffered, but her own vicious streak was always apparent as she toppled subordinate rulers, having two kings of Zhao killed and replacing ministers at court with her own appointees. She issued documents under her own name, stamped with a jade seal bearing characters usually reserved for an emperor. She increased the power of her clan by having relations married into the imperial family, and distributed perks to nobles to keep them quiet. Before her death, she made six of her kinsmen marquises, contrary to Gaodi's original ruling that no-one outside the Liu family could hold noble rank.

The dowager has been blamed for the deaths of four princes whose claims to rule were more legitimate than hers, although as always these accounts may have been motivated by writers under subsequent rulers who wanted to paint Lü in the worst possible light. To buttress state power, she established centralized law courts and sought to protect the country by strengthening the Great Wall. As a widow, she attracted a proposition of marriage from a Xiongnu ruler which she rejected, but her plea for China to be spared by the nomads showed how vulnerable the Han felt.

For all Lü's ruthlessness, her period of power saw a dramatic weakening of China at the hands of neighbouring states. Not only did the Xiongnu encroach on territory in the Gansu corridor of the northwest, but there was also a big rising of the Nanyue people in the southern delta region. Their leader, Zhao Tuo, even set himself up as an emperor on his own, and moved out of his remote southern region to attack present-day Hunan.

Wendi and Jingdi

The death of Empress Lü in 180 BC led to uprisings by representatives of the three surviving strands of Liu Bang's original royal grouping: Qi, Huainan and Dai. The king of Qi took the initiative by attacking the imperial capital. The battle was

'I am a lonely widowed ruler, born amidst the marshes and brought up on the wild steppes of the land of cattle and horses. I have often come to the border wishing to travel in China. Your majesty is also a widowed ruler living a life of solitude. Both of us are without pleasure and lack any way to amuse ourselves. It is my hope that we can exchange that which we have for that which we are lacking.'

XIONGNU NOMAD RULER TO EMPRESS LÜ, LATE SECOND CENTURY BC

FOOD FOR THE AFTERLIFE Relics and records found in the
tomb of Lady Li, wife of an early noble under the Han dynasty, give a unique insight
into what the élite ate in this period of imperial history. The tomb inventory lists the
food and drink she would enjoy in the afterlife.

The principal dish for well-off people was a stew of meat and vegetables cooked to the consistency of a thick soup. Possible ingredients included beef, deer, dog meat, rice and celery. This dish could be prepared in 13 different ways, the meat being carefully cut into perfectly square cubes. Remains of rice, wheat, barley, millet, red beans and soybeans were found in the tomb. There were also two kinds of beer, varying in alcoholic strength.

Although meat figures prominently in Lady Li's posthumous diet, most people in China at the time had to make do with rice or wheat with other vegetables.

something of a non-event, with no-one having much of a stomach for a fight. What counted was the succession decision that would follow. Their experience of Lü led people to oppose the king of Qi, whose mother was thought to be too influential. The king of Huainan also had a forceful mother and was still a minor. That left the king of Dai, Liu Heng, who became emperor under the reign name of Wendi, apparently without any major disagreement from the other potential candidates. Wendi's time on the throne, from 180 to 157 BC, has been remembered for its stability. He was the first Han to occupy the throne for longer than ten years, and so was able to consolidate power. His 23-year reign and the peaceful accession of his son Jingdi, who would rule for another 16 years, spared China yet another succession crisis.

Economic development allowed taxes to be cut. Farmers were given financial incentives to encourage output. An early history of the Han reported that grain depositaries were full and that the state treasury *'had surpluses of wealth of all kinds'*. Disaster relief schemes were instituted. Imperial spending was reduced, although excavation of the royal tombs has shown that the dead were not stinted but were sent into the afterlife with a dazzling array of gold, jade and bronze objects, the finest silks, and terracotta armies modelled on the one that guarded the spirit of the First Emperor.

Some of the harshest laws were abolished, such as the one which dictated that the entire family of a criminal had to be punished along with him. But legalism still remained strong as an underlying force for the regime. (See Modernizers versus Reformers, page 73.) Other Qin practices, such as conscription and the use of mass forced labour, also continued.

There were recurrent raids by northern nomads, one of which got to within 80 miles (130 km) of the capital, but the big southern rising ended after an imperial envoy persuaded its leader to submit and declare himself a subject of the Han. Confucianism took deeper root, and the counsel of ministers trained in the ancient texts was heeded by the ruler. The Taoist system of geomancy was introduced to court under the influence of the empress Dou, one of its most famous practitioners.

THE HISTORIAN SIMA QIAN

Our knowledge of early imperial China would have been far poorer had a Han court historian by the name of Sima Qian (*c.*145–90 BC) followed the conventions of the time and killed himself rather than suffering castration after being found guilty of treason.

Born to a low-ranking noble family in present-day Sichuan, Sima Qian attracted attention for his fine poetry. He followed his father's work as a historian and astrologer under the rule of Emperor Wudi, travelling widely to collect information about the past. He was a diabetic and he created a stir by running off with the recently widowed daughter of one of the richest businessmen in China. Disgraced, the couple was reduced to poverty, but her father finally relented and gave them large sums of money.

Sima showed his free-thinking spirit once again by daring to defend a general, Li Ling, who had been condemned for his surrender and defeat in an expedition to the north. This was taken to be an attack on the imperial family, and Sima was sentenced either to pay a large fine – for which he did not have the money – or to be castrated. The tradition was that, rather than suffer such humiliation, a man of his class should commit suicide. But Sima decided to accept the punishment and, as he put it, '*cling to life, burying myself in filth without protest*',

ABOVE *Sima Qian was historian and astrologer to the emperor. This illustration of Sima is taken from the Chinese encyclopedia* Illustrations of the Three Powers, *first published in 1609.*

because he was determined to finish his historical work.

'*If it may be handed down to men who will appreciate it, and penetrate to the villages and great cities, then, though I should suffer a thousand mutilations, what regret should I have?*'

The resulting text, running to half a million characters, was written privately, but became the main source of information on the development of China up to the first century BC. As well as the narrative, which is brought alive with anecdotes and character sketches, it contains a wealth of tables, charts, calendars, economic information and accounts of rituals.

The politics of the time intruded, since the Han wished to depict themselves as the greatest of Chinese rulers, and Sima was no doubt aware of the need to 'spin' his accounts accordingly. But without him we would be far more dependent on archaeological discoveries and we would be robbed of vivid first-hand sketches of the protagonists of the early empire and their deeds.

These 39 years under Wendi and Jingdi have gone down in imperial history as a kind of golden age after all the upheavals which preceded them.

Revolt and reaction

However, during his boyhood, Jingdi had made a determined enemy. When he was about eight years old, he had been playing a game with the young son of the ruler of Wu, one of the subordinate kingdoms of the empire. An argument broke out between them and the imperial heir grabbed a floorboard and bludgeoned the other boy to death. The king of Wu waited until Jingdi had been on the throne for three years before launching a revolt in 154 BC from his domain on the east coast (in present-day Zhejiang and Fujian). He enlisted the support of six other kings and drew on strong separatist sentiment in his home region. But the central power was ready, and the rising was soon put down.

Grabbing his chance to assert central power, Jingdi divided up the old kingdoms and placed 14 of his young (and easily controllable) sons in charge of the reduced territories. Then, in 145 BC, he stripped the highest ministers in all the kingdoms of much of their power and abolished many other posts. The kingdoms became shadows of their former selves. Some of their ruling families died out, and sons of the Han moved in to take control.

Wudi

When Jingdi died in 141 BC, the throne was taken by the last of the great Western Han emperors whose long reign lasting to 87 BC would encapsulate, in a single life, the cycle of rise and fall usually attributed to whole dynasties. At the peak of his power, Liu Che, who took the reign name of Wudi, was powerful enough to proclaim a 'Grand Beginning' from which years were counted. A dozen years later, he was forced to flee his capital as enemies of his wife attacked. Great though his achievements were, his death was followed by a century in which seven successive emperors sat on the throne, and the Western Han went into a decline that ushered in a new but short-lived dynasty.

Wudi came to the Mandate of Heaven at the age of 15. Initially, power was exercised on his behalf by his uncle, the imperial chancellor, and the ardently Taoist dowager empress Dou. Her beliefs put her into conflict with Confucian officials, who urged the young man to sideline her. Dou mounted an investigation which came up with damning allegations that caused the ruler to sack two of the senior Confucians, who subsequently committed suicide. Dou then strongly promoted her creed as a unifying force for the country, getting the emperor to take part in a

206 BC Gaodi (Lui Bang) founds the Han dynasty

200 BC China is divided into 10 subordinate kingdoms and 15 commanderies

195 BC Gaodi is killed in a frontier war. Empress Lü begins her bid for power, which lasts effectively until 180 BC

180 BC Wendi ascends the throne

165 BC Introduction of written examinations for the civil service

141 BC Wudi takes the throne, reigning for 54 years

139 BC Imperial envoy Zhang Qian makes a 12-year expedition to Tibet and Central Asia. After this, the Silk Road trading route is developed

119 BC To pay for wars, imperial monopolies are established for salt and iron

104 BC A Chinese army marches as far west as the Ferghana Valley (present-day Uzbekistan)

100 BC A Chinese calendar is introduced, with 30- and 29-day months

87 BC Wudi dies, having named his eight-year-old son as heir

31 BC The emperor's title 'Son of Heaven' is officially promulgated

1 BC Wang Mang becomes regent and takes the throne in AD 9

particularly significant sacrifice to heaven on a holy mountain in eastern China. But her death in 135 BC checked the official propagation of Taoism, while the demise of the chancellor four years later left Wudi to exercise power on his own.

His 54-year reign buttressed the philosophy that underpinned the empire. (See Dong and the Single Cosmic System, page 55.) It was a period of enormous expansion for the empire. It was also marked by the pursuit of reforms, including strengthening the bureaucracy through the establishment of schools for civil servants and holding imperial examinations to select only the best and brightest of the land to become officials. Wudi encouraged efficient agriculture and undertook major infrastructure projects, including the repair of the Yellow River dykes and the building of an 80-mile (130-km) canal to bring grain to the capital of Chang'an.

The 'martial emperor'

Under Wudi, the throne pursued the idea that China's special role in the cosmos gave it a divine right to invade 'barbarian' territories, whose inhabitants needed to have the benefit of its civilizing imperial rule. Expressing this superiority, an edict from Wudi – which presents an early example of information spin that would be perpetuated across the millennia – proclaimed how he had *'pacified the world and spread peace throughout China'*. He then listed 'barbarians' who had striven to offer him tribute; *'stretching out their necks and raising up their ankles, they would gasp to compete to be loyal and righteous, all wishing to be my subjects and concubines, even though the road is long and the mountains are high'*. After this fanciful statement, a more realistic note entered the document as it stated, *'those who did not agree were executed'*.

ABOVE *An earthenware model bullock and cart. Agriculture prospered during the first century of Han rule, partly as a result of technological changes, such as the increased use of oxen and horses as draught animals.*

Despite his soubriquet of 'martial emperor', Wudi never accompanied his troops on their campaigns, but he was constantly seeking to expand his realm in all directions.

TRADE AND THE SILK ROADS The expansion of China under Emperor Wudi opened up international trading routes that passed through the deserts of central Asia and on to the Middle East.

A minister described goods from the northern frontiers coming into China on an unbroken line of mules, donkeys and camels all carrying furs, rugs, carpets and precious stones, and accompanied by prancing horses. Western products arrived along the routes that would come to be known as the Silk Roads.

'Foreign products keep flowing in while our national wealth is not dissipated', the minister added. *'National wealth is not being dispersed abroad, the people enjoy abundance'*. Orthodox Confucians, on the other hand, looked down on merchants, and regarded commerce as incitement to commit crime.

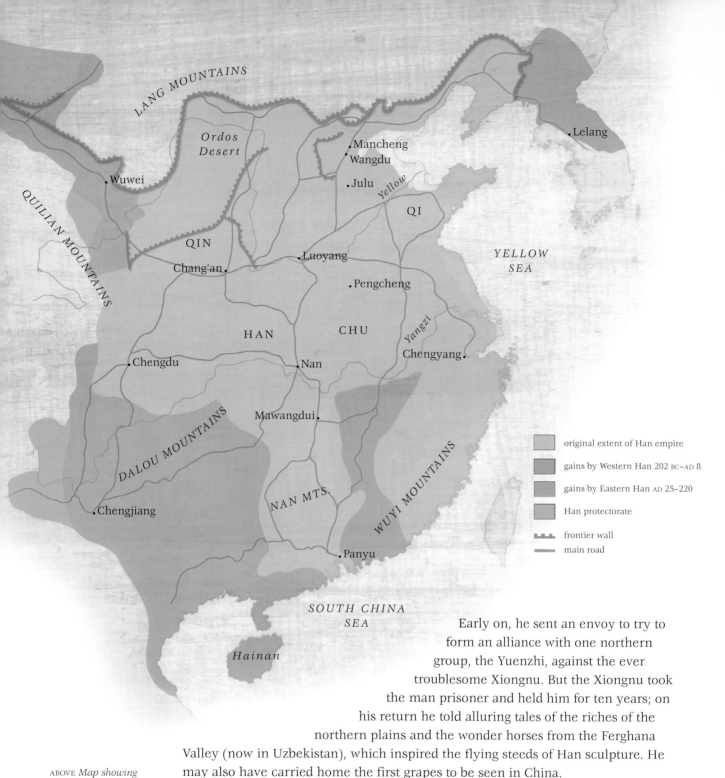

LANG MOUNTAINS

Ordos
Desert

QUILIAN MOUNTAINS

•Wuwei

•Mancheng
•Wangdu

•Julu

•Lelang

Yellow

QI

QIN

YELLOW
SEA

Chang'an •

•Luoyang

•Pengcheng

HAN

CHU

Yangzi

•Chengdu

•Nan

Chengyang•

DALOU MOUNTAINS

Mawangdui•

NAN MTS.

WUYI MOUNTAINS

•Chengjiang

•Panyu

SOUTH CHINA
SEA

Hainan

original extent of Han empire

gains by Western Han 202 BC–AD 8

gains by Eastern Han AD 25–220

Han protectorate

frontier wall

main road

Early on, he sent an envoy to try to form an alliance with one northern group, the Yuenzhi, against the ever troublesome Xiongnu. But the Xiongnu took the man prisoner and held him for ten years; on his return he told alluring tales of the riches of the northern plains and the wonder horses from the Ferghana Valley (now in Uzbekistan), which inspired the flying steeds of Han sculpture. He may also have carried home the first grapes to be seen in China.

To the south, Wudi dispatched forces to subdue vast tracts of territory that had previously been beyond Han rule, stretching down to the South China Sea and Vietnam. In the east, China conquered Korea. In the west, imperial forces took Gansu, which was colonized by 700,000 Chinese and protected by a new section of the Great Wall. Armies forged into the desert expanses of present-day Xinjiang and crossed the Pamir Mountains into Central Asia, reaching the former Greek kingdom of Sogdiana, where they won a battle 2000 miles (3200 km) from home against an army that included captured Roman soldiers.

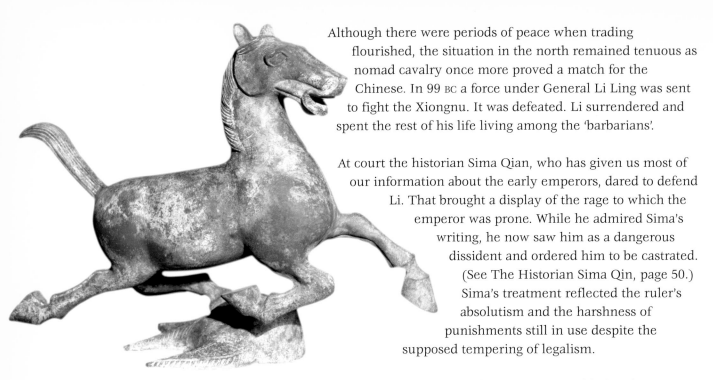

Although there were periods of peace when trading flourished, the situation in the north remained tenuous as nomad cavalry once more proved a match for the Chinese. In 99 BC a force under General Li Ling was sent to fight the Xiongnu. It was defeated. Li surrendered and spent the rest of his life living among the 'barbarians'.

At court the historian Sima Qian, who has given us most of our information about the early emperors, dared to defend Li. That brought a display of the rage to which the emperor was prone. While he admired Sima's writing, he now saw him as a dangerous dissident and ordered him to be castrated. (See The Historian Sima Qin, page 50.) Sima's treatment reflected the ruler's absolutism and the harshness of punishments still in use despite the supposed tempering of legalism.

ABOVE *Hearing reports from one of his generals of 'blood-sweating horses' from the western region of Ferghana, Wudi vowed to possess some of these thoroughbreds. They became status symbols and were immortalized by Han craftsmen as bronze statuettes known as 'celestial horses'.*

Wudi chose his own men for senior posts rather than favouring noble families. Although he cut down the power of regional barons, he also encouraged the growth of large estates – acquired either through free trade in land or as imperial favours – to facilitate tax collection and reward loyalists. But he ordained that, on the death of the holder, such estates were to be divided among his sons, thus blocking the growth of hereditary bastions that might challenge central rule. Turning his back on his grandmother's Taoist beliefs, he promoted Confucianism. He recruited scholars to select the five most important texts by the sage, which became the core of the Confucian canon that gave the empire its philosophical structure. But there was an in-built tension between the sage's teachings and the legalistic heritage that was still needed to bind the state together.

In the early period of Wudi's rule the economy had flourished, and imperial finances with it. But the rolling sequences of major military campaigns and the sovereign's many other schemes required funding, and money became short. Under his

❛ Li Ling's troops numbered fewer than 5000 when he led them deep into the territory of the nomads. They marched to the khan's court and dangled the bait in the tiger's mouth. They boldly challenged the fierce barbarians, in the face of an army of a million ... For 1000 miles they retreated, fighting as they went until their arrows were exhausted and the road cut. The relief force did not arrive. Dead and wounded lay in heaps. But when Li Lang rallied his men with a cry, his soldiers rose to fight, with streaming tears and bloody faces. ❜

THE HISTORIAN SIMA QIAN, ON LI LING'S EXPEDITION TO THE NORTH IN 99 BC

DONG AND THE SINGLE COSMIC SYSTEM

Dong Zhongshu, a Confucian scholar and imperial adviser to Wudi, laid down the tenets of rule which were to continue through the centuries.

According to Dong, who lived from c.175 BC to the end of the century, the emperor was to serve heaven through sacrifices and by setting a moral example, to serve earth by symbolic acts such as ploughing at appropriate festivals and to serve mankind through the establishment of schools and the enlightenment of the people. If the ruler failed in his duty, this would become apparent through portents engineered by the gods. If these were ignored, other, stronger signs would appear. If the ruler still did not mend his ways, calamity would ensue.

A single cosmic system governed man, earth and heaven. Different forces and elements moved up and down in an ever-changing pattern; sometimes light, heat and activity predominated, only to be replaced by darkness, cold and inactivity. As soon as one of the five elements of wood, fire, metal, water and earth predominated, it would start to decline, and another would begin to rise. In other words, there was constant flux, a notion which applied to the affairs of the empire as well as to the cosmos and nature.

predecessors the land tax had been cut from one-fifteenth of the value of what it produced to one-thirtieth. Increasing it could provoke discontent. So the state decided to raise additional finance by setting up monopolies on salt (see Salt Monopoly, page 120) and iron, followed by copper, bronze and wine fermented from grain. Prices rose, causing widespread distress and anger as the emperor neared the end of his life.

A powerful family, the Li, capitalized on this by raising a revolt in 91 BC. Their special target was Wudi's wife, Wei, whom he had taken as a concubine after being charmed by her singing and dancing at a banquet. The existing queen conspired to kill Wei and her family. When Wudi learned of the plot, he reacted by raising Wei to high concubine rank, and had his wife jailed. He took Wei to replace her, and their son was named as crown prince.

Magic and plots

Following Empress Lü's example, Wei had relatives promoted and arranged power-generating marriages. But she encountered increasing hostility, and members of her family were implicated in a sensational witchcraft case that occurred in 92 BC. Wudi had always been superstitious, seeking the elixir of everlasting life and designing his hunting parks so that they would attract helpful spirits. He took the counsel of magicians, rewarding one with the rank of marquis, presiding over a large domain. As he aged, the emperor grew convinced that shamans and witches were hiding in his main estate to do him harm. The place was searched for ten days, with no results. Then two high officials were arrested on an array of charges, including employing shamans to burn images of the ruler along roads leading to the imperial summer residence, and offering up prayers to wish Wudi ill. They were duly executed.

Empress Wei's name was also mentioned. Her clan became extremely vulnerable. Wudi withdrew his trust in the crown prince, who hanged himself after fleeing from the court. The Li faction took the opportunity to launch an attack on the capital. The emperor was forced to take refuge in the countryside. The Li family wiped out the Wei family and the empress hanged herself. Wudi remained on the throne, but his power was broken. In 87 BC, he died. His eight-year-old successor, Zhaodi, who had been picked as heir apparent only two days before the emperor's death, was chosen largely because he had no links with either the Wei or the Li clan.

Zhaodi and Xuandi

The subsequent reigns of Zhaodi (r.87–74 BC) and Xuandi (r.74–49 BC) saw a victory for the reformists. Despite the name given to these activists, they argued for a return to old principles, seeking to achieve greater harmony and care for the population. They reduced spending, cut taxes and further alleviated the punishments of the legalistic code. But they also had to cope

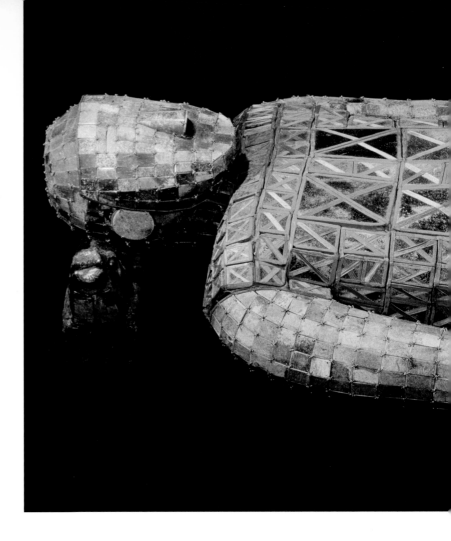

ABOVE *Jade burial suit of Han princess Tou Wan, who died around 140 BC. Nobles were buried in jade suits, as it was believed that jade had properties that ensured immortality.*

with the financial black hole left by Wudi's spending. On top of this, powerful families reasserted their power and there was a new succession struggle after Zhaodi died in suspicious circumstances. A young grandson of Wudi, named Liu, was put on the throne by a faction that controlled him. He lasted for 27 days before another grandson, 17-year-old Xuandi, was named by rival factions as his replacement.

The new ruler was lucky to be alive, since his grandmother had been Empress Wei. Arrested by the Li rebels in 91 BC, he had been saved by a friendly prison warder. Around 66 BC, his court was rocked by a scandal involving an extremely powerful family, whose head, Huo Guang, had played a major role since Wudi's death and had acted as regent. His associates commanded the imperial guards, while his son and great-nephew held high office. When the time came for Xuandi to choose his consort, the Huo clan promoted one of its young ladies. However, the emperor insisted on Xu Pingchun, the daughter of one of Wudi's ministers, with whom he already had a son.

Although Xuandi imposed his choice, Huo's wife Xian did not give up. When Xu became pregnant again, Xian had her poisoned. She died in agony on 1 March, 71 BC. Huo Guang's daughter took Xu's place, but Huo died (of natural causes) in 68 BC; as a sign of his very high rank, he was buried in a suit of jade, and a settlement of 300 families was established to care for his tomb. With the patriarch gone, voices soon started to be raised against the family he left behind. Many of the Huo clan were stripped of their rank. When the emperor learned how his favourite, Xu, had died, he

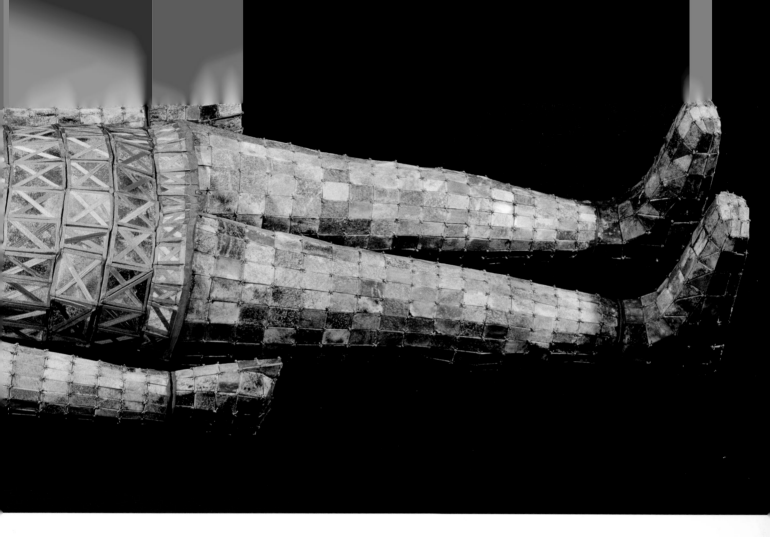

was furious, leaving the Huos with two choices – to stand and fight or to commit mass suicide. They chose revolt. But word of their plans reached the ruler and he had them all arrested before they could act. The entire family was exterminated and Xuandi's consort committed suicide. To show his feelings for Xu, the ruler bestowed on her father the rank that had been Huo Guang's, and named their son as his heir.

Yuandi

When the son of Xuandi and Xu Pingjun ascended the throne in 49 BC, the need to do something drastic about the economy and lighten the burden on the population was inescapable. Instructions were issued for court expenses to be slashed; how effective this was given the strength of entrenched interest is questionable. However, banquets were banned, and meals given to the tens of thousands of people worshipping at imperial shrines were reduced. The tradition of forcing farmers to undertake unpaid labour on building projects in lieu of monetary taxes was ended, but it was not clear how the work would be done. When state monopolies on salt and iron were abolished, the financial loss was such that they were reinstated. The Yuandi reign was serious in its intentions, but its measures were limited in their effect. As it turned out, it could be seen as the calm before the storm.

Chengdi

The next emperor, Chengdi, took the throne in 33 BC. A dissolute young man who preferred watching cock fights to running his realm, he deposed his wife and then

WESTERN HAN EMPERORS

Gaodi	206–195 BC
Huidi	195–188 BC
Lü Hou (regent)	188–180 BC
Wendi	180–157 BC
Jingdi	157–141 BC
Wudi	141–87 BC
Zhaodi	87–74 BC
Xuandi	74–49 BC
Yuandi	49–33 BC
Chengdi	33–7 BC
Aidi	7–1 BC
Pingdi	1 BC–AD 6
Ruzi	AD 7–9

had two sons by other women, who were killed after he fell for a concubine of low birth.

In the third year of his reign the capital, Chang'an, was thrown into panic. Sustained heavy rain had caused the dykes in the Yellow River to burst, flooding large areas of central China, killing thousands and devastating property. Nineteen other provinces were also affected by flooding at the same time. This was a clear portent from heaven expressing divine displeasure at a dynasty. A minister, Yin Zhong, was blamed and executed. As panic took hold of the capital's citizens, a nephew of the dowager empress, called Wang Mang, came to the rescue, arguing that there was no reason why heaven should want to destroy the Han. More practically, he mounted a full-scale relief operation, using 500 boats to reach those stranded by the Yellow River floods and a conscripted labour force to erect barricades and dig channels to divert the water.

A pretender emerges

Wang Mang's reassurance to the dynasty hardly seemed borne out by events. Chengdi failed to produce an heir. He introduced religious changes that offended important officials. After his death in 7 BC, three short reigns were marked by an aggravation of problems, notably the difficulty of maintaining such a far-flung empire. This brought a partial withdrawal from Korea. Taxation bore more and more heavily on ordinary people, while intrigue at court made things worse.

Chengdi's immediate successor, Aidi, who took the throne at the age of 17, was obsessed with his male lover to the point of handing him the imperial seals and offering to abdicate in his favour. After Aidi's death at the age of 23, the flood relief manager Wang Mang emerged as the dominant figure at court, placing an eight-year-old boy, Pingdi, on the throne and betrothing his daughter to the emperor. When he died six years later, Wang chose a two-year-old, Ruzi, as the new ruler.

Wang's clan had come to prominence when one of its female members had risen at court to give birth to the emperor Chengdi. Intrigues sidelined him for a time, but he was soon back with even greater power as regent to Pingdi and then Ruzi. By now there was a widespread feeling that the dynastic cycle of the Han – whose 200-year span as imperial rulers was unprecedented – had, indeed, entered its downward phase. It must be time for change.

Reports of bad omens multiplied. Stones with unpropitious inscriptions were found. Wells were said to be opening up of their own accord. The story spread that Wang was descended from a mythical founder of China, making him the obvious candidate to take on the Mandate of Heaven. Having put down several revolts, he faced no real opposition. On 10 January, AD 9 he had the Han dynasty declared defunct and made himself emperor of the Xin (New) dynasty, the shortest lived of the empire.

CHANG'AN – CAPITAL OF THE WESTERN HAN

In its heyday the Western Han capital of Chang'an (meaning 'Perpetual Peace') may well have been the biggest city in the world. Lying 1.9 miles (3 km) northwest of present-day Xi'an in Shaanxi province in the northwest of the country, it was at the eastern end of the Silk Road on a tributary of the Wei River, and developed into a thriving commercial centre as well as the political focus of the empire.

After Chang'an was chosen by the first Han ruler as his capital in 202 BC, a series of imposing palaces was built, facing one another in the middle of the city. Huge walls 16 metres (52 ft) wide were erected, stretching for 15 miles (24 km). Inside, the streets followed straight lines on a north–south axis to accord with the alignment of the cosmos. Imperial tombs were constructed nearby.

The city's location between two mountains was regarded as a strategic advantage since its troops could control the passes. But if the enemy got over them, the city could become a trap, which was the fate of the 'usurper' Wang Mang who ruled between the two periods of the Han dynasty. When he was defeated in 23, the city was sacked. The returning Han then moved east to Luoyang, leaving Chang'an to decline.

In the early fourth century a chronicler reported that not more than 100 families lived in Chang'an, with just four carts between them, while 'weeds and thorns grew as thickly as in a forest'. But the city was not finished. In the seventh century

the Tang restored it as the imperial capital, turning it back into a metropolis of a million people during the period known as China's 'Golden Age'.

A rubbing taken from a stone tablet (stele) depicting the city of Chang'an. Over 3000 such tablets exist, dating from the Han to the Qing dynasty.

THE GREAT WALL OF CHINA *'I think that you would have to conclude that this is a great wall and that it had to be built by a great people'.* **Thus spoke Richard Nixon, as president of the United States, after visiting China's most famous monument in 1972. For all that it is a very tangible relic of the past, the wall has become shrouded in mythology and has given its name to innumerable Chinese products from wine to computer software. It is also a major tourist attraction – long held to be the only man-made landmark that could be seen from outer space – a Chinese astronaut has shot down that particular myth.**

In fact, the wall is not a single barrier but a series of structures stretching across more than 3000 miles (4800 km) of northern China, and generally taken to mark the northernmost border of the Han domain. Its extent as it snakes along mountain ridges and swoops down into valleys makes it one of the wonders of the world, but its real history is a good deal less impressive than the aura surrounding it.

Construction began in 214 BC, though earlier rulers had thrown up earthworks to protect their kingdoms. After the First Emperor's great commander Meng Tian had led a huge army to defeat northern enemies living in the upper reaches of the Yellow River, according to the historian Sima Qian the general *'built a long wall, constructing its defiles and passes in accordance with the configurations of the terrain'*. His main aim was to link up fortified cities on the Yellow River, along the natural line of the mountains and valleys. A huge army of forced labourers and convicts was employed to press ahead with the project. A more fanciful explanation of the speed with which it was built told of a magic whip or shovel wielded by the emperor himself. Another story had it that a dragon had been flying over China and, becoming tired, flopped to earth, where it turned into a wall.

Work on the wall continued through the centuries as dynasties sought to bolster their defences against the nomads of the steppes, who represented a constant threat to imperial China and, in some cases, took the throne. The founder of the Han dynasty had repaired the Qin wall during the wars that led him to the throne. Once his successors had restored the empire's fortunes, they threw up large stretches of fortifications across their northern lands, but faced constant problems in dealing with the tribes of the steppes. Some of these tribes which settled in China proper also adopted the national habit of wall-building.

Seventeen hundred years or more after the first sections were put up, some of the best-known and most visited parts of the wall, north of Beijing, were erected under the Ming. The early stretches of the wall were probably made from tamped earth. The technology improved steadily under the different dynasties until the final sections were constructed of bricks and stone.

Symbol of oppression

The defensive network was not particularly efficient, and some modern historians have seen the wall as a symbol of the way in which Chinese rulers sought to contain their people – that is, as a symbol of autocracy as much as a practical defensive line. Raiders from the north frequently breached it or passed through stretches of terrain not covered by the wall. Despite a burst of major construction in the mid-sixth century, Turkic cavalry rode into central China, *'leaving not a single human or animal [alive] behind them'*, according to a contemporary account. Later the Mongols simply skirted the wall in their great attacks before founding their own dynasty, the Yuan, in the 13th century. (See The Yuan, pages 154–65.)

Though it is now praised as a symbol of national endeavour, the wall long stood in the people's mind for the oppressive demands of the state as armies of forced labourers were sent to work in often extreme climatic conditions, driven on as little more than slaves.

'Can't you see? The Long Wall
Is propped on skeletons'.

QIN-ERA ODE

A celebrated folk story tells of a wife making her way to the wall during the Qin era with warm winter clothes for her husband. When she arrives, she finds that he is dead of cold and exhaustion. Her lamentations cause the structure to open in front of her, exposing his bones together with those of a multitude of other workers. Having reburied her spouse, she drowns herself – four rocks where the wall reaches the sea are said to be her tomb.

The Jin clan which moved into northern China after the fall of the Tang at the start of the tenth century developed wall-building technology, but a song from their era records that *'the wall was built, with cries of pain and sadness … if all the white bones of the dead had been left piled up there, they would reach the same height as the wall'*.

The soldiers who served along the wall to try to keep out the nomadic raiders lived harsh, dangerous lives, often dying in the attempt:

'We fight south of the wall, we die north of the wall.
If we die, unburied, in the wilds, our corpses will feed the crows'.

HAN-ERA VERSE

Neglect and defeat

Despite the building work that took place under the Ming, the wall was in poor shape by the 17th century, since no funds were provided for its upkeep. A commander described one stretch where the moats were filled with sand, which nobody bothered to dig out, and the walls were in ruin. Having been poorly treated by the emperors, the frontier troops were in no mood to fight when the Manchu advanced on China from the northeast in the early 1640s. Holed up in their garrisons, they underwent brutal sieges – in one, nearly 20,000 of the 30,000 imperial troops perished, and the officers ended up by killing their men to eat their flesh. In a final battle at Shanhaiguan, a Ming general changed sides, and the loyal imperial troops fled as the cry went up, *'the Tartars have come'*. The invaders became the last dynasty; the wall had failed to save China.

BELOW *The Great Wall of China began construction in 214 BC, continuing through the centuries as successive dynasties sought to protect their lands from the northern nomads.*

WANG MANG

AD 9—23 Orthodox Chinese history depicted Wang Mang's 14-year rule from AD 9 to 23 as a time of usurpation. In fact, he was a well-meaning, pragmatic administrator. Interlopers like him would never fare well in the official chronicles of the empire. His problem was that his policies led him into growing difficulties with the establishment élite inherited from the Han, and he finally faced a major natural catastrophe that contributed to his fall.

WANG WAS DESCRIBED BY THE MAIN ACCOUNT OF THE TIME, THE *HISTORY OF THE FORMER HAN*, as having a large mouth, receding chin, bulging eyes with brilliant pupils and a loud, hoarse voice. Whether or not this is a true description of the man we shall never know. Physiognomy was very popular among the Chinese of the time, and the description may have been designed to show that he was not worthy to occupy the throne.

Wang embarked on a series of ambitious policies, some of which were far-sighted but needed careful application. One was to take over all land and redistribute it in an attempt to equalize the size of holdings and do away with the big estates built up under his imperial predecessors. The sale of slaves was forbidden. Both measures proved too ambitious and had to be abandoned, however. Wang brought back the monopolies that had fallen into disuse and introduced state trading in grain, cloth and silk. Holders of gold were ordered to hand it to the state in return for coins. A 10 per cent tax was put on the commercial activities of merchants. The new ruler encouraged science, Confucian scholarship and the study of history.

Some of these steps were a continuation of previous Han policies, but others represented a break which aroused the hostility of the élite. There were also new challenges on the northern and western frontiers, which required the mobilization of fresh armies.

LEFT *Statuette of a fishmonger from the Han dynasty. Wang Mang's 14-year rule was characterized by a series of ambitious policies, including the introduction of the first Chinese income-based tax of 10 per cent on merchants. His far-reaching reforms caused a series of risings which ultimately led to his downfall.*

Undoubtedly, Wang tried to do too much too fast. The blow that ultimately ended his dynasty came from a natural cause – the shifting of the course of the Yellow River as it neared the sea. This brought huge flooding, mass migration and famine in the Shandong region. Bands of young unemployed men rose in revolt, painting their foreheads red to distinguish themselves from Wang's soldiers, thus becoming known as the Red Eyebrows. Two campaigns by imperial forces to suppress the rebels failed. By AD 22 the Red Eyebrows seemed invincible as they encouraged others to stage separate risings.

The scene was set for a Han bid to return to power. A gentry-led army staged a large-scale rising in what is now Henan province, south of Shandong, and reached agreements with other anti-Wang groups. This coalition took the city of Nanyang in southern Shandong in AD 23. A descendant of the Han rulers, Liu Xuan, was the new candidate to take the throne.

> The people could not turn a hand without violating some prohibition ... The rich had no means of protecting themselves and the poor no way to stay alive. They rose up and became thieves and bandits, infesting the hills and marshes, and the officials, being unable to seize them, contrived on the contrary to hide their presence ... Famine and pestilence raged and people ate each other.
>
> HAN HISTORIAN ON WANG MANG'S RULE

ABOVE *A painting in the*
Shaanxi Provincial
Museum in Xi'an depicts
the storming of the
Imperial Palace in
Chang'an by the Red
Eyebrow rebels.

In early October, AD 23, an anti-Wang army stormed Chang'an. The city became a trap for the defenders. Fighting continued for several days until the attackers broke into the palace, which was set on fire. Wang Mang was beheaded.

In the end, he had been unable to control the country or implement the decrees he promulgated. There was a deep irony in his fall. Wang had come to the throne on the back of the feeling that the Han had forfeited the Mandate of Heaven. But his own demise had its immediate roots in a natural disaster which could, equally, be taken as a sign of divine displeasure.

NATURAL DISASTERS Natural disasters were important to imperial China not only because of the devastation they caused in the countryside, but also as signs of divine warnings to the rulers that they were not living up to the Mandate of Heaven.

It was therefore appropriate that Wang Mang came to power on the back of one set of disasters and lost power after another. As well as the catastrophes which regularly hit China in the form of floods, droughts, earthquakes and plagues of locusts, portents in the skies – comets, eclipses and strangely shaped moons – were interpreted as messages from the gods. As late as 1898, a total eclipse of the sun at the Lunar New Year was regarded as a highly inauspicious sign for the last Chinese dynasty.

Gengshi and the sacking of Chang'an

The new emperor, who took the reign name of Gengshi, made a series of blunders. He refused to recognize the part the Red Eyebrows had played in the overthrow of Wang Mang. He kept Chang'an as the capital, against the counsel of his advisers, who pointed out that, while its position between two mountains meant that it appeared easily defensible, it could become a death trap – as Wang had discovered. Gengshi sent some powerful regional figures away from court but let them keep armies in their home territories, where they could only be encouraged to plot against the ruler.

One of those expelled from Chang'an was a bright and well-liked rival for the throne, a landowner from Henan called Liu Xiu. He was sent to travel as an envoy to the people of the steppes, giving him time and space in which to lay plans of his own. Liu raised an army and came to rule over a section of China almost as powerful as Gengshi's domains, drawing on the backing of the lesser gentry who identified him as their preferred candidate for the throne. A court faction rose against the emperor and sided with Liu. At the same time, the disgruntled Red Eyebrows marched in revolt.

Overthrow of Gengshi

It has been estimated that only a quarter of the population now owed loyalty to the ruler. Matters came to a head during the spring and summer of AD 24 as the capital was caught between the two advancing armies. In October the Red Eyebrows entered the city. Gengshi tried to flee on horseback, only to be captured. He was sent off to herd horses and cattle and was strangled not long afterwards. The Eyebrows avenged themselves by the sacking of the once mighty Chang'an.

1 BC Wang Mang becomes regent, first to Pingdi and then Ruzi

AD 9 Wang Mang takes the throne after Ruzi's death; he nationalizes land and sets up a gold monopoly

11 Major floods of Yellow River start

20 Plot against Wang Mang is uncovered and many of those involved are executed

23 Red Eyebrow rebels take Chang'an; fall of Wang Mang

THE EASTERN HAN

AD 25–220

In AD 25 the rebel leader Liu Xiu was crowned as Guang Wudi (New First) Emperor. His rule, lasting until AD 57, marks the start of the second period of Han rule. Guang Wudi moved the capital east from Chang'an to Luoyang in his home region, a city dating from 2200 BC, which had been the centre of the ancient Eastern Zhou kingdom. The transfer gave the dynasty its name of the Eastern Han.

Although it lasted for 32 years, Guang Wudi's reign did not start in peace. There were up to a dozen other contenders for the throne, and some leading figures were unwilling to give automatic allegiance. Guang Wudi had to win support.

His core backing came mainly from the lesser gentry, with important regional barons showing more reluctance. The Red Eyebrow bands proved less of a threat than they could have been, as they moved from the sacked Chang'an further west into the sparsely populated lands of what is now western Shaanxi and eastern Gansu provinces, where they met their match in a local warlord.

> ❝ In present times, it is not only the sovereign who selects his subjects. The subjects also select their sovereign.❞
>
> GENERAL MA YUAN UNDER EMPEROR GUANG WUDI

Most of the first decade of Guang Wudi's reign saw risings from Sichuan to Shandong. The Gansu warlord, Wei Ao, rose against the Han, forcing the emperor to ally with smaller local groups to bring under control mountain passes leading to the west of the empire. However, the most serious sustained challenge was from Gongsun Shu, a one-time adviser to Wang Mang, who established a power base as the king of Shu in Sichuan in the west, with Chengdu as his capital. In AD 25, he proclaimed himself emperor, safe in his inaccessible terrain that stretched from the Tibetan lowlands to the Three Gorges and north to the Jinling Mountains. Huge as his domain was, it was sparsely populated, and lack of manpower may have led him to refrain from attacking Guang Wudi when he was at his weakest.

The two men fought a long propaganda war involving the elements central to Chinese cosmology. Gongsun claimed to be taking over from his old master Wang Mang; Wang's element had been earth and his colour yellow, so it made sense for

RIGHT A traditional-style house in modern-day Chengdu. Gongsun Shu, Guang Wudi's main adversary, declared himself emperor in AD 25 and ruled the inhospitable lands from the Tibetan lowlands to the Jinling Mountains, with Chengdu as his capital.

him to carry on with the next in sequence: metal and white. Because the compass direction for metal is west and Gongsun's power base was there, this made him appear to have the mandate to rule. Guang Wudi took the line that the old Western Han element of fire (red) had not been over-ridden, but had merely died down and was now again in ascendancy. This meant that, like Wang Mang, Gongsun was a mere pretender to the throne.

In AD 34, having dealt with his other enemies, Guang Wudi launched a campaign against Sichuan. It was a long and bitter fight; imperial ships moved up the Yangzi to combine with land forces. Finally, Chengdu fell on 25 December, AD 36 and Gongsun was beaten. Guang Wudi was master of China.

Conquest and reform

Even so, fighting would continue on other fronts, with recurrent risings in the south where the immigration of Chinese alienated the aboriginal inhabitants. In AD 40 the people of the Red River Delta in present-day Vietnam revolted against Chinese overlordship, led by two sisters, one of whom proclaimed herself queen. A prominent general from the northwest, Ma Yuan, was sent to Guangdong in early AD 43 to organize suppression of the uprising. As his army marched through the difficult terrain, a fleet of supply ships sailed along the South China Sea coast. When the two joined up, the revolt was put down and the sisters beheaded.

After the years of internal war, Guang Wudi faced a major task in reconstructing the country and rebuilding imperial administration. There is evidence that population levels had fallen, probably mainly as a result of the frequent wars. At the start of the new millennium, China was estimated to contain 57 million people; by AD 140 this had dropped to 48 million.

Within this total, there had been a substantial shift in distribution away from the north to other regions: in AD 2 the north housed 76 per cent of the population, while in the middle of the following century the figure was 54 per cent. The changing balance was caused by several factors, primarily lower crop yields in the north than in the south, which made it harder to sustain large families and led to infanticide.

Guang Wudi brought in economic measures that restored stability, including the usual reductions in imperial spending. He reformed taxes and raised funds through a return of the monopolies. He developed imperial examinations to provide civil servants. Transport

LEFT *A sculpture of a civil official. Guang Wudi's attempts at reconstructing a country ravaged by years of internal warfare included providing more civil servants to rebuild imperial administration.*

routes were improved. Cash increasingly replaced payment in kind for wages. Trade flourished.

To start with, Guang Wudi abolished the old system under which sons of the ruler had been named as kings over specified territories. But in 41 he reverted to this practice, and then enlarged it by creating kingdoms for his nephews as well. This produced alternative regional power bases. Some became centres of intellectual and artistic achievement. Others were magnets for adventurers, intriguers and opponents of the ruler. Some kings engaged shamans and wizards to conjure up spells against the emperor. A number of the local rulers appear to have been mentally unbalanced. Three were accused of treason; two of them committed suicide.

Nomads and factions

A strong Confucian, Guang Wudi encouraged education by establishing state institutes of learning. In his bid to unite the country and hailing from central China himself, he had picked a wife from the north. But the north became less threatening when the emperor reached a pact with the southern branch of the nomadic Xiongnu peoples of northwest China. In 50, two Chinese envoys went to visit the chief and told him to prostrate himself. After hesitating for a moment, he did so, and was rewarded with valuable gifts and a golden seal.

The nomad people were given permission to occupy a large area of northwest China. Since they already held the land, the decree seemed rather pointless, but the chief was facing internal rivals and needed formal Chinese backing. The emperor was urged by his generals to build on the alliance by staging a campaign against the northern Xiongnu, but he chose not to – perhaps a major error, since he would then have had a good chance of marginalizing the nomadic threat altogether.

Since the north was now less important, the emperor dropped his first empress in favour of a woman from his harem, who hailed from his own region in central China, and with whom he already had five children. She was raised to the rank of empress. In the way of court politics, she became the focus of factionalism, primarily among a group from the emperor's home region, another that brought together officials, and a third under the victor of the southern campaign, General Ma, which had a stronger military component.

When General Ma died of fever after conducting another successful campaign against rebels in the south, posthumous accusations of corruption and wrongdoing against him flowed in at court. With their leader unable to defend himself, or them, his

ABOVE *Pottery figure of a court entertainer from the Eastern Han dynasty. The emperor Hedi abolished court performances to pay for drought relief.*

followers rapidly lost ground. The dead commander was relegated to the rank of a commoner, and his widow did not dare to have his body buried in the ancestral grave. The emperor refused the family's request for a pardon, but after receiving six memorials (petitions) from them, he finally allowed the corpse to be interred in the tomb. This still left the court deeply factionalized when Guang Wudi died in 57 at the age of 62.

Mingdi and Zhangdi

The rule of the next Han emperor, Mingdi, which lasted from 58 to 75, was marked by the continuation of faction fighting inherited from his father's reign. The prime question at the start of his reign was which clan the ruler would honour by choosing from among its daughters a girl to be his wife. In the end, he picked a woman from the Ma family, thus marking its return to power at court. But his nine sons came from less important concubines. This left Mingdi free to choose his successor. A deal was struck in which the boy's mother would receive an equal share of royal privilege along with Empress Ma.

ABOVE *A group of bronze horsemen and carriages from the Eastern Han dynasty, found in a tomb.*

These years were seen by many at the time as being needlessly chaotic and an example of too much power being given both to the immediate faction surrounding the empress and to the eunuchs – the latter were noted for the way in which they conspired with different groups at court and plotted against targeted enemies. Far from the capital of Luoyang, many border lands came under the command of ineffectual delegates, while other areas were controlled by oppressive overlords.

There was, however, a successful campaign on the steppes in 73, in alliance with the southern Xiongnu nomads against their northern rivals. This paved the way for a series of expeditions over the following 16 years, culminating in a decisive victory by a force of imperial cavalry and chariots. That dispersed the northern Xiongnu into Central Asia, but they still remained a potent force, deeply hostile to China and lurking out of reach.

In the dynasty's heartland, Mingdi employed engineers to repair the collapsed Yellow River dykes, a project which cost a small fortune and took most of the year 69 to complete. Nevertheless, it was a major achievement for the Han, as the lack of attention to the dykes had been a source of local resentment for decades. That same year was proclaimed to be one in which the world – that is, the Middle Kingdom – was at peace. A series of good harvests ensured plentiful grain supplies, conscription of peasants for forced labour diminished, sheep and cattle roamed in the fields; the official declaration of good times noted. Still, central rule was seen as harsh. Ministers were often scolded publicly by the emperor, the most famous example being the treatment of a senior adviser, Zhongli Yi, who was given a thrashing by Mingdi for daring to raise concerns over the money spent on a project to build a northern palace.

THE POWER OF PAPER

AD 105 is often cited as the crucial year in which paper was invented and developed on a national scale; although archaeological discoveries suggest that forms of paper may have existed on a local scale in Gansu in the northwest two centuries earlier.

The relatively low cost of paper and the convenience of this new medium made it an essential part of the bureaucratic and cultural development of the Han empire, from where it spread to the rest of the world. Its invention is commonly attributed to a civil servant called Cai Lun, who received sponsorship from the court. Traditionally, the pages of Chinese books had been made of silk, bamboo or wood. Paper now allowed knowledge to become accessible to people further down the social scale.

At first, paper was made from hemp waste, which was later supplemented with bark, bamboo and plant fibres. Improvements in the moulds in which paper was produced led to the creation of smoother surfaces, while dyes were used in its manufacture, to repel insects.

The spread of paper westward came in the mid-eighth century after a Chinese army was defeated by a Muslim force at Talas in present-day Kazakhstan. Captured soldiers were taken to the great cities of Central Asia, bringing paper and knowledge of its manufacturing technology with them. Once it had arrived in Central Asia, paper helped Muslim publishing to find its feet,

and quickly spread to Damascus, Baghdad and Cairo, and from there on to the Muslim cities of southern Spain.

The European nations were sceptical about a substance they viewed as bound up with Islam but, with the advent of printing a few centuries later, paper would revolutionize Europe too, allowing new, anti-élitist movements to grip the continent: the Reformation, the Renaissance and, in time, the Enlightenment.

BELOW *Early forms of paper were made from vegetable material, pulped with water in a trough. The pulp was then spread onto a fine mesh or screen, and the water drained away to leave behind a criss-cross pattern of matted fibres which dried to form a sheet of paper.*

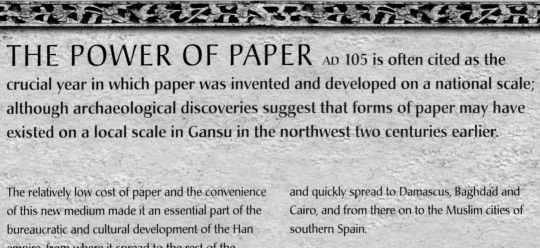

The end of Mingdi's reign and the first years of his successor, Zhangdi, who ruled from 76 to 88, saw major transport links being put into place in regions such as Fujian that were still foreign and exotic for the rulers. An acceleration in canal and road building meant that, while travelling was still dangerous, it was now at least possible. For the most part, land south of present-day Nanjing had only a token attachment to the Chinese empire, but the better transport links did bring Han culture much closer to far-flung regions. In addition, military successes in the far north enabled the empire to re-occupy oasis towns along the Silk Road. China had re-established itself geographically, but the dynasty was embarking on a downward path as tension rose at court and challenges to its authority increased.

Hedi, Shangdi and Andi

Of the next three emperors, only the last had a meaningful impact. The reign of Hedi, from 89 to 105, was plagued with the problem of a powerful family called the Dou, which had retained a presence in court circles since the restoration of the dynasty. In 89 one of their number, Dou Xian, pestered to be allowed to lead an attack on the Xiongnu tribes of the northern steppe. As the Xiongnu had been defeated by both the Chinese and another tribe, the Xianbei, many ministers saw this as unnecessary. Ren Wei, the minister of works, and Yuan An, the minister of finance, both raised concerns about the pressure such a campaign would put on the male population through conscription. The views of the ministers were, however, ignored in favour of the Dou, and incursions were made into Xiongnu territory, but with only limited success. The matter of the 'sinicization' of the north weighed heavy on the emperor's mind. In 101 he changed the rules of the civil service exams to allow a larger quota of northerners to pass.

BELOW *Modern-day Dunhuang in western China. Attacks on the early settlement by the nomadic northern tribes of the Xiongnu resumed during the middle period of the dynasty – partly as a result of Guang Wudi's earlier inaction.*

MODERNIZERS VERSUS REFORMERS

The eminent historian of the Han dynasty, Michael Loewe, has suggested that the best way of looking at its political and philosophical development is to divide it into 'modernist' and 'reformist' schools.

The modernizers were the heirs of the legalists of the first empire. They wanted to get to grips with current problems using contemporary methods. The reformists, on the other hand, wanted to use Confucianism to return society to an ideal situation which they believed had prevailed at some time in the past.

Although the harsher elements of legalism were diminished under the Han, the modernizers still remained in the ascendant, developing the Qin bureaucracy. This process reached its apogee during the reign of Wudi. In reaction, the reformers then gathered strength, notably during the interregnum of Wang Mang. Thereafter, Confucianism would generally hold the upper hand, but the legalist tradition continued – and admiration for its hard rule would emerge many centuries later under the Communist leader Mao Zedong (Mao Tse-tung; 1893–1976).

From 103 the court suddenly seemed to become aware of the need to cut back on expenditure. This was prompted by droughts that gripped the country that year, requiring savings to pay for relief. The court pulled in its belt. The caravan that brought a delectable cargo of exotic southern fruits up from Fujian, Jiangxi and Guangdong was cancelled. Private dance and drama performances at court ended, and imperial musicians were assigned to guard duties.

Eunuch power

When Hedi died in 105, his successor, Shangdi, was a baby who passed away seven months after ascending the throne. He was followed by 12-year-old Andi, who ruled from 106 to 125. The situation bred further factionalism and weakened the authority of officials in the face of the dowager empress, court favourites and the growing influence of eunuchs. Memorialists mourned the trend, pointing to the way in which powerful families such as the Dou and the dowager's relatives, along with the eunuchs, were undermining imperial authority. One outspoken critic was arrested after a campaign against him orchestrated by eunuchs. In prison, he was advised to commit suicide. He refused, saying that he wanted to make his views known even if he had to do so at his own public execution. He was freed.

In 109 the dowager fell ill. Special prayers were read out for her. Their content shocked her as they seemed to hint at the demise of the Han. In her anger – and perhaps out of fear that the prayers might be true – she cancelled all parties at court for that year and halved the 120 youths needed to perform religious exorcisms. Further savings were introduced in 110 by reducing all official salaries.

The final major event of this period of Han history was brought about by renewed attacks by the northern nomads of the Xiongnu on the settlement of Dunhuang in the

25 Guang Wudi founds the Eastern Han dynasty, ruling until 57

39/40 The Trung sisters lead a four-year independence movement in the Red River Delta in present-day Vietnam

69 Major repair work of dykes along 250 miles (400 km) of the Yellow River

73–91 Imperial armies launch campaigns in northern steppes and into Central Asia, reaching the Caspian Sea

90 Invention of the wheelbarrow

Second century Paper is developed at the beginning of the second century

122 As China's international links increase, a troupe of Roman jugglers reaches the capital of Luoyang

132 Invention of a form of seismograph

146 The first of the 'bad emperors', Huandi, takes the throne. Taxation becomes more onerous

153 Major earthquakes and plague of locusts

184 Revolt of Yellow Turban rebels after flooding of the Yellow River

End of the 2nd century Rise of regional warlords

192 General Cao Cao, who had defeated the Yellow Turbans, seizes power; his attempt to conquer all China fails, and he and his son remain only kings of the northern Wei state

far west. While some ministers pushed for a full-scale retaliation, the emperor was advised that it would be unwise to commit large armies so far away. Instead, a crack garrison was deployed, and diplomatic channels were opened. The empire retained its allure for the people to the west; in 120, ambassadors from Central Asian kingdoms arrived to pay respects – some may have come from as far away as Persia.

Shundi

The ensuing reign of the emperor Shundi from 126 to 144 was marred by natural disasters and rebellion. So much so that, only months after his death, vandals desecrated his tomb. A big earthquake which hit the capital in 133 had significant ramifications. Some ministers advised that it could only have happened because the dynasty was not sufficiently virtuous. In response, the ruler had many courtesans thrown out of the harem. Petitions to the throne took the opportunity to attack court factions and insist that the ruler should consult men of learning more frequently and listen to their advice. A decision to allow eunuchs to adopt sons, and so found family lines that could perpetuate the honours and privileges granted to them, aroused attacks by Han officials. The eunuchs showed their power to fight back by laying allegations against a prominent general who criticized them. He was saved only by the intervention of a senior ally at court.

Chongdi, Zhidi and Huandi

After Shundi's death in 144 at the age of 29, two boy emperors were declared. One, Chongdi, died in 145 at the age of two, after just five months as nominal ruler. The other, Zhidi, succeeded at the age of seven and died 16 months later. The next Son of Heaven, Huandi, was 14 when he ascended the throne. Ruling for 22 years, from 146 to 168, he was regarded as a 'bad emperor', who ushered in the fall of the Han.

Natural disasters multiplied. Another earthquake hit the capital; there were droughts and floods, and plagues of locusts. Disorder spread, with revolts and growing levels of banditry. A pretender set himself up in the southeast as the 'Black Emperor'; his rising was put down with the killing of some 4000 of his followers. A student at the Imperial Academy went as far as to blame the emperor personally for all the trouble, accusing Huandi of being isolated from the real world and ignorant of the extent of the people's oppression. *'The tigers and panthers lie in their lairs in the playground of fawns'*, he wrote. *'The wolves and jackals are nurtured in gardens where spring flowers bloom'*. He was realistic enough to add that he

THE DEVELOPMENT OF AGRICULTURE

'Without farming, there is no stability; without grain, there is chaos'.

TRADITIONAL SAYING

A brick from a tomb structure dating from the Han period showing ploughing with an ox-drawn plough. Confucius regarded farmers as more important than merchants.

Agriculture was at the heart of imperial China. The Confucian system lauded farmers as the bedrock of society, placing them far above merchants. When emperors spoke of the welfare of the people, they meant the inhabitants of the vast expanses of countryside over which they ruled. In countless villages spread across the country, the rhythm of the crop seasons dictated life for the inhabitants. The Grand Canal carried rice to the court, and the empire came to depend on the rural gentry to ensure stability across the nation.

During the first two millennia of known Chinese history, farmers used slash-and-burn techniques, moving on from one area to another after the crops were exhausted. Then a more settled form of cultivation evolved, and the taxes paid by farmers became a major source of revenue for the throne. The sevenfold increase in population under the empire posed a continual challenge, since the amount of land available to grow crops only doubled in the same period. On top of this, there were recurrent natural disasters.

But, from around 800, improved techniques generally enabled output to keep ahead of basic demand. New crops were introduced and land was opened up for farming in the northeast and by deforestation. There was a clear geographical distinction in crop patterns and soil and climate conditions – rice prevailed in the well-watered south with its patchwork of paddies, while wheat was the staple in the dry north with its big fields on the plains. Chinese farmers became highly skilled at irrigation, but farm tools remained primitive while the general ability to provide enough food stunted the impetus to introduce more efficient agricultural management methods.

knew he was offering *advice that does not accord with the time, at a court which bans criticism'*. He was indeed ignored.

Lingdi and Xiandi

Huandi died without an heir, and his wife, from the Dou clan, was declared dowager. She chose a 12-year-old boy – a great-great-grandson of Zhangdi – to become emperor, under the name of Lingdi.

EASTERN HAN EMPERORS

Guang Wudi	25–57
Mingdi	58–75
Zhangdi	76–88
Hedi	89–105
Shangdi	105
Andi	106–25
Shundi 1	26–44
Chongdi	144–5
Zhidi	145–6
Huandi	146–68
Lingdi	168–89
Xiandi	189–220

The struggle between court factions escalated as a group around the new ruler and within the imperial harem worked with eunuchs to out-manoeuvre the Dou clan and their allies. An eclipse of the sun was seen as a portent of trouble. The Dous called for the execution of all eunuchs, claiming they were an evil force at court. The eunuchs' foes prepared a long list of criminal charges against them, and had one eunuch arrested and tortured to provide evidence. The Dou group had an ally installed as chief of the court eunuchs and delivered to the palace a list of those it wanted detained. Some of the eunuchs discovered the list, and reading its contents, decided on a pre-emptive strike against their adversaries. They forced the appointment of one of their leaders to replace the Dou ally as head eunuch, and freed their tortured colleague. They then went to the dowager's quarters and seized the seals that were used to issue commands to troops, ordering the arrest of the Dou chief. The eunuchs enlisted an army recently returned from a successful campaign, and Dou soldiers defected in large numbers.

Now in charge of the regime, the eunuchs began to purge the administration and had themselves appointed to noble positions and important military posts, including that of commander-in-chief. But, as well as their long-standing enemies among officials, they faced regional opposition and difficult times: farm output stalled and natural disasters continued. The administration crumbled as positions and titles were sold. Instead of being divided between the public purse and the ruler's personal use, all revenue went into a single pot, which Lingdi and his circle could plunder at will.

A Taoist movement, known from its members' headgear as the Yellow Turbans, instigated a revolt in eastern China which mobilized 350,000 men. In Sichuan, to the west, another Taoist group, the Five Pecks of Rice sect, declared independence. With central power weakening steadily, regional barons raised their own armies and operated as local warlords.

Dynasty's end

When Lingdi died in 189 at the age of 33, a succession struggle broke out once more at court. A powerful warlord from Sichuan province intervened, marching on the capital of Luoyang, massacring 2000 eunuchs and burning the imperial library. A new emperor, eight-year-old Xiandi, was proclaimed. But real power lay with three major regional militarists.

The boy ruler was soon on the move, seeking safety in the old capital of Chang'an for a time with a ragamuffin court. Although the most powerful warlord, from the north, chose not to claim the throne (perhaps with the example of Wang Mang in mind), the Han were finished. In 220, Xiandi formally abdicated, dying 14 years later.

Legacy of the Han

The longest-reigning dynasty had produced great figures, set a Confucian template, and expanded China's reach greatly in the north, south and west. The final downward turn of the cycle had been a protracted process. In the end, the throne was lost through internal fighting at court and the sheer difficulty of keeping such a huge domain together. Looking back on the period since the time of Emperor Hedi at the end of the first century, the historian Ssu-ma Kung lamented that the power of the imperial relatives and the eunuchs meant *'rewards were without any rule, bribery was a public business, worthy men and fools were mixed together, right and wrong were confused'*.

The ensuing 350 years would see constant warfare, with some 50 rulers setting up in different parts of the country at the head of kingdoms or would-be dynasties. But, even in the chaos of division and civil war, some constants remained. Most importantly, the Qin and Han had asserted the importance of imperial rule, in principle if not always in practice, as the central organizing principle for China. A legitimate ruler had to have the Mandate of Heaven. Amid the disruption that would follow, the idea of empire and the importance of the throne as the centre of the Chinese universe lived on.

PERIOD OF DISUNION

220—581

'Empires wax and wane; states cleave asunder and coalesce … the government went quickly from bad to worse till the country was ripe for rebellion and buzzed with brigandage'.
The Romance of the Three Kingdoms, Luo Guanzhong.

WRITTEN IN THE 14TH CENTURY, *THE ROMANCE OF THE THREE KINGDOMS* IS PROBABLY THE greatest of Chinese sagas. The disastrous background against which the epic is set is that of China after the Han finally fell, an event that paved the way for three-and-a-half centuries known as the Period of Disunion. In the tale, what follows is a time of chivalry and stirring martial achievements by a cast of heroes – thinly veiled versions of the leaders who emerged from the ruins of the dynasty. The reality was, naturally, far more prosaic and, for many, tragic. The era was one of war, division, economic distress and mass movements of refugees, epitomized by the names given to its various struggles, such as the War of the 16 Kingdoms or the Rebellion of the Eight Princes.

> All down the ages rings
> the note of change.
> For Fate so rules it; none
> escape its sway.
> The kingdoms three have
> vanished as a dream.
> The useless misery is ours
> to grieve.
>
> FROM *THE ROMANCE OF THE THREE KINGDOMS*

The Three Kingdoms

One character in the *Romance* is described by a seer as '*able enough to rule the world, but wicked enough to disturb it*'. Such men now took charge of three huge domains within what had formerly been the united realm of the Han. In the west, Sichuan was under the Shu Han kingdom, headed by a tall warlord, Liu Bei, who developed public works, notably irrigation projects, and expanded into Yunnan in the far southwest. To the southeast lay the kingdom of Wu, with its heart in the Yangzi Valley, but stretching down over territory which was not still entirely sinicized. Its core consisted of a confederation of rich families that wanted to run their own affairs independently of an emperor in the north. Its ruler, Sun Quan, was famed for his courage.

The largest of the new power bases was the kingdom of Wei in the north. Although each of the three kingdoms claimed either to have inherited the Mandate of Heaven or to be continuing the heritage of the Han, Chinese historians generally view the Wei as successors to the Han. The realm was governed initially by Cao Pei, whose

RIGHT *A painting by the 19th-century artist Yoshitoshi of the third-century general Cao Cao on the eve of a battle he would later lose (the birds overhead signifying ill omens). Cao Cao had been the leading general in the final years of the Han dynasty; however, it was his son, Cao Pei, who was to take over leadership of the realm.*

百姿

南屏山昇月

曹操

Toba

Xiongnu

· Pingcheng

· Loulang

Dengzhou ·

WEI

Yellow

YELLOW
SEA

Chang'an (Xi'an) ·

Wei

· Luoyang

· Nanjing
· Suzhou

· Chengdu

· Hangzhou

SHU HAN

· Jiangling

Yangzi

· Yuzhang

WU

· Guangzhou

Hainan

Wei kingdom

Shu Han kingdom

Wu kingdom

Northern Wei state *c.*500

Northern Zhou dynasty *c.*560

Sui empire *c.*600

nomad invasions

migration of Chinese landowners,
fourth century

father, Cao Cao, had been the leading general of the final years of the Han, but had
not sought to make himself emperor.

Cao Pei maintained the style of an imperial court and took the imperial name of
Wei Wendi. The Wei kingdom was ruled as a centralizing autocracy, run on legalistic
lines. The government set up agricultural colonies, sometimes numbering 10,000
people, to tie the population to the land, and tried to form a professional army out of
the mercenaries, bandits and adventurers who formed its troops – it also assimilated
nomadic cavalry, with their skill as mounted archers.

After the Han fell in 220,
China was broadly divided
into three separate kingdoms –
the Shu to the west, the Wu to
the south and the Wei in the
north. The nation was united
once more in 589 with the
emergence of a new dynasty,
the Sui.

Initially, the Shu leader sided with the Wu to repel an attack down the Yangzi River by the Wei forces which were routed at the Battle of the Red Cliffs. But then, in 222, Liu Bei attacked his ally at the head of an army said to have been 200,000 strong, after the Wu king had executed one of his generals in a side quarrel. The attack went wrong and, though larger than its foe, the Sichuan army was defeated. The western warlord fled and a year later became ill and died. His son, Liu Shan, was a feckless young man who showed little interest in running the kingdom.

Battles for power

The dominant figure at the Sichuan court in Chengdu was the chancellor, Zhuge Liang, who has gone down as an exemplar of the cunning statesman. He concentrated on attacks against the Wei, seeing the north as the key to gaining the Mandate of Heaven. Though the kings who succeeded to the northern throne were weak, the repeated offensives from Sichuan all failed, in part because of the extended supply lines, at a high cost to the Shu Han.

In 263 a more competent Wei ruler, Yuandi, turned the tables and mounted an attack on Sichuan. His two main generals showed themselves to be brilliant strategists, and Sichuan was overcome. The Sichuan ruler tried to raise resistance, but failed and was killed. Victory did not preserve Yuandi, however. He was overthrown by a general who took the name of Wudi and set up his own dynasty, the Western Jin.

Wudi then turned on the Wu, who were now ruled by the dissolute grandson of their founder, a man said to have a harem of 5000 concubines. In 280 Wudi emerged victorious from the conflict during which he sent an armada of war junks down the Yangzi. China could now be said to be reunited, but its unity would prove fragile.

The Jin and the southern rulers

With his capital in Luoyang, Wudi, the Western Jin ruler from 265–89, proved to be an effective administrator who undertook public works and kept trade routes open. But the regime faced a familiar problem – the power of big landowners who had been granted estates in return for their services to the throne. This was not only a political matter, it also undermined the tax base. The central government could not force the great magnates to pay up; the result of this weakness, coupled with the effects of the wars, was that the taxable population in the Jin realm was put at only 16 million compared to 56 million under the later Han.

Wudi granted each of his 25 sons a domain. When he died, none could dominate the others. Widespread family strife broke out, with the successor to the throne, Huidi, forced by constant fighting to decamp from city to city. The situation was exacerbated by famine and incursions by northern nomads, some of whom were actually invited in by Huidi's successor, Huaidi, in a misguided attempt to use them against his own clan. By 316, when the next ruler, Mindi, was killed, a million people had emigrated from the Wei lands in search of security; tribal revolts had shaken the regime's fabric,

ABOVE A ceramic jar with figures from the Jin dynasty. The Jin period was characterized by weak government, powerful nobility and turmoil and strife amongst the peasantry.

ABOVE *The arts prospered in the southern capital of Nanjing. Classic river landscape painting flourished, an example of which can be seen in this detail from the later Jin period.*

and the anarchic state of northern China was an open invitation to the armies of the steppes to establish themselves inside the Great Wall.

In the centre-south, however, a new regime made up in part of refugees from the north, took shape under the name of the Eastern Jin. It claimed the Mandate of Heaven under 11 emperors who ruled from 317 to 419. They were not a distinguished group and, despite successful expeditions to Sichuan and Luoyang in 347 and 356, they failed in their attempts to restore their fortunes in the north. They also had the constant problem of dealing with extensive landed aristocratic families, which operated largely beyond central control and were the real holders of power.

The fertile Yangzi

The southern capital of Nanjing on the Yangzi was a prosperous city, its streets bustling with activity, its palaces famed for their splendour. The arts prospered with the development of classic river landscape painting. Calligraphy took a new, flowing form under a master whose characters were said to be '*light as a floating cloud, vigorous as a startled dragon*'. Buddhism had already spread in the north, and at the turn of the fourth century it made strides in the south, when a ruler converted to the foreign religion that had adapted to Chinese beliefs. (See Buddhism in China, pages 90–1.)

For the refugees from northern China, the luxuriance of the region was a revelation, encouraging the Taoist connection between man and nature, prompting the newcomers to forget about their harsher former homes and deepening the division of China along the line of its greatest river.

However, there was tension between the Eastern Jin and the longer-standing inhabitants of their territories. At the end of the fourth century the Eastern Jin faced a rising by a movement that claimed to have inherited the mantle of the Yellow Turbans of the late Han era. The revolt was led by Sun En – a pirate who was also an adherent of the Taoist Five Pecks of Rice sect. He recruited his men from among the sailors, fishermen and outlaws of the Zhejiang coast. They were also almost certainly in contact with the big landowners of the region, who saw the rising as a way of further weakening central authority as the rebel 'armies of demons' ravaged the shoreline from island bases and threatened Nanjing. The rebels were, however, put down in 402, causing a mass suicide in their ranks.

Dissolute rulers

One effect of this struggle was the emergence of military figures who became increasingly influential in the Eastern Jin regime. In 420 one of them, a general who had started out as a woodcutter and then fought well against the northerners, staged a coup and founded a ruling house of his own, the Liu Song, which held power from 420–79.

Under the new ruler Wudi and his son Wendi, the southern realm prospered further, expanding its territories and holding off attacks from the north – one of which got as far as the outskirts of Nanjing before being driven back. But the means by which Wudi had grabbed the throne meant the legitimacy of the governing house was always in question. On top of which, Wendi was succeeded by a string of incompetent rulers. One was a drunkard, another was so wild that his own officers killed him, a third (nicknamed 'the Pig') poisoned 33 members of his family, and a fourth amused himself by shooting blunt arrows at a target daubed on the stomach of a sleeping minister. (The latter was so enraged that he had the sovereign killed.) A fifth ruler, who came to the throne at the age of 13, was deposed within two years.

The new house, the Qi, which took over after a coup in 479 and governed until 501, expanded commerce and tried to reduce the power of the aristocracy. But only one of its five sovereigns could be counted as an able ruler, and there followed the familiar series of murders and young monarchs. The last, Hedi, who assumed the

286 Buddhist *Lotus Sutra* first translated into Chinese

366 Construction of the first of the Thousand Buddha caves at Dunhuang

414 Return from India of scholar-monk Fa Xian after a 15-year journey; he brings Sanskrit texts which become key to the spread of Buddhism

444 Northern Wei ruler persecutes Buddhists and advances Taoism. Buddhist monks flee to southern China, strengthening their religion there

450 Northern Wei army marches against southern rulers and reaches the walls of Nanjing, but is forced to retreat

451 Southerners stage unsuccessful counter-offensive against the north

502 Liang Wudi establishes the Liang dynasty in the south, promoting Confucianism and Buddhism

528 A Turkic army storms the northern capital of Luoyang. The young emperor is killed along with 2000 members of his court

548–56 The southern dynasty is pulled apart by bloody in-fighting

577 Expansion of the Zhou in the north, but then decline under a mentally ill ruler. General Yang Jian takes Luoyang and becomes regent before ascending the throne to found the Sui dynasty

throne at the age of 15, had six of his brothers killed, as well as the brother of his regent, who took his revenge by besieging Nanjing. Eighty thousand people were estimated to have died in the city before it fell to the regent, who founded a new dynasty. Hedi's guards decapitated him and sent his head, preserved in wax, to the new ruler.

Adopting the name of Liang Wudi, the former regent proved an able ruler at the head of the new Liang dynasty, which ruled from 502–57. A scholar and devoted Buddhist who stopped animal sacrifices and was reluctant to order executions, he also embraced Confucianism as a foundation for government. On three occasions he entered a Buddhist monastery, and only returned to power at the urgings of his ministers. His growing otherworldliness created a gulf between him and his people, however, while on the other hand he was criticized by Buddhists for paying too much attention to temporal affairs.

The Toba

In the anarchy that prevailed in northern China after the fall of the Western Jin, tribes from outside China proper moved across a wide arc stretching from Tibet in the west through Mongolia in the centre and on to the east. The first big threat came from the traditional enemy, the Xiongnu, who staged a successful attack on Chang'an. Though his men were still formidable horseback fighters, their leader, Liu Yuan, represented a break with the past. He had absorbed Chinese ways of thinking and wanted to establish a settled domain rather than follow the traditional nomadic pattern. At his court, Chinese ceremonials were performed and Chinese scholars were invited to enlist in his service as Liu sought to establish a claim to the Mandate of Heaven, invoking the marriages of the past between his predecessors and imperial daughters.

Liu died in 310. The next year, the Xiongnu took Luoyang and their leader proclaimed the dynasty of the Earlier Zhou, which survived for 16 years. But the ensuing tribal leaders were not interested in following the Chinese model of governance – or life. They went back to a nomadic existence, leaving the invasion role to Tibetans who swept over the north of China, recruiting local infantrymen to complement their cavalry and proclaiming yet another pretender dynasty, the Earlier Qin. After defeating a northern tribal federation, the Toba, the Tibetans carried on towards the Yangzi and the Eastern Jin lands in 383. But the terrain beyond the Yellow River was strange to them, and they were defeated.

> The Chinese are your slaves, the men farm for you, the women make your clothing, so they bring you what you eat and what you want, allowing you to be warm and full, why do you want to oppress them?

TOBA GENERAL SPEAKING TO HIS PEOPLE IN THEIR NATIVE TONGUE, XIANBEI

This gave a chance to the Toba, who had reorganized themselves. Bringing together several tribal groups, they developed an army, which forged westwards into Gansu to control the trade routes to Central Asia, and conducted successful campaigns against northern nomads. Having settled down, they decided to absorb China's methods of government, and sought to reconcile the nomads and the Chinese.

THE GLORY OF LUOYANG

In 493, the Northern Wei moved their capital south to a historic site at Luoyang, which could trace its roots back to before 2100 BC. After nine years, the metropolis grew to accommodate half a million inhabitants.

Palaces and official buildings were erected behind the thick protective wall. Nobles, officials, eunuchs and merchants occupied fine mansions with lofty gateways. Charitable donations paid for 421 Buddhist monasteries and convents. There was an exquisite Buddha Hall and a soaring pagoda.

After its years of glory, Luoyang was caught up in factional struggles that rocked the Northern Wei in the early sixth century. A white-skinned northern commander, Erhchu Jung, led an army into the Yellow River region and swept down on Luoyang. He summoned officials from the city to pay homage to his candidate for the throne; when they left the safety of the defensive wall they were butchered, and the empress dowager and her baby were thrown into a river to drown.

Erhchu Jung kept Luoyang as the capital for his puppet ruler, but the city went into sharp decline. Eventually, the ruler he had installed turned on the general, inviting him to the palace and killing him. Hearing the news, Jung's men went on the rampage, killing, looting and raping, and taking the emperor to their headquarters, where he was strangled.

In 534, a military strongman decided to move the capital from Luoyang for strategic reasons. In a few days the city and the surrounding region were emptied of people – perhaps two million moved. A poem written by the emperor who was strangled by Erhchu Jung's followers might stand as a lament for Luoyang's brief glory:

*'Full of regret I left Luoyang
behind;
Sadly, I now enter the land
of ghosts …
Nor more will that dark court
see light.
A bird sings pensively among
green pines
Amid white poplars mourns
the wind'.*

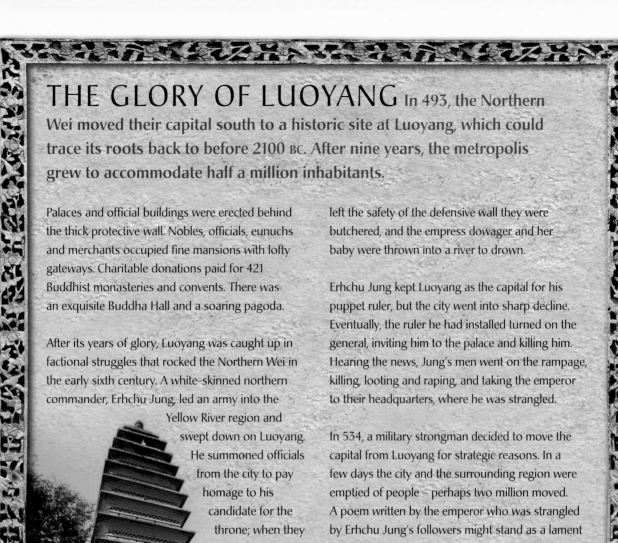

LEFT *The Qiyun Pagoda (Cloud-reaching Pagoda) in Luoyang is believed to be China's first pagoda. The original wooden pavilion burned down and it was rebuilt in brick in 1175.*

In the absence of a written script of their own, they adopted Chinese characters. Chinese scholars and officials were employed to institute a Confucian bureaucracy. A large palace complex was built in the capital of Pingcheng, in the far north of the Toba lands, along with residential areas to take the place of the nomads' traditional tents. But the relationship with China remained edgy for many, while a contemporary observer noted the differences between ways of life in the north and in the south:

> *'To the south of the Yellow River, the husband must cut a good figure in public, however impoverished the family may be. He would not scrimp on his carriages or clothes, even if his extravagance causes his wife and children to suffer hunger and cold. To the north of the Yellow River, it is usually the wife who runs the household. She will not dispense with good clothing or expensive jewellery. The husband has to settle for old horses and sickly servants. The traditional niceties between husband and wife are seldom observed, and, from time to time, he even has to put up with her insults'.*

> FROM THE *FAMILY COUNSELS OF MR YAN*, MID-SIXTH CENTURY

The Toba ran a tough, centralized regime, watching workers closely and making family groups responsible for the maintenance of order. The state assumed ownership of land and parcelled it out to the peasants in accordance with the number of men available for farm work. People were deported to populate the region around the capital on the edge of the steppes. Female infanticide was common.

But, as the Toba settled down, their attacks on other tribes diminished. Part of the motivation for the sinicization process they encouraged may have been that they wanted to diminish the power of the warrior chiefs around them and institute an administration which answered only to the throne.

Northern Wei

By the middle of the fifth century, when they constituted the most powerful group in China, the Toba had become sinicized as a new dynasty, the Northern Wei. Their ruler decreed that Pingcheng was a place from which to wage war, not to rule. So the capital was moved to Luoyang. The transfer took two years, with seven more required

❝ I had a distant relative in whose household there were many concubines. When any were pregnant and the time of delivery drew near, janitors and servants were set to watch. As soon as the birth pains were noticed, the watchers waited at the door and peered through the windows. If a girl was born, it was snatched away at once, though the mother screamed and cried, no-one dared to save it; one could not bear to listen. ❞

FROM THE *FAMILY COUNSELS OF MR YAN*, MID-SIXTH CENTURY

to rebuild it to sufficient size and grandeur: at its completion it had walls 30 metres (100 ft) thick, a water supply system, grain-processing machinery and a population that rose to 500,000. Buddhist monasteries and monuments sprouted in and around the city, making it the main centre of the religion in East Asia. Foreign relations flourished as envoys arrived at the Wei court and the southern Chinese established links in Southeast Asia. (See Links with the Outside World, page 89.)

Impressive as Luoyang was, it was far from the Toba's northern roots. There was considerable opposition at court to the move. Several senior figures staged a short-lived revolt in protest. The heir apparent tried to move back to the far north; his

TABLE OF DYNASTIES AND KINGDOMS

THE THREE KINGDOMS 220–80

Wei	220–64
Wu	222–80
Shu Han	221–63

PERIOD OF DISUNION 265–589

Western Jin	265–316
Eastern Jin	317–419
Liu Song	420–79
Qi	479–501
Liang	502–57
Chen	557–89

SIXTEEN NORTHERN KINGDOMS 304–439

NORTHERN DYNASTIES 386–581

Northern Wei	386–534
Eastern Wei	534–50
Western Wei	535–57
Northern Qi	550–77
Northern Zhou	557–81

father had him imprisoned, and then forced him to commit suicide. Nor were the tribesmen and nomadic warriors comfortable with the increasing influence of the Chinese. The end of their raids across the steppes meant that they no longer benefited from plunder. Sedentary farming was alien to them, however much their rulers enjoyed the claim to be emperors.

The Toba court also fell prey to another familiar aspect of Chinese dynasties – factional infighting. In 528, one group attacked Luoyang and sacked the city. The child emperor and the empress drowned in the Yellow River, and 2000 courtiers and aristocrats were slaughtered.

The realm was divided between one leader who kept Chinese traditions alive in his capital of Chang'an, and another who rejected sinicization. Two new dynasties followed, fighting one another until 577. By then the centuries of struggles across the huge expanse of northern China had finally taken their toll, and it was time for a unifying force to emerge which could bring together the north and south.

The Chen

In Nanjing, meanwhile, Liang Wudi's son rose against his father, egged on by a northern ally. They took the southern city after a bitter siege. Wudi greeted them with suitably understanding Buddhist words: '*You have campaigned long. You must be tired*'. His life was spared. The dynasty then careered downhill, weakened by its own internal rivalries and by drought, famine and a plague of locusts. The new ruler was soon murdered by his northern ally, who was attacked by another member of the family and cut into pieces, which were thrown to the mob.

The next sovereign, Yuandi, another of Wudi's sons, was a man of great cruelty, who starved opponents to death in prison. He was a firm believer in the magical charms of Taoism. When he was overthrown by troops under a grandson of Wudi, he burned his library of 200,000 books and left the hall in a white mourning robe, abdicating in favour of one of his sons. The latter was then killed at the age of 16 by another rival, Chen Wudi, who took the throne in 557 to found his own dynasty.

After a year, the new ruler of the Chen gave up power to enter a monastery, and the familiar succession struggles erupted. In 583 the mantle passed to a particularly incompetent figure, described as a drunk, dissolute, extravagant and superstitious wastrel who left government to the eunuchs. But by then, a new power was rising that would end the centuries of disunion and re-unite the empire.

LINKS WITH THE OUTSIDE WORLD

Although it was a time of great chaos and upheaval, the long Period of Disunion saw China establishing links with the outside world and exploring its own more remote regions.

Between 553 and 578, embassies arrived at the northern courts from Persia and the states of Central Asia. There was tribute from lands across the Pamir Mountains. For a time, a Chinese presence was re-established in Korea. One fleet sent to help Manchurian rulers was said to have numbered 100 ships, carrying 8000 men.

Peoples from Tibet, Mongolia and Manchuria settled in Chinese territory, took Chinese names and begat families that became prominent in the re-unified empire. While the Toba regime adopted Chinese ways, the newcomers brought fresh ideas with them to both the northern and southern portions of China, making this a time of intellectual debate – when there was time for it amid all the fighting.

The southern dynasties maintained relations not only with Central Asia but also with Southeast Asia and the islands of Japan. Envoys were sent to the Mekong Delta and Cambodia. Between the fourth and six centuries, ambassadors came from India, Ceylon and Java, while Nanjing housed diplomats and traders from as far away as Iran.

In China itself, travellers explored the wild regions of the southwest and crossed into the Red River Delta of Vietnam. in the southeast. Two major works were compiled on the flora, fauna, products and customs of these areas, inhabited mainly by aboriginal minor tribes.

Divisions at home therefore did not prevent China from playing the regional role which its size and population merited, or from finding out more about itself.

Earthenware sculpture of a foreigner riding a camel, dating from the mid-sixth to mid-seventh century. It was during this period that China established many links with the outside world.

BUDDHISM IN CHINA
There is a certain irony in the way that the otherworldly religion of Buddhism flourished in China during the Period of Disunion, when rulers were engaged in recurrent material struggles. Its appeal to the rulers of the north was that it was, as one put it, a 'barbarian' religion which offered them an alternative to Chinese Confucianism.

Buddhism had first reached China long before the Period of Disunion, both along the trading routes that linked the Middle Kingdom with Central Asia and India, and by sea. A monk who had been sent to explore these far-off lands returned with word of the religion, and Han generals who fought campaigns in the far west brought further news. Some Buddhist teachers appear to have started working in China in the first century BC. In the next century, Emperor Mingdi was recorded as having sent an envoy to find out about the religion after dreaming of a man with a glowing head:

'There is a current tradition that Emperor Ming dreamed that he saw a tall golden man, the top of whose head was glowing. He questioned his group of advisers and one said: "In the West there is a god called Buddha. His body is 16 chi [5.3 metres/17.5 ft] high and is the colour of true gold". To discover the true doctrine, the emperor sent an envoy to Tianzhu [northwestern India] to inquire about the Buddha's doctrine, after which paintings and statues appeared in the Middle Kingdom'.

THE LATER HAN CHRONICLE

Temples and missionaries
The emissary returned in AD 67 with two priests and sutras containing 600,000 words. A Buddhist worshipping place, known as the White Horse Temple, was erected outside the gates of the Han capital. Mingdi showed interest in the religion, but did not actually convert.

The Buddhist presence advanced after the arrival in 148 of a Parthian missionary who set up temples in Luoyang and translated sacred texts into Chinese. But it still occupied a marginal place and initially existed in the shadow of Taoism, with which it had some similarities. Its original central beliefs, such as spiritual enlightenment, monastic life and chastity, were at best alien to the Chinese and, more probably, seen as actively threatening the basic tenets of Confucianism, including filial piety and devotion to the emperor. Nirvana must have appeared a useless, abstract aim in life to the practical Chinese élite, soldiers and gentry.

The process by which this foreign faith became a central belief system for China depended on several factors. Buddhism, as propagated in China, was adapted to stress elements likely to appeal to the local people, such as Indian sutras exhorting fealty of children to parents, while Buddhist missionaries argued that their beliefs could strengthen the imperial state. A text stating that *'Husband supports wife'* and *'Wife comforts husband'* became the more Chinese *'Husband controls wife'* and *'Wife reveres husband'*. Local gods were not rejected and were absorbed along with Taoist teachings.

The non-Chinese rulers who established themselves in the north during the Period of Disunion provided the vital material boost, seeing the advantages of a religion that enabled them to establish a separate identity. They might employ Confucianism for affairs of state, but Buddhism offered an alternative spiritual path which could be used to bind their disparate peoples together, independently of the old Chinese aristocracy or the bureaucracy. They could aspire to be the 'wheel-turning kings' who distinguished themselves by piety and, as a result, governed well.

'We were born out on the marshes and, though we are unworthy, we have complied with our destiny and govern the Chinese as their prince … Buddha being a barbarian god is the one we should worship'.

NORTHERN KING, c.335

These rulers gave large sums to build Buddhist monasteries and to have sacred texts translated from Sanskrit into Chinese. The nomad chief who conquered Luoyang in the early fourth century was introduced to a Buddhist missionary just before the final attack on the city. In an account set down two centuries later, the missionary *'took his begging bowl, filled it with water, burned incense, and said a spell over it. In a moment, there sprang up blue lotus flowers whose brightness and colour dazzled the eyes'*. That event made the ruler give the Buddhists the right to build monasteries, and Luoyang became one of the religion's main centres in China.

On a cliff face outside the city, enormous Buddhist sculptures were carved in a direct response to the great monuments of previous dynasties. In this way the heirs of the northern nomads used the new religion to set out their stall in massive shape at the heart of the domain of the Han. Artistic politics, a recurrent factor in imperial history, was rarely more impressive.

The afterlife

In southern China, Buddhism took hold somewhat later, under the Liang dynasty. So complete was its founder's conversion that he retired three times to a monastery. For peasants in both north and south, the religion appears to have been attractive in offering solace in hard times. Its vision of the afterlife, with the possibility of positive reincarnation, was a lot more appealing than the Chinese prospect of a netherworld filled with suffering. A further attraction was that because Buddhism could be adapted to local customs, a peasant could adopt it but still worship local deities.

The work of influential, persuasive teachers helped the process further during the fifth century. The self-denying way of life of Buddhist monks could only strike a chord with oppressed peasants fearful of dying in wars or natural disasters. The way in which these monks moved about among the ordinary people was something new in China, a grass-roots contact, which contrasted with the élite world of Confucian officialdom.

Naturally, the Buddhist communities were not blameless, and were accused of amassing land and riches from the donations given to them. Some northern rulers, in search of targets as their own authority came into question in the sixth century,

turned on them, confiscating their land. But, by the end of the Period of Disunion, Buddhism was established as a major religion in China and could only grow further as its savvy adaptation to national beliefs enabled it to embrace ideas from Confucianism, Taoism and other Chinese doctrines. Its Chinese manifestation would continue for so long that the last major ruler of the empire would be known as 'the Old Buddha'.

A bronze cast of a contemplating Buddhist monk. Although Buddhism might at first appear at odds with the established principles of Chinese Confucianism, subtle changes to some of the sutras made it more relevant to the Chinese way of life, and Buddhism took hold in China during the Period of Disunion.

THE SUI

581–618

Although their rule lasted for less than 40 years and their reputation was assailed by their successors, the three Sui rulers re-established the basis for a national empire after their northern founder, Duke Yang Jian, displaced the boy emperor and took the throne, assuming the reign name of Wendi.

BORN IN A BUDDHIST TEMPLE IN 541, YANG WAS A FORMIDABLE FIGURE. HE CAME FROM A long-established aristocratic family in the far west of the Yellow River plain, and was raised by a Buddhist nun until the age of 12. Enrolled in an academy for the sons of the nobility, he absorbed the skills of horsemanship, hunting, archery and military tactics. His contemporaries regarded him as aloof and unapproachable.

Establishing himself among the northern élite, Yang gained a dukedom and took part in a series of campaigns that brought the region under the control of a single dynasty, the Northern Zhou, ruled by Emperor Wu. The 27-year-old aristocrat-soldier became one of the dominant figures at court, despite the official proscription of Buddhism, which he practised. His position was reinforced when the crown prince, Yuwen Pin, married Yang's eldest daughter.

But when Emperor Wu died and was succeeded by Pin, Yang fell under the suspicion of his son-in-law, a violent, abusive man who at one point threatened to liquidate his clan. Its leader survived, however, and when Pin died in 580 after having abdicated in favour of his son, Yang made his power play. Two of his allies forged documents giving him control of the armed forces of the Northern Zhou. He eliminated opponents at court and sent an army to defeat dynastic loyalists. The infant successor to Pin – Yang's own grandson – was murdered, together with 59 members of his family. In 581 Yang had himself proclaimed emperor at the head of the Sui dynasty, taking the name of Wendi.

River wars

Having gained the throne at the head of a united northern China, Wendi forged south in 588–9. His forces were said to comprise half a million men in eight armies stretched out from the Yangzi gorges to the sea. They faced only 100,000 troops of the

RIGHT The first emperor of the Sui dynasty was Wendi, who ruled from 581–604. He usurped the throne and the rightful claimant, the boy emperor, was murdered. Wendi's reign was a period of great economic prosperity for China.

southern Chen rulers. The Sui made thorough preparations, drawing on the united resources of the north and an array of capable, experienced generals. Canals were built, granaries established and 100,000 horses collected for the cavalry. Wendi legitimized the attack with an edict listing the crimes of the southern Chen ruler, to seek to establish that he had no claim on the Mandate of Heaven and that it was his duty to overthrow him. Three hundred thousand pamphlets relaying the edict were supposedly distributed in Chen territories. The Sui also made alliances with minority groups in the far south, including one led by a woman warlord.

The Chen were divided and lackadaisical. A major city fell as its defenders lay about drunk. The Chen ruler was said to have left unopened an urgent message warning of a river crossing, and to have been discovered hiding in a well with two concubines by troops who took his capital.

SUI DYNASTY EMPERORS

Wendi	581–604
Yangdi	604–17
Gongdi	617–18

Armadas conquer China

The Sui built a large fleet in Sichuan, in western China, to sail down the Yangzi and fight in concert with land forces. It was dominated by huge vessels known as 'five-toothed' warships; with five decks reaching to an overall height of 30 metres (100 ft) from which archers fired at the enemy. The boats could carry 800 men and were armed with six 15-metre (50-ft) spiked booms. Sailing down the Yangzi to the Wolf's Tail Rapid by the Three Gorges, the fleet found 100 southern warships blocking its path, while Chen forts lined the river banks. Under cover of darkness the Sui fleet slipped past the forts, the men on board

biting on sticks to ensure silence. It then attacked the enemy vessels, while Sui infantry and cavalry successfully stormed Chen positions.

Continuing downriver, the armada was blocked by three strong chains that had been strung across the Yangzi between fortified positions. Three daylight attacks against the shore failed, at the cost of 5000 Sui lives. There followed a night raid combined with a land attack, in which the defenders were overcome and the chains removed. At a final battle on the river near Jingmen Mountain in what is now Hubei province, four Sui warships used their spiked booms to smash enemy ships. This was followed by a general assault that carried the day and destroyed Chen resistance in central China. By the end of 590 the south was conquered, and the Sui ruled, albeit somewhat uncertainly, over the whole of China.

The new order

Ruling from 581–604, Wendi gained the backing of the Confucian scholarly élite and sought to legitimize and cement his rule through social, bureaucratic, religious and military reforms. The northern capital was reconstructed, and the philosophy of the new dynasty was formed with Buddhism as its central pillar. Nepotism was partially suppressed and the bureaucracy reformed to create a simpler, more loyal and efficient service.

RIGHT *Statuette of a warrior from the late Sui/early Tang period. The first Sui emperor, Wendi, was an intelligent and cunning war strategist, who conquered his enemies north and south to rule over the whole of China.*

581 Foundation of the Sui dynasty in the north by Emperor Wendi

590 Sui re-unify China

600 Japan sends the first of four missions to study the Chinese system of government

601 Major programme to build Buddhist stupas across the empire

604 Emperor Yangdi ascends the throne; the Grand Canal is developed

608 A two-year mission strengthens links with Southeast Asia

609 Census puts the population of China at 50 million

613–14 Two invasions fail to establish Chinese authority over Korea, while putting strain on the imperial treasury

616 A bridge on the Grand Canal is built with 1000 one-tonne stones

617 Government authority fragments and the situation is compounded by flooding of the Yellow River and a Turkic invasion in the north; General Li Yuan leads revolt, takes Chang'an and instals a six-year-old as Emperor Gongdi

618 Li Yuan captures Luoyang. The previous emperor, Yangdi, is strangled by the son of a disgraced official. Li Yuan declares himself emperor and founds the Tang dynasty

Forcing local armies to disband, the first Sui ruler re-imposed central government, rebuilding the Great Wall to keep out nomadic invaders, introducing a common currency, establishing granaries and implementing land reform. Waterways, including the Grand Canal in eastern China, were developed to move food around his domain, and a new capital was established a short distance south of the former Han capital of Chang'an, near present-day Xi'an. Hard-working and austere, Wendi evolved an effective administrative system and conciliated southerners by giving them guaranteed positions. The law was applied equally – even to the emperor's son.

His son Yangdi (r. 604–17) was a devout Buddhist, much influenced by time he spent in the south. He encouraged Confucian studies, built huge libraries, but lost the backing of the northern nomads. He constructed a new second capital at Luoyang and extended his father's canals so that they reached almost every part of the empire. For a ceremonial progress on the Grand Canal, he had a boat built with four decks and 120 rooms for his concubines – 80,000 men were used to pull the imperial fleet along the waterway. Before long, his extravagance exhausted the treasury.

Korean adventure

Equally serious was the effect of repeated unsuccessful attempts to conquer Korea. One campaign was recorded as involving more than a million troops and 3000 warships. Another Chinese army was so enormous that it took 30 days to leave its base, its columns stretching over 300 miles (500 km). The Koreans were tactically superior, harrying the extended supply lines and bringing the skills of their archers to bear with bows that were said to be able to fire arrows up to 600 metres (2000 ft). Chinese soldiers froze in the extreme winter cold; only a tiny proportion returned home from the defeats, sometimes taking years to regain their homes. When the emperor ordered conscription to raise a new army, peasants and urban dwellers hid.

Heavy taxation and conscription to pay for the wars in Korea, together with the emperor's projects and the wars themselves, sparked widespread anger. Flooding of the Yellow River set off a wave of revolts which the imperial forces put down ruthlessly, setting off more protests. A northern military adventurer exploited the discontent to lead an army to take Chang'an in 617. Yangdi fled southwards, where he was strangled by the son of a minister he had expelled from court. His grandson Gongdi succeeded to the throne, but power lay with the regent, Li Yuan, who defeated opponents to take Luoyang. In 618 Li Yuan had himself declared emperor, founding the Tang dynasty which would rule until 907.

CHINA'S CANAL SYSTEM The Sui emperors developed
an extensive network of canals radiating out from their capital of Luoyang,
which thus became the hub of a major transport system.

The dynasty's first waterway, the Guangtong Canal, which stretched for around 120 miles (190 km) from Luoyang to the confluence of the Wei and Yellow Rivers, compensated for the poor navigability of the silt-choked Wei River. Much more important was the Grand Canal, which was made of two branches – northern and southern. The longest stretch amounted to 600 miles (1000 km) and, counting all its tributaries, totalled some 1800 miles (2400 km).

It ferried grain and supplies, and played an important military role in enabling the emperors to

The Grand Canal running through the city of Suzhou in southeastern China. When the Grand Canal was completed, Suzhou was at the heart of a major trade route. The city then became a centre for trade and industry.

move troops swiftly across the country. In national terms, the canal system was instrumental in joining together the wheat-growing north and the rice-rich south. A writer under the Tang dynasty looked back to the *'intolerable sufferings'* inflicted on those drafted in to labour on the project, but added that it had *'provided endless benefits'* to the next rulers.

TANG DYNASTY: THE FOUNDERS

618—49

After overthrowing the Sui, the Tang dynasty ushered in a golden age of Chinese history. Once the new regime was consolidated, it embarked on a programme of expansion that reached from Korea deep into Central Asia. As its prestige soared, neighbouring countries acknowledged China's overlordship. Tang China was considered the greatest political and military power on earth and provided a model for government and culture that was widely copied in East Asia.

THIS WAS AN ARISTOCRATIC REALM, BUT A STRONG OFFICIAL CLASS ALSO EMERGED. THE DYNASTY sought to impose uniform control from the centre. Land holdings were reorganized. The later part of the Tang era saw an unusually brilliant period marked by a great flourishing of the arts, including poetry, essays and the characteristic sculpted horses and female figures. Porcelain became a Chinese speciality. (See Chinese Porcelain, page 173.) The dynasty's capital of Chang'an, near present-day Xi'an, was the greatest walled city ever known, and a magnet for foreigners. Its two great markets dealt in grain, timber, tea, salt, horses, slaves, silks and jewels. (See The Markets of Chang'an, page 103.)

Buddhism grew in strength. In the later seventh century, China had its only female emperor, the extraordinary Wu Zetian. But, as so often, the dynasty faced growing internal flaws that were heightened by a long rebellion in the middle of the eighth century, which left the dynasty seriously weakened. In 907 a military governor took the throne, ushering in a new period of short-lived competing dynasties before China was united once again.

The Early Tang – Gaozu

A northern general, Li Yuan, who had led a defensive campaign against northern nomads for the Sui, decided to rebel in 617, reportedly at the urging of his son. He

RIGHT Li Yuan, the first emperor of the Tang dynasty, from a portrait painted in the 18th century. He took the reign name of Gaozu, meaning 'High Progenitor'. He lowered taxes, redistributed land among the people and reformed the harsh rule of law established by Emperor Yangdi of the Sui.

marched on the capital of Chang'an to seize the throne the following year under the name of Wudi, although he is generally referred to by his posthumous temple title of Gaozu ('High Progenitor'). The new dynasty took its name from the title of the duke of Tang, which had been granted to his grandfather.

The new emperor, who would rule until 626, came to the throne at a difficult time, when the weakening of the Sui – exacerbated by the strain of its expedition into Korea – had encouraged revolts in northern China. On top of this, there was a pressing danger from the eastern Turkic peoples, who had attacked Shanxi. Li led the foreigners to think that he might become their vassal, thereby gaining their support for his attack on the Sui, after which he made it clear that he was going to be his own man.

Once enthroned, Li had a suitably august family tree drawn up to link him to the Han. In fact, he came from a mixture of Chinese, Turkic and northern nomad stock – a familiar product of the unsettled times in the north of China during the previous turbulent centuries.

TURKESTAN

TIBET

Tang empire

temporary Tang expansion, seventh century

A new foundation

Like many dynasty founders, the new sovereign's first concern was to deal with rivals and rebels in order to consolidate his position. Although his son and successor would have him described as a second-rate ruler with a weakness for music and women, Gaozu was actually efficient. By the time of his death he had succeeded in imposing the new dynasty on China, thus laying a solid foundation for the glories to come. He also built on the infrastructure improvements of the Sui, notably canals.

Instead of eliminating his predecessor, the emperor sought to win over the Sui family and its officials by sparing their lives and issuing amnesties. The administrative system implemented under the Sui was maintained, both at central and local levels. A new coinage was introduced. Confucianism was revived. Defences were erected on the northern borders.

The empire was divided into ten large regions which were put under the authority of inspectors. In agriculture, the aim was to achieve an equal distribution of land among citizens who acted as farmers during times of peace and as soldiers during wartime. The plots were held only for a single lifetime, after which they reverted to the empire to be re-distributed. The system was designed to facilitate collection of taxes, since the authorities would know who owned what, and where. How well it worked in a society dominated by military and court aristocrats is uncertain. It appears to have been applied particularly in the north and west, and to have proved more tricky to implement in the rice lands of the south, which were difficult to split up. Two capitals were established to span the empire, one in Chang'an and the other in Luoyang. Higher education

EARLY TANG EMPERORS

Gaozu	618–26
Taizong	626–49

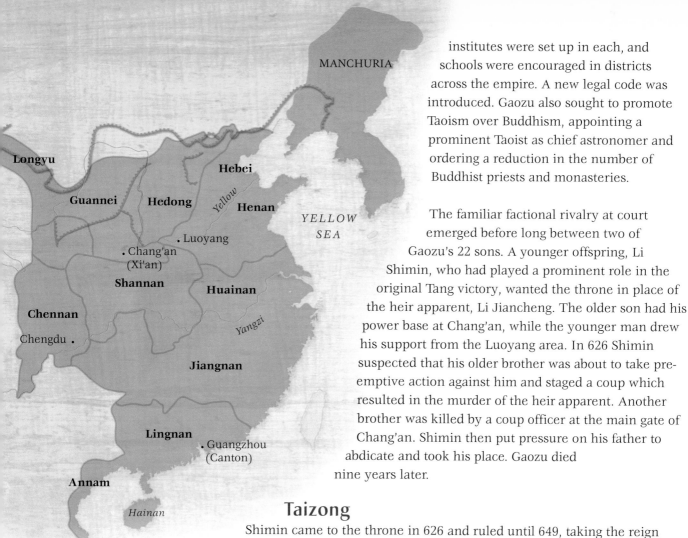

MANCHURIA

Longyu

Hebei

Guannei   Hedong   Yellow   Henan   YELLOW
                                           SEA

. Luoyang

. Chang'an
  (Xi'an)

Shannan   Huainan

Chennan

Chengdu .   Yangzi

                Jiangnan

        Lingnan
          . Guangzhou
            (Canton)

Annam

    Hainan

institutes were set up in each, and schools were encouraged in districts across the empire. A new legal code was introduced. Gaozu also sought to promote Taoism over Buddhism, appointing a prominent Taoist as chief astronomer and ordering a reduction in the number of Buddhist priests and monasteries.

The familiar factional rivalry at court emerged before long between two of Gaozu's 22 sons. A younger offspring, Li Shimin, who had played a prominent role in the original Tang victory, wanted the throne in place of the heir apparent, Li Jiancheng. The older son had his power base at Chang'an, while the younger man drew his support from the Luoyang area. In 626 Shimin suspected that his older brother was about to take pre-emptive action against him and staged a coup which resulted in the murder of the heir apparent. Another brother was killed by a coup officer at the main gate of Chang'an. Shimin then put pressure on his father to abdicate and took his place. Gaozu died nine years later.

Taizong

Shimin came to the throne in 626 and ruled until 649, taking the reign name of Taizong ('Supreme Ancestor'). The manner in which he ascended the throne caused some shock, even in a country and an age that had seen much blood-letting at the various dynastic courts. A myth arose that Taizong had been obliged to explain himself to the King of the Dead who, on hearing Taizong's claim that he had had to *destroy his family in order to save the kingdom*, allowed him to return to the land of the living. However, his earlier role in the campaign to take the throne on behalf of his father earned him a high military reputation, which he sought to burnish by having court writers deliver their unflattering account of Gaozu's abilities. Clearly, Taizong was a man who would brook no rivalry.

Judged by his achievements, however, he was genuinely one of the great rulers of China, showing an acute awareness of the realities of governance as he compared himself to a ship and the people to the surrounding waters. It was, he reasoned, in his interest to maintain calm and contentment and to avoid the storms of angry mobs. Accordingly, he lightened the load of forced labour on peasants, reduced taxes and juggled Confucianism, Taoism and Buddhism in search of a consensual form of rule.

The new ruler was intensely focused, well read and hard-working – documents were pasted to the wall around his bed so that he could work on them if he awoke during the night. He knew the value of good subordinates.

唐高祖

姓李名淵 祖虎事後周封唐國公

代隋目女傳位太子號太上皇在位九年

壽七十一

The empire expands

Apart from the stability he brought at home, Taizong's reign was celebrated for an enormous expansion of territory controlled by the empire. He undertook a series of successful offensives in Mongolia and the far west, allowing his armies to penetrate into Central Asia and India. To the east, Chinese forces won several victories in Korea, but also suffered a defeat there in 645.

States in present-day Vietnam acknowledged the suzerainty of the Tang. Chinese cultural influence became strong in Japan. Expansion opened trade routes, and foreign goods flowed into Chang'an. So did exotic customs, religions and clothing.

Polo was imported from Persia and the sport became popular among the aristocracy in a society in which horses were treasured. (See The Horse – Symbol of Wealth and Military Might, pages 106–7.) China felt so confident that it actively embraced influences from abroad instead of fearing or rejecting them.

ABOVE *The Tang empire was at its pinnacle under the emperor Taizong. He brought peace and stability, while greatly expanding the territory under his control.*

❝ With bronze as a mirror, one can correct one's improper appearance; with history as a mirror, one can understand the rise and fall of a nation; with good men as a mirror, one can distinguish right from wrong. ❞

TANG EMPEROR TAIZONG

Balance of government

This early period of the Tang dynasty was one of aristocratic, military dominance while, at the same time, the administration became increasingly mature. At the centre there was a balance between court factions, the families of the empresses and the eunuchs. Ministries in the Department of State Affairs dealt with administration, finance, the military, public works and justice. The chancellery checked and distributed decrees. The grand secretariat produced official texts. A council of state brought together the ruler, major figures and the heads of the ministries. On top of this, the court of censors was charged with detecting abuses and receiving complaints. Other departments were responsible for palace services, waterways, arsenals, the university, the palace guard and the imperial library.

The structure for imperial administration was thus set. The ruler was acutely aware of the extent to which he depended on competent subordinates. '*Sometimes I remain sleepless until the middle of the night, considering the capabilities of various officials*', Taizong revealed. '*I list their names on the screen and review them, marking good deeds under the doers. Being isolated in the palace, my contacts do not extend far; thus the prosperity or degeneration of the empire depends upon them'.*

The civil service examination system was further developed to pick the brightest young men, with the addition of a new subject, poetry, which the Tang cherished and which flourished as a result. Another characteristic of the administration emerged which was to be present to the end: the small number of imperial officials sent out to administer the provinces. The central authority did not want to see a substantial group of decentralized functionaries, and the theory was that it was enough for the throne to issue instructions for them to be followed. In practice, this meant that the men sent out to run the empire on the ground were heavily dependent on their local staffs and on the co-operation of the gentry in the region to which they were posted.

THE MARKETS OF CHANG'AN The two big markets of the Tang capital of Chang'an were at the centre of a transport system of roads and canals, and served as the eastern end of the Silk Road.

In keeping with Tang control mechanisms, the markets were highly regulated under directors who made sure that the rules were followed, inspected goods and produce for their quality and checked weights and measures. Because of a shortage of the bronze used for coins, silk was the main currency for commerce. The directors watched price movements and acted to stop big traders cornering a commodity.

The Eastern Market contained both accommodation for students preparing for the imperial examinations and official brothels, which prostitutes could only leave if a

The markets at Chang'an were a place where every commodity could be bought and sold – including women.

customer posted a bond with the madams, who posed as the girls' mothers.

The Silk Road brought many foreigners through Chang'an. While their commercial activity was allowed, the government kept a close watch on them, ensuring that their travel documents were regularly inspected and that they had proof of legal ownership of their goods, animals and slaves.

IN SEARCH OF BUDDHIST TRUTHS

In 629 a monk called Xuan Zhang began one of the most famous journeys in Chinese history: to seek the truths of Buddhism in India.

A Tang dynasty fresco showing the transportation of the golden image of Buddha. Buddhism continued to grow during this period.

At the time, Emperor Taizong did not approve of the Buddhist religion, and the monk's 10,000-mile (16,000-km) trip was made secretly, since Buddhists were forbidden to leave the country. On the way, Xuan Zhang experienced many perils – he was threatened with death by his guide and nearly died of thirst in the Gobi Desert. On his way west, he was captured in the deserts of present-day Xinjiang by a king, who was so impressed by the monk that he freed him to continue on his way, offering him assistance.

In India, the monk sailed on the Ganges, where he was captured by pirates, who planned to sacrifice him to their gods. Xuan Zhang told them that he had no objection to their using his 'miserable body' in this way but warned them that he had not yet achieved enlightenment: *'I fear that if you were to sacrifice me now, it would be more likely to bring you bad luck than good'*. A storm then blew up which made the pirates think that he might be right, so they released him. The monk went on to see the tree under which Buddha was said to have attained enlightenment. He spent time at a leading temple and gained such fame that an Indian emperor bowed before him. At an 18-day convention, the monk won arguments with the greatest Buddhist scholars of the day.

In 645 he returned to China with 657 sutras packed into 520 cases. Though he could not know it, this helped to preserve such teachings when Hinduism sought to supplant Buddhism in India. Zhang had great knowledge of the religion and experience of lands unfamiliar to most Chinese. The emperor greeted him and offered support for his translation work on sacred texts, ensuring the growth of Buddhism. By the time Xuan Zhang died in 664, he and his associates had translated 73 of the sutras. He also left a book, *Records of the Western Regions*, which became the basis for one of the great classic sagas, *Journey to the West*.

Taoism versus Buddhism

In the early years of his reign Taizong appeared more friendly towards Buddhism than his father had been, ordering a moratorium on the closing of the monasteries. But then he delivered a broadside against Buddha as *'nothing more than a crafty barbarian who deluded his own countrymen'* and whose teachings had been dressed up by ill-intentioned men in China in *'bizarre and mysterious language'* to mislead the uneducated masses. *'Buddhism offers no benefits to our people'*, he declared. *'On the contrary, it is injurious to the state. It is not that I do not understand Buddhism, but rather that I despise it and refuse to study it'.*

However, he showed his awareness of the hold the religion from India had achieved by continuing to leave in abeyance the purge ordered by his father on priests and monasteries, and by allowing some new buildings to be put up. In keeping with his metaphor on governing, it was best not to agitate the sea of Buddhism around him. But Taoist ceremonies were accorded precedence, and legal sanctions introduced, designed to restrict Buddhists to their own establishments and stop them proselytizing. He changed his mind, however, after the return to China of Xuan Zhang from an epic journey to India, which greatly impressed him. (See In Search of Buddhist Truths, left). Taizong took Xuan as his spiritual mentor and authorized the ordination of 18,500 Buddhist clergy.

Turkish roots

Seeking to avoid the frequent succession disputes, Taizong named one of his 14 sons as his heir early in his reign. But the young man had a homosexual affair that horrified his father, who ordered his lover to be killed. After that, the prince developed a fixation with the dynasty's Turkic roots, insisting on speaking Turkish rather than Chinese, wearing Central Asian clothes, living in a tent and stealing sheep which he cooked over a camp fire. He also plotted against a brother whom Taizong favoured for a while. In the end, both men were disgraced and exiled, and a younger son, Li Zhi, became the official heir.

Deeply affected by the death of his wife in 636 and troubled by the succession struggle, Taizong became a remote figure, embodying many of the dangers he had seen in his more lucid days. He grew cranky on a grand scale, ordering the demolition of a large palace because he decided that the location was too hot and the building too ostentatious. He planned a new military expedition to Korea to avenge the defeat there in 645. But he died in 649, his death ending the earlier Tang dynasty and opening the way for the rise of a concubine who would become China's only woman emperor.

618 Emperor Gaozu founds the Tang dynasty

624 Tang legal code is drawn up

626 One of Gaozu's sons becomes emperor as Taizong, after pushing his father to abdicate and murdering a rival brother

630 Major campaigns re-establish Chinese influence in Central Asia

634 Taizong marries his daughter to the king of Tibet to try to bring the territory under Chinese control, but Tibet remains a potent threat from the north

635 Gaozu dies. The first Christian church is opened by a Nestorian monk in Chang'an

638 Envoys from Persia and Byzantium come to China seeking help against Islam, but are refused aid

645 China makes another unsuccessful attempt to subdue Korea militarily. Xuan Zhang brings back 657 Sanskrit manuscripts (sutras) and Buddhist relics from India, and becomes the ruler's spiritual mentor

649 Taizong dies while preparing a new attack on Korea; his heir soon comes under the influence of his favourite concubine, Wu Zetian

THE HORSE – SYMBOL OF WEALTH AND MILITARY MIGHT

Under the Tang dynasty, horses came to play a central role in imperial military strategy, as well as being a favourite subject for the famous equestrian sculptures and paintings of the era. The élite loved riding, and imported the game of polo from Persia.

Elaborate equestrian displays were laid on for the rulers. The first steeds were small, squat Mongolian ponies, but taller, slimmer horses were brought in from Central Asia and the Middle East.

When the Tang ascended the throne at the beginning of the seventh century, they had only some 5000 horses at their disposal, according to contemporary texts. But stud farms were established which, by the middle of the century, produced 700,000 horses living on vast pasture lands in present-day Shaanxi, Shanxi and Gansu. Many belonged to soldiers, who were expected to provide their own mounts. The aristocratic military élite owned many steeds which were used in imperial expansion, particularly in the northwest. However, invasions and raids by Tibetans and Turkic peoples at the start of the eighth century disrupted the stud farms, and the number of horses dropped to about 240,000. But the breeding establishment resumed business, and horses were bought from inhabitants of the steppes in return for silk and precious metals – the total varying between 300,000 and 400,000 in the mid-century.

There was a further decline as the result of damage caused by Tibetan attacks, and the dynasty was obliged to buy tens of thousands of animals from nomadic merchants and private citizens. After helping the Tang against the Tibetans, the Uyghur people of the far northwest gained a virtual monopoly on the horse trade and began to sell sub-standard mounts; in 815, a fine horse could fetch 10,000 rolls of silk, but by the end of the century Uyghur horses were being sold for only 40 pieces of the material.

Horses would continue to play a sometimes decisive role in the empire – but not to the advantage of the Han Chinese. The nomadic raiders who were a recurrent threat to the rulers were skilled horsemen. None more so than the Mongols, who took the throne to establish the Yuan dynasty in 1279 – their advance in China was checked only when they reached the Lower Yangzi region, where fields and waterways impeded their cavalry. In the 17th century, the Manchu rode from the northeast to grab the throne in the chaos of the late Ming era.

Green-glazed funerary figure of a horse. The horse was one of the most popular animals to be found in sculptural form within Tang burial chambers. Artefacts found in such chambers reflected what the wealthy would need in the afterlife.

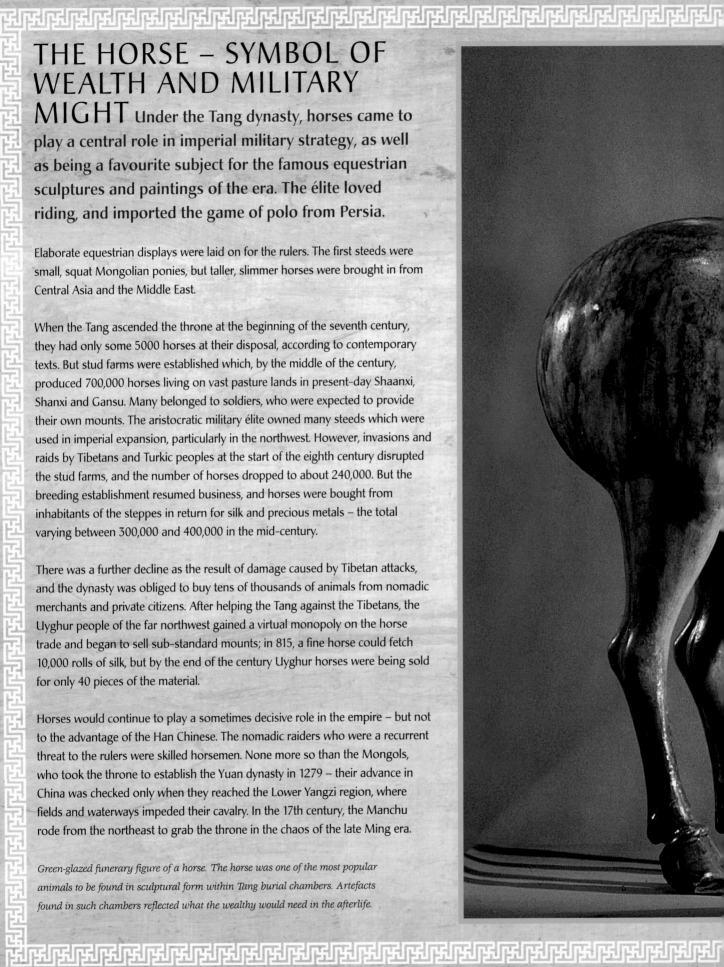

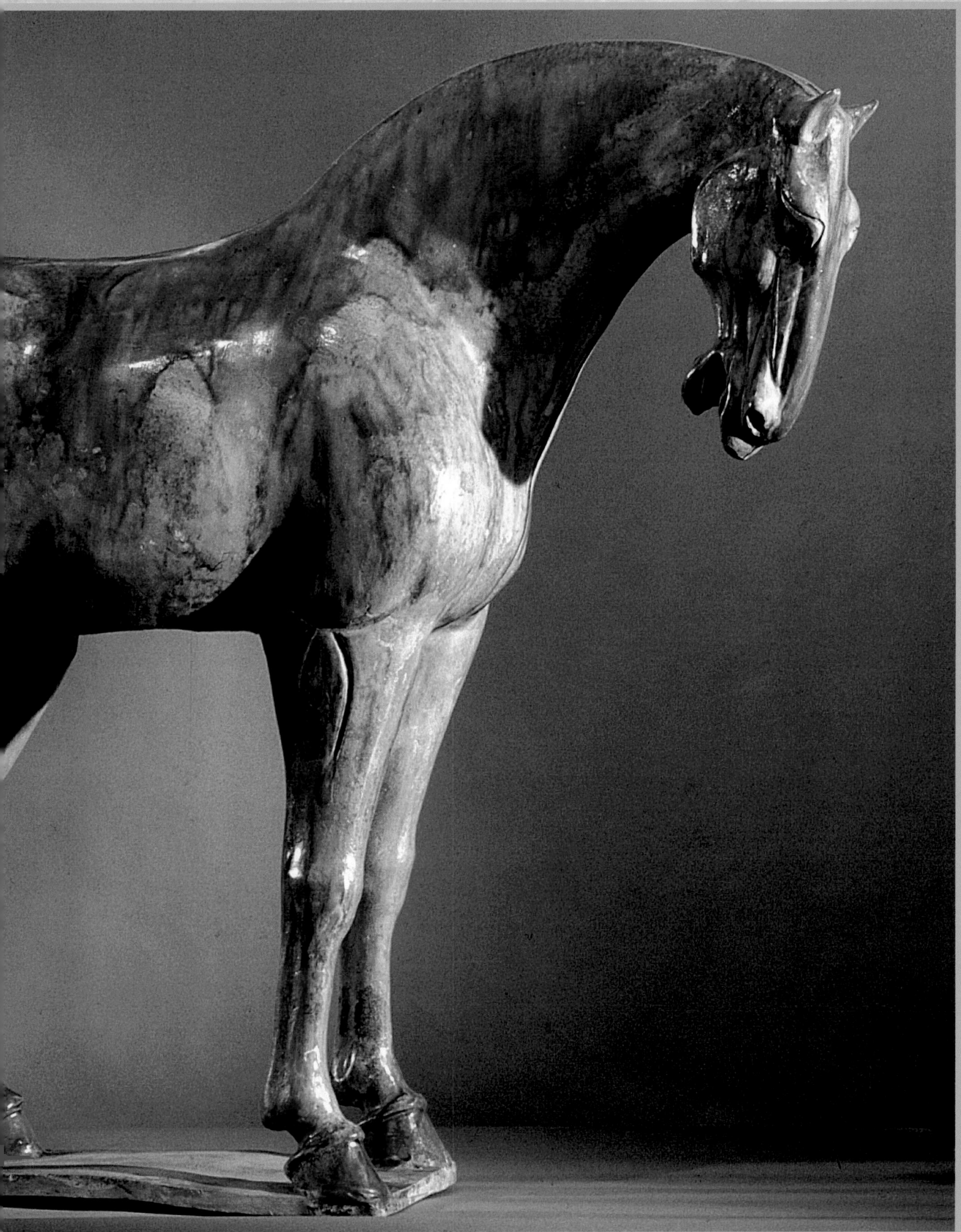

THE ERA OF WU ZETIAN

649–705 China's only female emperor and the founder of her own dynasty, Wu Zetian, was the most extraordinary woman to appear in the centuries of imperial rule. Melding ruthlessness and great acumen, superstition and quick-wittedness, she was a unique figure. Her deadly treatment of opponents struck fear into those who opposed her. She employed an army of spies. As she grew older, she was said to have become addicted to aphrodisiacs, which made her grow additional teeth and eyebrows. She conferred too much authority on two brothers who were her lovers, and was dethroned in 705, dying a broken old woman a year later at the age of 80.

THE TRADITIONAL VIEW OF WU ZETIAN WAS ARTICULATED BY AN ENEMY, THE REBEL LEADER Luo Binwang, who staged an unsuccessful rising. '*With the heart of a serpent and the nature of a wolf, she gathered sycophants to her cause and brought destruction to the just*', he declared. '*She slew her sister, butchered her brothers, killed her prince and poisoned her mother. She is hated by men and gods alike*'.

But, as with some of the other major figures of imperial China, there are two questions that have to be taken into account before condemning Wu as a she-devil incarnate. The first is the familiar one – many of the denunciations of her and accounts of her extreme cruelty were written under later rulers whose interests were served by painting a terrible picture of her. The other is that, for all her undoubted ruthlessness, she was in some ways a progressive figure.

She introduced sensible reforms and promoted officials of ability, even if some argued with her. Rejecting the subsidiary position attributed to women in the Chinese system, she was an early advocate of women's liberation. As for her personal life, if male emperors had an army of concubines, why should she not take beautiful young men to bed? Despite this, while her emperor husband was alive, the couple may have actually offended against the belief that men gained strength from sleeping with many women by remaining faithful to one another, leading to accusations of an unspecified sexual transgression that could, in fact, have simply been fidelity.

RIGHT *An 18th-century painting of Empress Wu, China's only female emperor, who ruled the country from 690–705. Empress Wu has perhaps suffered an unfair press from her later chroniclers. She was certainly a progressive figure who advanced the cause of women's rights.*

649 Third Tang emperor, Gaozong, ascends the throne

655 The concubine Wu gives birth to a daughter. She smothers the baby and blames the empress, who is put to death. Wu becomes empress

656 Wu gives birth to a son and increasingly takes control at court after the emperor suffers a stroke

666 Wu leads a group of women to conduct rites on a sacred mountain normally only performed by men

668 Successful invasion of Korea

680–3 Crown prince is poisoned and other rivals killed at Wu's behest

683 Gaozong dies and Wu engineers a coup against the heir, Zhongzong, when he comes under the influence of his wife. She ensures one of her sons, Ruizong, is made emperor

690 Wu persuades her son to abdicate and has herself proclaimed emperor

694 Wu declares herself the reincarnation of the Maitreya Buddha

705 Wu's two young lovers are murdered and she steps down, dying later the same year at the age of 80. Zhongzong and Ruizong compete for the throne, with Wu's daughter, Princess Taiping, trying to emulate her mother as power broker

In her world there was no place for mercy or softness. As she said to those around her after one rebellion: '*They [the rebels] conspired, and still I destroyed them. If your abilities surpass theirs, then make your play. Otherwise, change your hearts and serve me, to save the empire from further ridicule*'.

Born probably in 625, Wu followed the classic path of the beautiful concubine who rose to power and married the emperor, though her career was on a scale not seen before or since. She seduced two emperors, ruled in the name of one and got rid of her own sons when they threatened to become rivals. She was said to have used poison with a will. Having cleared the way for her own accession to the throne, she used omens interpreted by a mountebank monk to proclaim herself the Sage Mother of Mankind, blessed by conveniently discovered sacred texts and thus entitled to found a new dynasty, which died with her.

A fearsome reputation

Had she been prepared to play by the accepted rules, her ascension would have stopped when her first imperial swain, Taizong, died in 649. By convention, the 24-year-old Wu should have retired to a nunnery. But she managed to stay on at court and became the favourite concubine of the next ruler, Gaozong. Aged 21, he was inexperienced, indecisive and physically frail, suffering from incapacitating dizzy spells. Wu soon dominated him, and pushed the empress to one side. According to the saga of her infamous deeds, she suffocated her own newborn daughter and managed to fix blame on Gaozong's wife to get her marginalized.

Becoming empress in her own right by marrying the ruler, Wu took over the reins of power and gave birth to a son. She showed her disregard for the gender conventions of the time by leading a group of women up the sacred Mount Tai to conduct rites previously performed only by men.

Her husband faded into the background, and suffered a stroke which reduced him to near blindness. Wu's power increased further as a result. She was said to have had her predecessor as empress executed, along with a concubine she regarded as a rival – accounts had it that their arms and legs were amputated and they were either thrown into a river or a vat of wine, or eaten by pigs.

For most of China, naturally, life went on as usual far from the bloody intrigues at court. However, Wu's desire for expansion resulted in activism abroad. China's forces defeated the Koreans, who had so successfully fought off a number of Chinese offensives during the Sui dynasty. The peninsula became a vassal state. Other

armies forged into Central Asia, but conquering Tibet proved more difficult as the mountainous territory managed to resist the imperial advance.

When her husband neared death in 683, Wu made her preparations. Fearing that he could prove independent of her, she had the crown prince poisoned, and banished others who might oppose her. Her third son was declared the heir. A will attributed to her husband was produced, stating that the successor was to refer all important matters to Wu as she ruled from behind a curtain by the throne.

Complete power
But she had miscalculated. The dominant influence on the new emperor, Zhongzong, who took the throne in 684 at the age of 36, was not his mother but his wife. He

ABOVE *Detail of a painting from the tomb of Princess Yung T'ai of the Tang dynasty, showing court ladies wearing distinctive hairstyles.*

❛ Whenever the emperor held court, the empress attended behind a curtain. There was no matter of state, great or small, which did not reach her ears. All true power under heaven resided in her: demotion or promotion, life or death, reward or punishment. The Son of Heaven sat with folded hands. In court and country, they were called the Two Sages. ❜

THE *OLD BOOK OF TANG*, BOOK 5

LENDING AND BORROWING An insight into Tang-era commercial activities is provided by 13 contracts found preserved in the tomb of the merchant Zhou Chongxi in the oasis town of Turfan in far western China.

Seven of these concerned loans of money or of pieces of silk cloth, which were used as currency. One was for a 15-year-old slave, another recorded the purchase of 90 bundles of hay, and four were for the rent of land from poor people. The texts reproduced similar legal forms, with individual insertions for each case. Those borrowing money from Zhou had their finger joints traced on the documents as a form of identification and agreement.

In one case, starting in 668, Zhou seems to have encouraged a farmer to get increasingly deep in debt to him, perhaps with the aim of taking over his land-holding. First, he loaned the farmer 20 silver coins at a monthly interest rate of 10 per cent, with a vegetable field and all the borrower's household goods as surety.

Two years later, Zhou rented a field from the same man. Then he loaned him 40 silver coins at the same interest rate. The documents do not say how this relationship ended.

Zhou had the documents buried with him so that he could use them if he was brought to court in a dispute in the afterlife or if he wanted to pursue his debtors from beyond the tomb. As well as the papers, he was recorded as having been buried with five slaves, 30 pecks of silver, 50,000 piculs of grain, 10,000 pieces of silk and the figure of a woman described as 'Wife Heduan'. In *The Open Empire* the historian Valerie Hansen adds that the 'silk' in the tomb may in fact have been paper facsimiles of the genuine article, which would have been burned at the merchant's funeral.

appointed his father-in-law as his prime minister. Still, Wu had sufficient authority to get Zhongzong replaced – on the grounds of treason – by a younger brother.

Wu's power was now complete. The new emperor, Ruizong, who was 22 when he took the throne in 684, was put under what amounted to palace arrest; he was not allowed to live in the imperial apartments or to show himself at state functions. Instead of concealing herself behind a curtain or screen as was the custom for women, Wu received ministers face to face. Her enemies were purged, however well connected they might be. Trusted officials replaced Confucian dignitaries and informers had their expenses paid to travel to Xi'an to deliver denunciations of enemies.

EMPERORS OF THE ERA OF WU ZETIAN

Gaozong	649–83
Zhongzong	684
Ruizong	684–90, 710–12
Wu Zetian	690–705

In 690 Ruizong's abdication was arranged. In customary humble form, Wu three times refused the suggestion that she should ascend the throne. Then she accepted, embarking on a campaign to sweep away the old establishment and replace it with a dependable new class of loyalists. Scholars were persecuted if they were suspected of free thought.

Throughout her career, she assiduously collected auspicious titles and merged these with her constant campaign to elevate the status of women, or, at least, not to let the male dominance of the system stand in her way. She was the 'Heavenly

Empress' and the 'Sage Mother' sacred to Taoism. She built temples dedicated to her ancestors, and had her mother proclaimed the dowager empress.

To give her divine backing, a supposedly ancient sutra, which was almost certainly forged by her monkish confederate, was produced forecasting the birth of a woman of such merit that she would become the universal leader. Under this goddess, harvests would be bountiful and joy limitless, while *'the people will flourish, free of desolation and illness … The rulers of neighbouring lands will all come and offer allegiance'*. A huge statue Wu had made of the Buddha of the Future bore facial features similar to her own.

In 697 Wu took two young brothers as lovers, allowing them to act as they wished at court. Their excessively corrupt and dissolute conduct alienated those around her, who were also probably emboldened by her advancing age. In 705 a group of courtiers killed the brothers. It was a sign of Wu's declining power that she was unable to save them. The following day she left the throne, and went off to die.

Nearly 1300 years later, another woman who fought her way to the top in China, Madame Mao Zedong (Jiang Qing; 1914–91), would be likened to Wu by her critics. As so often in Chinese history, the past had resonances for the future.

> 〝 The Sage Mother comes among men – an imperium of eternal prosperity. 〞

PROPHECY USED TO JUSTIFY WU'S TAKING OF THE THRONE

BELOW *Guardian statues near the tomb of Empress Wu at Xi'an. Empress Wu was China's only female emperor and, despite her ruthlessness towards rivals, promoted the status of women.*

THE LATER TANG

705–908

The final two centuries of Tang rule saw steady dynastic decline, though with some periods of effective governance and hope for the ruling house. If the sovereigns were steadily losing the Mandate of Heaven, they managed to hold on to the throne for longer than might have been expected.

THE RULERS LOST CONTROL DECADE BY DECADE, FOLLOWING A MAJOR REVOLT IN THE MIDDLE OF the eighth century by a military rival and another a century later by a huge army of peasant insurgents. China became militarized with three-quarters of a million men under arms. Regional barons grabbed power and acted with virtual autonomy of the court. Peasants left their land to seek shelter on the great estates.

Many late Tang rulers were weak. Their revenues were insufficient for the job of running such a large realm. To preserve their power, they were obliged to seek the help of Uyghur mercenaries from the far west, while Tibet became, for a time, as powerful militarily as the dynasty. Foreign rulers who had courted the Tang in the days of their glory now thought it not worth sending missions with tribute to the court because of the weakness of the dynasty and the decentralization of its power.

But there were bright spots. Some strong officials pioneered tax reform, getting more revenue from the Yangzi Valley region. Grain transport was improved. For all its vicissitudes, the administration of the empire continued to function, and central authority was maintained on paper, if not necessarily in practice. Historians who have a less pessimistic view of the period regard it as evidence of how strong the Chinese system of government had become, as the country did not fall into the long era of chaos that had followed the collapse of the Han dynasty 500 years before.

Zhongzong, Ruizong and Xuanzong

At the end of her reign Wu called Zhongzong back to become crown prince, and he was restored as emperor when she left the throne in 705. He was a weak ruler, overshadowed by his empress, Wei, and her nephew-lover who indulged in enormous corruption. Zhongzong died after five years, allegedly poisoned by Wei who then installed his 15-year-old son on the throne, only for the youth to be overthrown two weeks later by a daughter of Wu, Princess Taiping. She put another of her mother's

RIGHT *Pottery figures of two Tang princesses, embellished with painted and gilded detail. The foreign-inspired floral designs on the robes, the turned-up lotus-form shoes and the voluminous sleeves were the height of fashion at the Tang imperial court.*

victims, Ruizong, on the throne. The new ruler was not a happy man and abdicated in favour of his son, Xuanzong, a much stronger character.

But Wu's daughter exercised her authority over Ruizong, and had him declared 'retired emperor', which enabled her to keep him on the throne under her influence, while Xuanzong was reduced to formal appearances. However, Princess Taiping went too far when she tried to get rid of Xuanzong altogether. Her coup having failed, she sought refuge in a Buddhist monastery and then returned to the palace to kill herself. Thereafter, Ruizong was finally free to give up affairs of state and hand over full power to his son.

LOVE STORY A story written at the end of the eighth century but set 50 years earlier tells of a young student, Yuande, son of an imperial governor, who falls in love with a prostitute in the Eastern Market of Chang'an, called Li Wa. He moves in with her and her madam for about a year. After spending all his money, the two women flee.

Yuande becomes so depressed and ill that he is left for dead, but the staff at a funeral parlour revive him. He then works as a professional mourner, and wins a competition held for members of his new profession. But his father, the governor, comes across him in Chang'an and whips him nearly to death. Horribly disfigured, Yuande scrapes a living as a beggar.

In the snowy street one day he meets Li Wa, who cares for him and buys her freedom from her madam. He resumes his studies, enjoys brilliant success in the imperial examination, becomes an official and marries the prostitute, who bears four sons. The story shows the different social strata that existed in the Tang capital and, despite the young woman's initial conduct, ends with an observation by the author: *'How remarkable that a woman of the courtesan class should manifest a degree of loyalty and constancy such as is rarely exceeded by the heroines of antiquity! How can such a story fail to provoke sighs of admiration?'*

Early eighth-century funerary sculptures of Tang dynasty officials. Yuande is the son of an imperial governor who falls from grace and becomes a beggar before attaining distinction in his imperial examinations and becoming a high-ranking official himself.

The new ruler, Xuanzong, had the longest reign of any of the Tang – from 712 to 756. His main task was to pull the country out of the disarray into which it had been plunged by the last year of Wu and the confusion that followed her death. The reign began with the emperor taking revenge on those who had stood in his way during the turbulent years before his accession. That achieved, he could relax. Known as the Kaiyuan era, the first two decades of his reign are thought of as a golden period for the Tang.

The emperor was hard-working and intelligent. Scholar officials were picked to replace military aristocrats – the most celebrated of these, Yao Chong, overhauled the civil service and increased the authority of the chief minister. Another, Zhang Jiuling, was said to have been so austere that on the ruler's birthday he offered him a collection of pages of moral advice instead of the usual lavish gift.

A golden age

The Grand Canal was repaired to improve the flow of food to the capital from the rich Yangzi valley. State granaries were established to combat recurrent famines. Taxes were lightened for ordinary people, and collection made more efficient with a new register of citizens. The legal code was applied less severely. Treaties were reached with regional powers. Nine military commands were set up to ensure security, and there were imperial victories in the northwest.

ABOVE *China's poets flourished under the Tang. Most of the emperors were patrons of poetry, if not poets themselves. Li Bo was a leading figure of poetry in the Tang era.*

As arts and literature reached new heights, the emperor's love for his concubine, Yang Guifei, was widely celebrated by poets. She had been the wife of his son, but Xuanzong engineered the declaration of a divorce so that he could take her as his partner, building an elegant hot springs resort outside the capital where they could spend time together. Painting and sculpture flourished, while silk decorations, porcelain, pottery, jewels and metalwork showed the influence of Central Asia and beyond. A colloquial form of drama and story-telling sprouted, dealing with everyday events. (See Love Story, left.)

Some 50,000 poems were composed by 2000 writers in the greatest outpouring of verse China has known. One of China's best-loved poets, Li Bo, a Taoist, was valued at court before falling from imperial favour and spending the rest of his life living in the Yangzi Valley. Other great poets of the era represented Confucianism and humanism. Some idealized rustic life, although one noted how farmers had their *'feet burned by the hot earth they tread, [their] backs scorched by the flames of the shining sun'*. One of the most striking writers, Li He, laid out visions bordering on the apocalyptic.

As Mao Zedong (Mao Tse-tung; 1893–1976) would remark, the Xuanzong reign was *'half bright, half dark'*. The military aristocracy tried to claw back its former position, led by a member of the imperial clan, Li Linfu. He introduced some sensible reforms but became increasingly power hungry. His cause was helped by the fact that the emperor had begun to neglect his duties in favour of religious pursuits and was infatuated with Yang Guifei, who was clever and artistically accomplished as well as beautiful, but who was also busy getting members of her family promoted in the traditional way of favoured consorts.

The power struggle at court coincided with defeats at the hands of the Tibetans, the Qidan tribes of the northeast and Arabs who beat the imperial army in the Ferghana valley of present-day Uzbekistan. The Silk Road was cut. The decline in trade and loss of territory hit the empire economically. On top of this, the system of regional military commands set up at the beginning of Xuanzong's reign was leading to the emergence of warlords in the border areas. Between them they had almost half a million men and 64,000 horses. Some could muster more forces than the emperor. In 755, one of these commanders, the illiterate and extremely fat An Lushan raised the most serious revolt of the century.

Suzong, Daizong, Dezong and Shunzong

During the An Lushan revolt, the emperor abdicated in favour of his son, Suzong, who ascended the throne in 756 and ruled until 762. Xuanzong died that same year after being kept as a virtual prisoner in the palace. (See An Lushan, pages 124–5.)

Even though the Tang had at least recovered the throne, the rebellions went on through Suzong's reign. The dynasty's position was extremely weak. The ruler relied on mercenaries to maintain the throne and was obliged to declare an amnesty for the rebels. Eunuchs became increasingly powerful at court, headed by Li Fuguo, who was put in charge of imperial finances and military affairs.

LATER TANG EMPERORS

Zhongzong	(restoration) 705–10
Ruizong	710–12
Xuanzong	712–56
Suzong	756–62
Daizong	762–79
Dezong	779–805
Shunzong	805
Xianzong	805–20
Muzong	820–4
Jingzong	824–7
Wenzong	827–40
Wuzong	840–6
Xuanzong	846–59
Yizong	859–73
Xizong	873–88
Zhaozong	888–904
Aidi	904–7

Towns and agriculture had been badly damaged by all the fighting. The control systems which the dynasty had implemented as the foundation for its rule decayed – in 760 only one-quarter of households were included in the imperial register. Tax revenue declined. The weakness of the central authority handed power to regional warlords, who often withheld taxes, reducing imperial income, and acted as virtual sovereigns in their domains.

The capital and the surrounding region grew increasingly dependent on grain brought up the Grand Canal and other waterways from the Yangzi Valley and from the revenue from land taxes imposed there. To raise money, the court increased duties and sold salt monopolies to merchants, which came to produce half of all government income by 779. The twice-yearly collection of agricultural taxes was introduced, with quotas from each province that had to be paid in currency to the centre by local governments. Peasants, however, continued to settle their bills in kind.

Despite its difficulties, the Tang survived – although recruitment of officials fell, the imperial examination system was maintained. But the eunuch power was becoming a menace at court. Eunuchs were

blamed for murdering the empress and, soon afterwards, Suzong himself died of a heart attack, leaving the throne to his 25-year-old son, Daizong. He was a devout Buddhist, who reached into the treasury to fund monasteries and strongly encouraged the ordination of clergy.

Eunuchs and warlords

The eunuch Li Fuguo tried to restrict the new emperor's authority, but Daizong hit back, having Li and other leading eunuchs killed. Daizong thus established his position at court, and the last remnants of the An Lushan rebellion were liquidated, but there was a threat from another direction. In 763 Tibetan forces stormed Chang'an and pillaged it for a fortnight before withdrawing, only to return regularly during the next two decades.

When Daizong died in 779 his eldest son, Dezong, took the throne. In stable times he would have been a more than adequate ruler, introducing financial reforms and streamlining the bureaucracy. But during his 25-year reign, he faced recurrent revolts by regional aristocrats and military commanders. Seeking a source of loyal support, Dezong gave eunuchs military commands, which they used to build up their position at court. After fleeing another rebellion, he recognized the position of the warlords, which, in some cases, only encouraged them to show even more autonomy.

ABOVE *Cave painting at Dunhuang of Tang military ranks. During the Tang era, horses played an important role in military campaigns, but were also used for leisure activities, such as polo-playing.*

SALT MONOPOLY

To augment its revenue from land taxes, the Tang court used an imperial monopoly on the production and distribution of salt to raise more money. It licensed salt merchants who, in return for payment, were the only people allowed to sell this staple of life.

In addition, imperial officials slapped a supercharge on the salt it sold to these merchants for distribution across the nation. This indirect form of taxation boomed to the point at which, in 770, more than half of imperial revenue came from the salt monopoly. Monopolies were tried on other commodities, including tea, but these were generally less successful.

The officials who ran the Salt Commission became extremely important. The salt merchants prospered, developing into one of the richest classes among Chinese business people. The sufferers were, as

Detail of a brick from a burial tomb. In the foreground is a simple crane used in the salt-mining process, along with pans for evaporation. The Tang court imposed a very successful imperial monopoly on the production and distribution of salt, resulting in the mineral becoming a scarcity for the general population.

usual, the poor who found the price of salt raised above their means – peasants used salt very sparingly, and salt-smuggling became a major outlaw occupation while, as late as the 19th century, the salt merchants of Tianjin flaunted their wealth by rising to take breakfast in the afternoon.

From Dezong, the throne passed in 805 to his son, Shunzong, who had been disabled by a stroke and who abdicated after a year in favour of his own son. The dynasty still held the Mandate of Heaven, but it needed a strong figure to re-assert itself in the face of all the challenges that confronted it at the start of the ninth century.

Xianzong and lingering collapse

The new ruler, who came to the throne at the age of 27 in 805 and ruled for 15 years, was the last major figure of the Tang dynasty. Emperor Xianzong improved tax collection to pay for armies that defeated regional barons in a series of campaigns. At the centre, he brought in fresh bureaucratic reforms to improve efficiency. But this was not to last – Xianzong was followed by nine rulers in the space of 83 years, none of whom could restore the Tang to glory.

Between 820 and 827 the throne was occupied by two wastrels, Muzong and Jingzong, who paid little attention to government, preferring instead the pursuits of drinking, horse riding, court festivities and alchemy. The regional barons re-asserted their authority. Corruption increased.

Muzong died after a polo accident in 824, and eunuchs killed Jingzong three years later. The eunuchs' authority increased steadily. The new ruler, the serious but ineffective Wenzong, mounted a coup against them, but word seeped out, and the ruler was detained by the eunuchs, while senior officials who opposed them were executed. When Wenzong died in 840, the eunuchs picked the next ruler, his brother Wuzong.

The new emperor succeeded in reducing the power of the eunuchs and his army managed to hold back a fresh offensive by the Uyghurs. But imperial finances were in mounting trouble as regions refused to pay taxes and the campaign in the northwest drained the treasury. An ardent Taoist, Wuzong decided to raise money by plundering Buddhist monasteries. He also attacked Zoroastrianism, Nestorian Christianity and Manichaean groups. But the religious campaign was only a temporary financial palliative, and Buddhism would recover after his death, although the other three religions would not play a significant role in China.

The eunuchs showed that their power was not broken when they engineered the succession of the next ruler, Xuanzong, in 846. He was fortunate in that the threatening Uyghur empire

712 Xuanzong takes the throne and sets about trying to restore the country to order after the chaos that follows Wu's abdication

714 Attempted invasion of the Yellow River plains by Tibet is repulsed

736 Khitan and Xi tribes declare independence, but the revolt is crushed in 745

747 Chinese forces attack Tibet across the Hindu Kush

751 The imperial army is defeated by a Muslim force on the Talas River, losing Tarim Basin and major entrepôts on the Silk Road

755 An Lushan rebellion

757 An Lushan is murdered by one of his sons

763 A Tibetan army occupies Chang'an for two weeks and takes control of the Gansu corridor

779 Emperor Dezong ascends the throne and appoints court eunuchs to key military posts

820 onwards. Eunuch power at court increases steadily

842 Campaign launched against all religions except Taoism

874 Famine spreads, along with warlordism and revolts

879 Rebels sack Chang'an before being crushed in 884

907 A general, Zhu Wen, seizes the throne, but only controls part of northern China; as a result, the country fragments into disunity

fell apart during his 13-year rule and the Tibetan royal line died out, removing two major threats. As a result, his was a largely peaceful reign, during which Buddhism was allowed to revive. But the underlying weaknesses of the dynasty – notably weak central power and strained finances – were not dealt with. Xuanzong died in 859 from taking potions meant to guarantee eternal life.

Eunuchs again engineered the succession, this time of the extravagant, self-indulgent, indolent and hard-drinking Yizong. His spending depleted the treasury, and taxation was increased to pay the bills. This, together with natural calamities, fuelled peasant revolts. After Yizong's death in 873, the unrest gained in strength during the reign of his son, Xizong, who was 13 when he came to the throne and was dominated by the court eunuchs.

Losing the Mandate of Heaven

Famines in 874 set off outlaw rebellions in the classic bandit territory of Shandong and Henan, where disasters have always fuelled uprisings. Two salt smugglers took charge of the movement; one of them, Huang Chao, gave his name to the revolt. The bandits attacked towns along the Yellow River and then headed south to the Yangzi. They branched out into Anhui and Zhejiang and, in 879, reached Canton, where they killed foreign traders. Turning north, they marched through Hunan and Jiangxi.

BELOW Residence of the Tang emperor Xuanzong, who reigned for 13 years. His rule was characterized by general peace and a revival of Buddhism.

Now numbering 600,000 men, the rebels took Luoyang and then occupied Chang'an in 881, burning and pillaging the capital as the emperor fled to Sichuan, just as his predecessor had done during the An Lushan rising. Driven out by an imperial force, the insurgents regrouped and staged a

GIFTS AND OFFERINGS Missions from other parts of Asia brought a flow of valuable, exotic products – and human offerings – to the Tang court in the years of the dynasty's greatness.

After a hiatus caused by the weakness of the later Tang empire, the flow of tributes resumed to their successors, the Song.

A 12-page compilation by the historian Edward Schafer includes 122 elephants, 11 rhinoceroses, large quantities of fragrant woods, spices, teas, jewels, precious metals and stones, as well as five young black men and two black girls, female musicians and 'one black slave from Pagan (rejected)'.

The Indonesian territory of Srivjaya sent pygmies, girls, musicians, five-coloured parrots, elephant tusks, rhinoceros horns, golden lotus flowers, coral trees, silver, a rock-crystal Buddha, rings, pearls, opaque glass pictures, drugs and ointments, frankincense, rosewater, sugar, camphor and mineral oil. In return the Chinese offered silver and copper coins, porcelain, robes, belts, caps, lacquered and silver vessels, silk, cotton, copper and horse trappings.

A clay tomb figure of a kow-towing Persian trader. When the Tang empire was at its greatest, it received delegations offering gifts from throughout the Asian world.

counter-attack that further devastated Chang'an in an orgy of destruction, looting, murder and cannibalism. When the Tang army finally gained control, a historian recorded that *'thorns and brambles filled the city, foxes and hares ran everywhere'.*

The Tang court moved to the retaken city of Luoyang, which had been less damaged. But the rulers were impotent politically, subject to the dictates of the military barons. The Huang Chao revolt had destroyed the dynasty's last claim to be able to exercise the Mandate of Heaven while, to combat the rebels, it had been forced to allow local militias that further weakened its hold.

Xizong left civilian affairs to the eunuchs, and his successor Zhaozong, who ruled from 888 to 894, was no more able to assert himself on an increasingly fragmented empire. He was deposed by eunuchs, restored and then murdered by one of the military governors, Zhu Wen, who put Zhaozong's 12-year-old son, Aidi, on the throne as his puppet in 904.

Three years later Zhu had ministers loyal to the Tang killed and assumed the title of emperor himself, poisoning Aidi in 908. The often glorious but fatally flawed Tang era ended after 289 years of rule. Another period of disunion would follow, but the legacy of the Tang's finest achievements endured in the areas of administration and the arts, making the bright spells of their rule one of China's golden ages.

AN LUSHAN

Dynasties always had to watch out for powerful military figures who might nurture ambitions to claim the Mandate of Heaven and ascend the throne. The frequency of warfare and continuing border fighting meant that the emperors needed good commanders, but the danger was that the loyalties of the generals (and of the men they led) could prove unreliable, as the independence they enjoyed when campaigning translated into a thirst for political power.

The Tang system of appointing military governors to enforce imperial rule led, bit by bit, to the growth of decentralized power exercised by generals. The greatest of these, in the middle of the eighth century, was An Lushan, an extremely corpulent illiterate of Central Asian origin whose parents had settled in the Xinjiang capital of Urumqi. While working in a market, he was accused of sheep stealing, and sentenced to death. He escaped and joined the imperial army, fighting well in frontier wars, after which he was appointed military governor of present-day Hebei province and was then also given command over Manchuria. An Lushan enjoyed the support of the ruler and of Xuanzong's favourite concubine, Precious Consort Yang Guifei, who had him ennobled and given even more authority in the north at the head of very large forces.

His ascent provoked rivals at court to conspire against him, while his own view of his status became greatly inflated. In 755 he refused an imperial summons to attend the wedding of one of the ruler's sons. Four months later, pretending that he had to 'liquidate bandits' at court, An launched a revolt from his northern power base. His army of 150,000–200,000 men, with 30,000 horses for his fast-riding cavalry, took the city of Luoyang in a lightning campaign. But then he halted his advance, enabling his foes to gather their forces and inflict a defeat on him. However, a poorly conceived imperial attempt to recapture Luoyang failed badly, and the court was forced to abandon the capital of Chang'an as well. This led An Lushan to declare himself emperor at the head of the Greater Yan dynasty. (It is not recorded as such in Chinese history books, and An remains an unrecognized usurper.)

Attempts have been made to find the roots of the revolt in difficult economic conditions for peasants, particularly after heavy floods in Hebei in 724, and in the divisions between rich and poor, which resulted from the increase in trade and business. The latter was certainly a factor in sapping social cohesion. However, the depiction of An Lushan as the leader of an agrarian movement does not carry weight. No doubt starving peasants did rally to the rebel flag but, like many rebellions right up to the 20th century, it was primarily a military exercise by an ambitious commander with a strong regional power base, who calculated that his forces were better than those of the ruler and who was aided by factionalism at court.

There was blood-letting in the imperial hierarchy as the ruler fled to the southwest, a journey immortalized in one of the finest paintings of the epoch (later copied in the tenth century) which shows the emperor on a black horse, its mane tied into three plaits, followed by women wearing riding trousers and hats. The chief minister, Li Linfu, had been succeeded by Yang Guozhong, a cousin of the favourite concubine Yang. He was blamed for the defeat and executed, together with his family. The general in charge of the emperor's escort and his soldiers demanded that the 'precious consort' should also die. The emperor was forced to acquiesce, and she was strangled with a silk cord by the chief eunuch.

Xuanzong then set up his court in Chengdu in Sichuan while his heir apparent headed for the northwest to raise resistance there, eventually usurping the throne from his weak father. An Lushan grew increasingly suspicious and oppressive. He was himself killed by his son in 757, and the rebels split in two – one group headed by the son, the other by a rival commander. With help from Central Asian mercenaries, Xuanzong's third son recaptured Chang'an and proclaimed himself Emperor Suzong in 756, but the revolt continued until 763. The event is generally regarded as marking the start of the decline of the Tang, although the dynasty would last for another century and a half.

RIGHT *Painting depicting Emperor Xuanzong along with the precious consort and his imperial entourage fleeing the advance of the An Lushan rebel army. The painting follows the Tang style of fairy-tale pinnacles and wispy clouds.*

FIVE DYNASTIES AND TEN KINGDOMS

907—60

Like the previous long-lived dynasty, the Han, the decline and fall of the Tang was followed by a period of chaos, with dynasties and kingdoms succeeding one another in quick order. The anarchy was briefer than after the Han but five separate dynasties ruled in northern China between 907 and 960, while ten kingdoms carved up the south between them. Although the northern emperors changed place with great rapidity, much of the social and administrative structure remained intact beneath them. Their reigns may have been short, but they introduced measures which would be taken up when China was re-united. Despite this being a time of great upheaval, it would pave the way for another lengthy dynasty under which China would prosper once more.

THE FOUNDER OF THE FIRST POST-TANG DYNASTY WAS ZHU WEN, WHO HAD MURDERED EMPEROR Zhaozong and then usurped the throne from his successor after a three-year interval. He was the son of a ruined landowner and had worked as a farm labourer before joining the great Hua Chao revolt of the late ninth century. Deserting the rebels for the imperial forces, he marked himself out as a fighter and rose to command a key garrison on the Grand Canal around 882. The following years saw Zhu engaging in a series of manoeuvres, betrayals, murders and assertions of force, which ended with him assuming the throne in 907 as the first emperor of the Later Liang dynasty under the reign name of Taizu, with a new capital by Kaifeng on the Yellow River.

The historian, Ouyang Xiu, writing in the following century, refers to him ironically by another of his names, Quanzhong, meaning 'Wholeheartedly Loyal'. More to the point, he describes Zhu as 'evil', 'depraved' and 'despised by the world'.

We lament! The Liang was depraved to the extreme! Beginning in its rise through roguery and culminating in its purge of the Tang dynasty, its legacy poisoned the entire world ...

OUYANG XIU, *HISTORICAL RECORDS OF THE FIVE DYNASTIES*, CHAPTER 13

If the commander of one of Zhu's units died in battle, his men were slaughtered for cowardice. The ruler amassed a harem of hundreds of women and raped the wife and daughter of a loyal commander. In the end, Zhu himself was murdered by one of his sons after three years on the throne. The young man became the next emperor under the name of Modi and held on for a dozen years.

Amid this era of extreme violence, the Liang still succeeded in instituting reforms. Eunuch power was bridled. The military structure was reorganized, though this led to the defection of an important army that allied with a rival of Turkic origin. The latter then grabbed the throne in 923 and established the Later Tang dynasty, which ruled north and western China for 13 years under three emperors – Zhuangzong, Mingzong and Feidi.

Nomadic emperors

Its multi-ethnic army, combining Chinese and non-Chinese forces, extended the later Tang's control beyond that of its predecessor and the new ruling house suggested modernizing by collecting taxes in cash rather than grain. True to their nomadic roots, the emperors moved about between six capitals, showing themselves to their people and exerting personal rule. They shocked the Chinese by their lack of respect

ABOVE *The Temple of the Chief Minister in Kaifeng. Kaifeng became the capital of the first post-Tang dynasty, the Later Liang, under the emperor Taizu. Kaifeng reached its zenith during the era of the Later Song. The temple itself is one of the most famous Buddhist temples in China. Kaifeng was unusual in being home to a long-established Jewish community.*

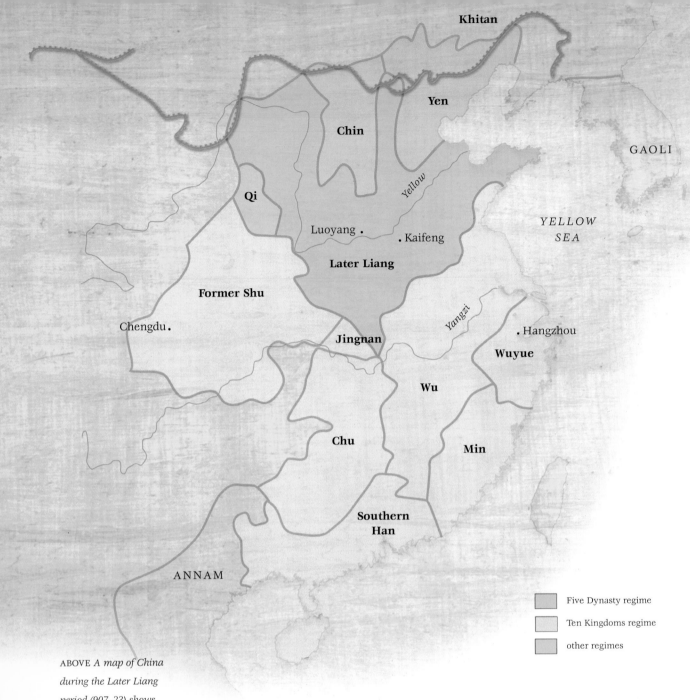

Khitan

Yen

Chin

GAOLI

Qi

Yellow

Luoyang .

. Kaifeng

YELLOW
SEA

Later Liang

Former Shu

Yangzi

. Hangzhou

Chengdu .

Jingnan

Wuyue

Wu

Chu

Min

Southern
Han

ANNAM

Five Dynasty regime

Ten Kingdoms regime

other regimes

ABOVE *A map of China
during the Later Liang
period (907–23) shows
how the previously
united empire was now
divided into smaller
dynasties and kingdoms.*

for rituals. Zhuangzong razed his own altar of accession to make way for a polo field
and adopted hundreds of sons, in the tradition of his northern ancestors.

An extravagant, romantic personality with literary as well as military gifts, he
surrounded himself with 1000 actors and, it was said, 2000 women. He also brought
back the eunuchs, which helped to set off a coup against him by the second Later
Tang ruler, Mingzong, who purged them from court. For all his disdain for the period,
the historian Ouyang Xiu acknowledges that Mingzong's eight-year rule (starting in
926) was a time when '*wars had abated and harvests were bountiful*', with a ruler
who knew the benefits of looking after his people.

But there were severe earthquakes and floods, as well as eclipses and falling stars,
which could only be bad portents. Mingzong's successor, Feidi, was not up to the

LEFT *Tang dynasty wall painting depicting polo players on their steeds.*

job, retreating to the clan's heartland in Shanxi and losing the throne to a commander in the Imperial Guard, who established the Later Jin dynasty in 936 under the name of Gaozu. He tried to strengthen the government and ordered an end to the practice of collecting taxes several years in advance. But, in part because of this reform, there was never enough money, and the Later Jin were hit by both a string of natural disasters and incursions by the Khitan people of the northeast, one of a series of regional tribal confederations that challenged the Five Dynasties.

Exiled leader

The Khitan chief had proclaimed himself as a Chinese-style emperor, and the dynasty was so weak that Gaozu was obliged to swear him allegiance and give up territory. The Khitan authority was such that its chief decided who would be Gaozu's successor – a dim figure known as Chudi, who took the throne in 944. He alienated his own people by reverting to tax collection in advance, disturbed convention by marrying the widow of his uncle, fell out with powerful figures at court, and so antagonized the Khitan that he was exiled.

The northeasterners overran the capital of Kaifeng but this provoked resistance led by a military governor. When the

THE FIVE DYNASTIES

LATER LIANG 907–23	
Taizu	907–11
Modi	911–23
LATER TANG 923–35	
Zhuangzong	923–6
Mingzong	926–34
Feidi	934–5
LATER JIN 936–47	
Gaozu	936–44
Chudi	944–7
LATER HAN 947–51	
Gaozu	947–8
Yindi	948–51
LATER ZHOU 951–60	
Taizu	951–4
Shizong	954–60

907 General Zhu Wen proclaims himself Emperor Taizu, founding the Later Liang dynasty. The dynasty controls only central northern China and, elsewhere, local warlords take power

911 The Later Liang emperor Taizu is assassinated by his son, who takes the throne

923 The son of a Turkic general founds a new dynasty, the Later Tang, which expands its control in the north

935 Another Turkic warlord sets up a new dynasty, the Later Jin

938 China faces a major incursion by the Khitan people and a revolt that makes Vietnam independent

947 Another coup by a Turkic leader establishes the Later Han dynasty

951 The fifth of the dynasties, the Later Zhou, is set up

960 To block the empress dowager, the mother of the infant heir to the throne, Later Zhou generals offer the throne to a Chinese general who founds the Song dynasty

Khitan evacuated their forces during a crisis of their own, this governor established the Later Han dynasty, which lasted for just four years under two rulers, one of whom, also called Gaozu, died within a year of acceding to the throne. His successor, the shy 16-year-old Yindi, was said to have *'frolicked within the palace with petty men'* from whom he took advice. In 950 he had a group of senior officials murdered, leading the main military commander to rebel. He killed Yindi, installed a puppet successor and then took the throne himself at the head of the last of the five dynasties, the Later Zhou, which held on from 951 to 960.

Its founder, Emperor Taizu, was recorded as having been a drinker and gambler in his youth but once in power he proved to be both a good ruler and an excellent military commander. He outsmarted the Khitan, provoking the assassination of their ruler, and gained the support of the empress dowager from the previous dynasty. In failing health, Taizu died in 954, but was succeeded by another powerful figure, Shizong. Despite the doubts of some of his advisers, he insisted on expanding in a new direction, to the south, against the Ten Kingdoms there. He felt that their often sybaritic ways had weakened them, whereas the northerners had been toughened by their half-century of struggle.

Like the northern rulers, the southern kingdoms had been spawned by the disarray of the late Tang era, led by upwardly mobile men of humble origins who made the most of their opportunities. The monarch of Sichuan was a former bandit, as were the Wang brothers who ruled in Fujian. The king of the Wu-Yueh domain on the east coast was a farmer who had enlisted in a militia. A monarch, who reigned on the Middle Yangzi, had been a slave, and the Prince of Chu started life as a carpenter before becoming an outlaw.

Strength in the south

The southern ruling families were more stable than the dynasties of the north, and some of the kingdoms developed economically, for instance Sichuan, where paper currency, known as 'flying money', was introduced. Printing expanded in Chengdu and Hangzhou. The division of China meant that their taxes and grain no longer headed north. They did not suffer from the recurrent raids by nomads from the northeast and northwest that plagued the Five Dynasties. There was extensive artistic patronage. Seaborne trade flourished, encouraging advances in shipbuilding, and both porcelain production and the tea businesses prospered.

Yet, when the test came, it would be the northerners who triumphed under the Song dynasty that re-united the country and ushered in an under-rated era of peace and prosperity.

THE DEVELOPMENT OF PRINTING

Printing in China dates back to the eighth century AD, some 700 years before it was seen in Europe. During the early stages of its development, printing was confined mainly to Buddhist sutras. But under the Northern Song dynasty (960–1127), it became more widely used and there was a flourishing of printed texts.

The earliest and longest-lived printing method used carved woodblocks, with a whole page generally put onto one slab of wood. Another technique required small, individual blocks for each character, but this involved the complex task of finding and arranging characters from thousands of little blocks.

The first step involved a handwritten text. With the ink still wet, the text was placed – ink side down – on a slab of wood, which was covered in a thin layer of rice paste. The rice paste held the paper onto the slab as it was rubbed with a rounded cloth-covered pad. The ink seeped through to stain the wood. After the paper was removed, the wood was carved away to leave raised characters standing.

The raised words were then smothered in indelible ink made from gum mixed with soot from lamps. The slab was covered with paper fashioned from bark or hemp, and then brushed. All that was left to do was to peel off the paper and sew it with other pages into a book.

Although printing revolutionized the way people wrote and read, it had its opponents. A leading 12th-century Confucian scholar, Zhu Xi, was horrified at what he saw as a cheapening of the written word. Before printing, handwritten books transcribed by scribes were personal possessions, beyond the reach of all but a tiny élite. Most scholars had to memorize texts. Zhu thought this method of learning should continue, rather than allowing the democratization brought about by printing. He feared that students would look at portions of a book once or twice without absorbing its full meaning. His opposition did not prevent the growth of printing in his own time and afterwards. But rote learning by recitation also continued; in the late 20th century, children in some primary schools were still chanting texts, with their backs turned to the blackboards on which they were written.

The world's earliest surviving printed book – a woodblock-printed version of the Diamond Sutra. *The sutra consists of sheets of printed text with a frontispiece illustrating the Buddha and disciples.*

THE NORTHERN SONG

960–1126
The Song dynasty was once portrayed as a weak house notable mainly for presiding over achievements in philosophy and the arts. Its three centuries on the throne saw a reduction in the area under imperial control. It accepted humiliating terms to buy peace with raiding armies from the north and west. But, after extending its territory for the first two decades of the dynasty, the Song claimed to govern almost 1.5 million square miles (4 million sq km) and a population of 100 million. At its height, it found a new equilibrium for the Middle Kingdom away from the constant warfare of the north and west – if only this could be preserved as the basis for a re-formulated China after so many centuries of armed conflict.

THE POTENTIAL FOR CHINA'S FUTURE WAS SHOWN IN THE MAJOR ADVANCES MADE UNDER THE dynasty. Agricultural output grew, including the cultivation of tea. Textile production expanded, as did manufacturing, mostly in small enterprises but also in a few factories that had several thousand employees. Urbanization was a feature of the Song dynasty, along with the expansion of the empire to the south. Commercial development, the spread of printing and the development of ceramics went hand in hand with the growth of seaborne trading links and river and canal communications. A monetary economy took root, and there was a major attempt to introduce reforms that could have given the whole system a sounder base. In the end, the dynasty was unable to withstand the challenge from the northern nomads culminating in the Mongol armies of Genghis Khan (c.1162–1227) and Kublai Khan (1215–94), but the Song era marked a major stage in the long-term development of imperial China.

Several relatively lengthy reigns created stability. The fact that the dynasty did not try to expand into Central Asia, Manchuria or Mongolia, and that it was blocked in the southwest by a powerful kingdom in Yunnan and by militarily strong Vietnam, gave its rule a cohesion within China proper.

'A period of civility'
The Song era saw a rise in the importance of civilian life and business, and centralized rule – backed by extensive instruments of state power – in a strange combination with increased individual liberty (not unlike the China of the early 21st

RIGHT *Portrait of Taizu, the first Song emperor, who seized power over northern China in 960 in a relatively bloodless military coup. His diplomatic skills set the tone for the Song years, which brought China a prolonged spell of prosperity and peace.*

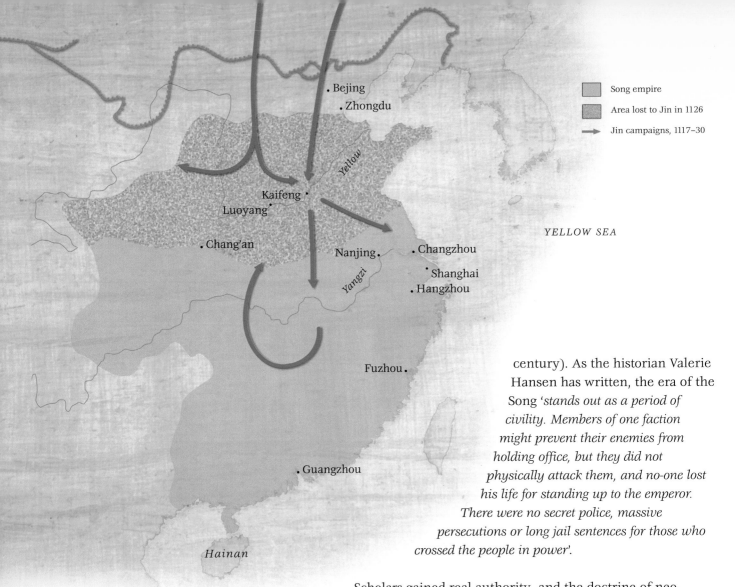

Bejing

Zhongdu

Yellow

Kaifeng

Luoyang

YELLOW SEA

Chang'an

Nanjing

Changzhou

Shanghai

Hangzhou

Yangzi

Fuzhou

Guangzhou

Hainan

ABOVE *Map showing the Song Empire at its peak and the division into the Southern Song after the Jin invasions from the north.*

century). As the historian Valerie Hansen has written, the era of the Song '*stands out as a period of civility. Members of one faction might prevent their enemies from holding office, but they did not physically attack them, and no-one lost his life for standing up to the emperor. There were no secret police, massive persecutions or long jail sentences for those who crossed the people in power*'.

Scholars gained real authority, and the doctrine of neo-Confucianism was evolved to re-interpret the sage's teachings for a different age. But conservative forces remained strong, and the court did not wish to undermine a system that had lasted for over 1000 years. The result, in the words of the historian E.A. Kracke, was '*change within tradition*'. The rulers included some of China's most sensible, far-sighted emperors – as well as others whose adventures and misjudgements provoked disasters.

Though learning in China was never as closely connected to utilitarian use as in the West, major inventions were put to practical use, including the magnetic needle for navigation, the chain treadmill, deep drilling rigs, piston bellows and breast straps and collars for horses. Mathematics and astronomy advanced. The arts flourished after the violence of the previous period of disunity, manifested at the highest level by exquisite painting and in popular shows performed in the growing cities. The wealth and cultural achievements under the Song were probably unequalled anywhere on earth at the time. (See Arts and Entertainment, page 138.)

Taizu, first of the Song emperors

In 959 the last pretender to the mantle of the Tang died, and the succession passed to an infant heir. The army rebelled, declaring its commander to be the true new emperor. The soldiers took over the capital of Kaifeng without resistance and the commander became Taizu, the founder of a dynasty, the Song.

The new emperor's family had been officials and, despite his military background, he proved to be very different from previous warlords who had originated from the north. Turning back the clock on an era in which rulers had ascended thanks to their military power, Taizu asserted the supremacy of civilian authority. Science was encouraged, and China's provinces were mapped as never before.

Taizu reorganized the military forces and focused on extending the influence of the new dynasty southwards, using diplomacy and treating the new parts of the realm well. This form of empire-building brought a decisive shift in its nature, taking account as it did of the growing importance of enormous territories far from the Yellow River – regions which previous dynasties had either ignored or regarded as barbarian lands to be either conquered or brought into fragile alliances.

Reduction in military strength

Kaifeng, surrounded by high walls and wide moats, with gates painted the imperial colour of vermilion, became the Song capital. Drawing on his links with other

BELOW Throughout Chinese history, scholars have influenced moral, political, social and religious thought. Song governments, like others before them, were mindful of their opinions. This detail is from a late Tang-era painting entitled Northern Qi Scholars Collating the Classic Texts.

ABOVE *Image of Emperor
Zhenzong, the third Song
emperor, first published
in China in 1609.*

military chiefs, Taizu was able to
persuade them to amalgamate their
forces into a single army – the
Imperial Guards – which came under
the ruler's control. There was no
conscription, but militia forces were
set up for local protection. The
Imperial Guards were smaller in
number than previous central forces,
totalling some 200,000 men, backed
by a labour corps.

The reorientation and running down
of the armed forces meant that the
Song in effect acknowledged the
power of the northern states, notably
China's old adversaries, the Khitan,
who had conquered 16 prefectures
around present-day Beijing under
their empress Chunqin in the later
years of the Five Dynasties. The
trouble with this policy was that it
depended on the northerners being
content to live in peace with the
Chinese, and showing a readiness to
halt their expansion to the south.

As it was, the statesman-like attitude
of the Song was not to find an echo
from the other side, spelling the long-
term doom of the dynasty when the threat to the empire from the northerners took
multiple forms, each more menacing than the last.

The exercise of reason and morality

The first Song had come to power by exploiting the weakness of the previous
ruling house when an infant ascended the throne. So Taizu passed over his own
young son and chose instead his scholarly brother Taizong (r.976–97) to succeed
him. Taizong, who was in his late 30s when he came to the throne, continued the
consolidation of the Song's southern influence and established a strong, centralized
administrative system based on the development of the imperial civil service. (See
Civil Service, opposite.)

At the centre, the growing strength of officials in the centralized Song state meant
that debates between them over policy replaced factional feuding at court. There
was now real intellectual argument between conservatives and those advocating
change about the way China should be run. Initially, these debates were fuelled by
discussions on how to deal with threats from the nomads of the northern steppes.

CIVIL SERVICE

Ruling over such a vast domain, the Song emperors depended heavily on the civil service to run the country. It was charged with performing multiple roles. In the capital, the most senior officials staffed the major organs of state, headed by the supreme council and major ministries. Others were responsible for bringing different strands of opinion to the attention of the emperor, so that he could be properly informed of what his people felt. Provincial governors and district-level magistrates imposed imperial authority across the nation.

For the Tang emperors, the civil service had been a useful counterweight to the power of the military élite. Selection of civil servants was developed under the Song to draw in as many bright young men as possible. They had to sit tests at three levels held in local prefectures, then in the capital and finally at court in the presence of the emperor. Those who obtained the highest degrees could be sure of joining the ruling élite. The tests were based on Chinese classical texts.

Some scholars would turn out to be reformers, but the result of their deeply classical grounding and the rote learning they underwent was that the majority of imperial officials were conservatives who saw their role as being to preserve what had gone before. Since the Chinese system was held to be perfect, the main task was to ensure that it worked properly, not to look for change.

This selection of the best men to administer the country reached its height under the Song when the mandarins who were selected largely displaced the traditional feuding court factions. But the system was not as open and fair as it might have been. Male relatives of officials were entitled to sit for 'shadow' examinations, which were easier and had a higher pass rate than the full tests. This did not entitle them to take the more senior jobs, but it meant they could enter the civil service and, if they so wished, subsequently sit the higher examination. During the first century of the Song, a network of 100 families based in Kaifeng specialized in filling official posts, intermarrying and helping family members to form a bureaucratic élite.

Under later dynasties the system degenerated as imperial degrees were sold to raise funds, or allocated on the basis of preferment. District magistrates became infamous for their corruption and the oppression of staff at their headquarters, known as *yamen*. But still the bureaucracy and the examination system remained at the core of imperial China, offering, in the words of a later poet, the chance for young men to be carried to Heaven:

'Parents, however much they love a child
Have not the power to place him among
the chosen few.

Only the examiner can bring the young
to notice
And out of darkness carry them to Heaven!'
YÜAN MEI, 18TH CENTURY

An 11th-century unglazed pottery figure representing a Song official. In his hand he holds a rectangular tablet.

ARTS AND ENTERTAINMENT
The Song era saw a flourishing of culture. The impressionistic landscape paintings produced under the dynasty were delicate in their brushwork and highly impressive in their scale, especially when unrolled as scrolls. Other schools of artists depicted people at work or focused on minute paintings of birds.

飛
鳥
似
怜
毛
羽
貴
徘
徊
如
飽
稻
梁
心

絢
膺
紺
趾
誠
端
雅
為
賦
新
篇
步
武
吟

製
作

弄

The growth of cities provided a ready audience for entertainment and contributed to the spread of popular culture. In Kaifeng, crowds went out in the evening in the 'pleasure quarter' with its 72 restaurants, the largest of which consisted of five three-storey buildings linked by passages and bridges. There were shows by acrobats and strange animals; storytellers kept Chinese mythology and history alive. In the 12th century there were references to moving lantern displays that showed riders on jumping horses. Meng Yuanlao, a contemporary writer, described a festival in Kaifeng:

'In the arcades along the broad avenue entertainers of every description plied their wares cheek by jowl, all displaying ingenious skills and wondrous talents. The singers, dancers and acrobats caused a din that could be heard miles away. Some of them demonstrated their skill at archery or kicking balls,

A great patron of the arts, Emperor Huizong encouraged artists at the Song Painting Academy to develop a realistic and meticulous style of painting that often included birds and flowers as its subject;this parakeet by the emperor himself is a fine example of the genre.

others walked on tightropes strung between tall bamboo poles. Wildman Zhao would eat and drink while hung upside down; Zhang Jiuge would swallow iron swords'.

The development of printing and the increased distribution of books went hand in hand as literary frontiers widened to take in more popular themes. Socially ambitious merchants set their sons to studying the classical texts in order to qualify for careers as officials. In such positions, they would be able to buttress the family fortune by access to administrative authority and perks.

Such acts of aggression would be a recurring feature of Song rule, however much the dynastic rulers tried to buy off the aggressors; China was simply too rich for them to leave it alone.

Although relatives of officials were granted privileged access to the civil service through an easier, albeit less highly regarded, system of examinations, the early Song era was a period when the mandarins for which the empire was famous reached their zenith. The evolving doctrine of neo-Confucian thought exalted reason as the faculty that separated man from other animals, enabling the human race to distinguish between right and wrong. Moral conduct was all-important.

The teachings of Mencius

The teachings of an early Confucian follower, Mencius, were adopted for the way in which they linked the moral order to natural law:

> *'The spirit is tremendous and strong'*, Mencius taught. *'If unobstructed and properly nourished, it will fill the whole universe. But it requires for its growth the steady pursuit of the sense of justice and truth. For without the sense of justice and truth, the spirit of man withers'.*

However far reality strayed from these principles, the dynasties had an updated version of an old creed to provide them with a secular system of ethics on which imperial rule could rest.

Yet half the Chinese remained strictly subordinated to the other half: the moral code promoted by the neo-Confucians did not bring any improvement in the lot of women. Increasingly in this commercialized age, girls were sold by their parents as brides or concubines. The practice of foot-binding also spread.

The Khitan push south

The first major challenge to the Song dynasty came from the Khitan, who rose to power beyond the Great Wall after the Uyghur peoples moved away from Mongolia. They blended the cavalry power traditionally associated with northern armies with the adoption of Chinese administrative and written skills.

ABOVE *This painting featuring a Khitan horseman was found on the wall of a tomb located near the site of Shangjing, the central administrative city of the Liao dynasty. It is thought to date from 959.*

Under a forceful leader known by his Chinese name of Abaoji, the Liao house – which ruled from 907 – embodied this unprecedented combination by founding two separate realms, one of which operated along traditional nomadic lines, while the other was modelled on the Chinese state.

Further attacks in the following decade made such inroads that the dynasty had to flee for a time from Kaifeng. A counter-offensive took the Song forces back

to the Yellow River, but the empire was exhausted. A treaty was concluded under which the northern ruler was acknowledged as a 'brother'. Heavy indemnities of silk and silver were paid.

Reforms under Renzong

The emperor Renzong (r.1022–63), suffered a similar fate at the hands of marauders from the northwest and was forced to agree to a heavy indemnity. That led the Khitan to demand more. The Song paid up, and bought peace. Though Renzong was no imposing ruler, he appointed good officials, notably the scholar, Wang Anshi (1021–86), who drew up a wide-ranging programme of reforms covering state finances to local organization. (See Wang Anshi and Sima Guang, opposite.) The appeal of his ideas was such that, despite the temporary triumph of conservative opposition at court, later emperors would revive them.

Wang Anshi was eventually displaced by anti-reform opponents and left the court, but his reforms brought some relief. The economy grew, and use of paper money spread. Irrigation projects improved agriculture. Schools were established and charitable foundations were set up to run hospitals, orphanages and hospices. Reserve granaries collected grain for bad times. Scholars who did not belong to the imperial élite sought new and often

ABOVE During the Northern Song, the technology of iron casting reached new levels of sophistication, allowing architects and builders to design elaborate structures made of cast iron, such as this sculpted incense burner.

interesting paths towards serving the people. But despite these measures and the development of the civil service to run the empire, by the middle of the 11th century the ruling house was heading for trouble. As with earlier and later dynasties, for Song emperors change had to be contained within the tradition on which they based the regime. The 'Song renaissance', as it is known, was an important stage in China's development, but it reached its limits when the élite that underpinned the regime felt their positions menaced.

On the northern frontier, success and imperial submission had reduced the Khitans' militancy as they opted for a more settled existence, subsidized by the Chinese payments. For instance, their practice of putting corpses in trees for three years

WANG ANSHI AND SIMA GUANG

Wang Anshi (1021–86), an outstanding scholar from eastern China, charted a path for reform that could have strengthened dynastic rule under the Song, had it not run into internal contradictions inherent in the Chinese system.

Wang spent his early adult years with his family rather than going to court. When he eventually graduated to the capital in 1069, he so impressed the emperor Shenzong that he was made a privy councillor, a position which gave him access to the central administration. He swiftly embarked on a far-reaching campaign of reforms.

Some, such as large-scale irrigation works, were highly practical. He called for the establishment of a national academy for civil servants, and regional colleges to teach law, medicine and military science. He urged that imperial examinations should focus on solving problems and elaborating policy. He advocated reorganization of state finances under a planning commission, extension of loans to farmers, and taxes to pay for local government staff. He introduced village units responsible for order, as well as military conscription, a drive against tax evasion and the stabilization of prices. Wang was also a great believer in the cash economy as a means of liberating farmers, in place of the old system of payment in kind.

It was a huge programme, somewhat akin to the proposals that would be advanced eight centuries later by Emperor Guangxu (r.1875–1908) during the Hundred Days of 1898. (See The Decline and Fall of the Qing, pages 234–43.) As would be the case with the Hundred Days, there were three major obstacles: the power of conservatives, the sheer scale of the changes and the necessity of obtaining the co-operation of the bureaucracy in order to implement them. The latter included many officials who feared that their privileges would be threatened by reform.

Thus, Wang faced massive opposition, which was headed by another eminent scholar, Sima Guang (1019–86) the son of a rich family in Shanxi. He had gained the highest imperial degree at the age of 20, and was said to have used a wooden pillow so that if he dozed off while reading at night he would be awakened by its hardness. Moving into official court circles, Sima made his mark with a series of histories of China since the start of the Warring States period in the fifth century BC. His work found great favour with rulers, and he was made a senior minister. But he opposed Wang's reforms at a time when they enjoyed imperial favour and, as a result, exiled himself from the capital to Luoyang, where he continued his historical work.

Famed for his moral uprightness, Sima believed that Wang's changes ran counter to the Chinese tradition; he was almost certainly also driven by personal rivalry. In particular, and rightly, he doubted whether the cash economy could be spread to the peasantry given the prevailing monetary conditions. Sima admitted that Wang had *'remarkable ideas and unusual powers of rhetoric'* but criticized him as *'a very self-willed man … [who] was so convinced that his own ideas were right that he would hold them tenaciously against all opposition'.*

In 1076 opposition forced Wang to retire and devote himself to literary pursuits for the last ten years of his life. In the following decades, his ideas would go in and out of fashion. The struggle he began between effective change imposed on the imperial system and the preservation of existing ways would reappear during the centuries to come.

GUNPOWDER Taoists first put together coal, saltpetre and sulphur to make gunpowder under the Tang – three centuries before the first mention of it in the West. A ninth-century text records that the resulting smoke and flames had burned the hands and faces of those who created the mixture, *'and even the whole house where they were working burned down'*.

It was under the Song that gunpowder came to be widely used for military purposes, prized initially for its ability to set off fires and emit frightening clouds of smoke. Then its destructive power as an explosive was appreciated, and imperial forces hurled gunpowder grenades from catapults against invading northerners.

By then the Chinese had also begun to use gunpowder as a propellant. Records from 1132 show flaming arrows being set at the mouth of a tube of thick bamboo in which gunpowder was lit to fire them at the enemy. Though the Chinese were well ahead of the Europeans in using gunpowder, they did not move on to firearms. In this, as in many other ventures, they were content to stop at the first stage of an invention without exploring its further possibilities.

The first description of a cannon in warfare was in the account of a battle fought in 1126, when the Song army used it against the invading Jurchens.

before burning the bones was replaced by burial in Chinese-style tombs. They evolved a written language, tilled fields, set up iron foundries and weaving shops and moved into walled towns. But their kingdom was hit by floods and drought; the ruling family became factionalized; the growing influence of Buddhism reduced the warlike spirit of their leaders; and other northern groups began to expand as serious rivals. The result was that, although the Song had tried to buy peace by agreeing to treaties and paying indemnities, the dynasty felt it could no longer abide by Taizu's 'small army' policy. Its forces mushroomed to well over a million men, putting an enormous strain on the treasury. Military innovations were introduced, including crossbows capable of firing a series of arrows, and gunpowder. (See Gunpowder, above.)

Treaty and trade with the Xia

One of the new groups to pose a threat, the Western Xia, emerged from the Tangut people to establish itself over a wide belt at the top of northern China, looming over

Gansu, Shanxi and Shaanxi provinces. Herdsmen who knew the value of commerce, the Xia occupied major trading centres in the far west and formally established their dynasty in 1038. Six years later they obliged the Song to sign a treaty, in which the emperor agreed to pay over large sums but gained no guarantees of non-aggression.

Trade flourished between the empire and this new power in the north; the Xia sold horses, camels, sheep, cattle, carpets and beeswax while the Chinese exported silk, ceramics, medicines, lacquer and incense. Smuggling of salt in contravention of the imperial monopoly provided another thriving trade for the northerners. Among the tribute items the Song committed themselves to supply every year were 135,000 rolls of silk, 72,000 ounces of silver and 30,000 pounds of tea.

The last early Song emperors

The last five rulers in the first phase of the Song dynasty enjoyed varied fortunes. The first, Yingzong (r.1064–7), was an invalid and left the job of running the empire to the dowager empress, who ordered an end to Wang Anshi's reforms and put the court on a conservative course. The next ruler, Shenzong (r.1068–85) – a serious man who saw the problems facing the dynasty – re-introduced Wang's plans but ran into opposition from the élite landlords and merchants who were threatened by his taxation proposals. His successor, Zhezong (r.1086–1101), was ten when he became emperor, and his dowager empress repeated the swing back to conservatism. After her death, Zhezong recalled some reformers, but he was an inconstant ruler and died at the age of 24 in 1101.

With a population of almost a million, the capital of Kaifeng was still a symbol of the wealth and power of China. It was not simply a matter of geographical expanse or population, however. Industry was also growing; in 1078 China produced some 115,000 tons of iron – a per capita output that would not be equalled in Europe for another six centuries.

A late-11th-century poet, Su Shi, described one enterprise in Jiangsu province which consisted of 36 foundries owned by rich families; the surrounding countryside had been stripped of trees for fuel and the iron works were now powered by coke. In Shandong, to the north of Jiangsu, farmers grew crops for half the year and then worked in iron smelters during the winter. They were so poor, an official reported, that they never stopped working. Much of the iron was taken to Kaifeng to be made into weapons, tools and construction equipment.

960 Emperor Taizu founds the Song dynasty, restoring the Confucian bureaucracy

971–9 Autonomous kingdoms are brought under imperial rule

979 The Khitan defeat an imperial army in the north

983 Publication of an encyclopedia sponsored by the throne

1004 Emperor concedes parity to the Khitan

1007 Merchants in Chengdu issue paper money, the printing of which is taken over by the government

1020 Population of China reaches 100 million

1038 Xia herdsmen formally establish their dynasty in western China

1041 Invention of movable type

1078 China produces an estimated 115,000 tonnes of iron

1116 With the weakening of the Khitan, the Jurchen people revolt and set up the kingdom of the Jin in the northeast

1126 Having overcome the Khitan, the Jurchen march south to take Kaifeng and establish their capital in what is now Beijing. Millions join the exodus to the south, where the Song establish themselves in a new, restricted realm

FUNERARY PREPARATIONS FOR A WEALTHY MAN

Great Master Zhao was an important landowner and perhaps also a merchant in the town of Baisha, in the Yellow River region around Luoyang.

When they died, Zhao and his wife were buried together in a miniature house, with five intricately constructed rooms. The mock windows had mock curtains. A door stood half-open with the figure of a servant girl looking round it.

Paintings on the walls showed how the Zhaos had lived, sitting in chairs at a table listening to musicians as they sipped wine, attended by servants bearing a dish of peaches and a spittoon. One painting features their cat; others depict servants bringing

A mural found in a tomb of around the same period as that of the Zhaos shows a group of servants watching a bird and catching cicadas.

the couple what they would need in the afterlife – money, grain and wine. An inscription records how much had been paid for the funeral plot: 99,999 strings of copper – three was the symbolic number for light, and three times three multiplied ten thousand times was a powerful answer to death.

On the other hand, those who benefited from economic expansion of the Song era grew extremely rich, as shown by archaeological excavations of their tombs (See Funerary Preparations for a Wealthy Man, left). This was a time of growth and a search for a peaceful empire; but it was not destined to fulfil its goals.

Defeat by the Jurchen

The early-12th-century emperor Huizong (r.1101–25) was an accomplished painter and calligrapher, and his court became a mecca for culture. He preferred to retreat into his love for the arts rather than confront the growing factionalism around the throne. When he did turn his hand to statecraft, the result was disastrous.

NORTHERN SONG EMPERORS	
Taizu	960–76
Taizong	976–97
Zhenzong	998–1022
Renzong	1022–63
Yingzong	1064–7
Shenzong	1068–85
Zhezong	1086–1101
Huizong	1101–25
Qinzong	1126

A new northern power had emerged in the shape of the Jurchen people from Manchuria, who menaced not only the Song but also the other northern groups. They were an egalitarian tribal grouping in which everybody in the army, from the commanders to the ordinary soldiers, ate the same food. When major decisions were to be made, they all went out into the wilderness and deliberated while sitting around the ashes of a fire. 'When the army returns after a great victory', one account says, 'another great reunion is held and it is asked who has won merits. According to the degree of merit, gold is handed out; it is raised and shown to the multitude. If they think the reward too small, it is increased'.

Initially the Jurchen were inferior to the Khitan, but then, in 1112, their leader Aguda refused an order from the drunken Khitan king to dance in front of him at a feast. The following year, the Jurchen launched the first of a series of attacks on the Liao dynasty. In 1116 they occupied the central Liao lands. The Song tried divide-and-rule tactics in the north by concluding a pact with the Jurchen against the Khitan. But the Manchurians did not need the Chinese to take their enemy's southern capital in present-day Beijing. Although Aguda died in 1123, they finally wiped out Khitan rule in 1125, and their ruling house acquired the name of Jin.

Next, the Jurchen Jin turned on the Song, launching an unstoppable offensive to the south, headed by their cavalry. Emperor Huizong fled, abdicating in favour of his son, Qinzong (r.1126). The Jurchen took Kaifeng in 1126, together with a string of other Song cities. A heavy indemnity was imposed; the treaty documents called the Jurchen ruler the 'elder uncle' while the Song emperor was only the 'nephew'. The captured Chinese rulers were taken north and forced to bow in front of a Jurchen altar. To humiliate them further, the Song ruler and his son were given the Chinese titles of 'Marquis of Muddled Virtue' and 'Double Muddled'. The Jurchen began to develop their government in the north, and their armies continued to probe southwards. The Song appeared to be done for, but it was time for a dynastic revival in new lands while the new rulers of the north began a mass emigration of three million people south from Manchuria.

145

THE SOUTHERN SONG

1127–1279
While Emperor Huizong and his heir were prisoners of the Jurchen, along with thousands of their followers, another of his sons escaped to keep the dynasty alive. It sought refuge first at Nanjing on the Yangzi River and then further east at Hangzhou. Despite the capture of leading members of the dynasty, there were still plenty of others to carry on the line – Huizong had 31 sons and 34 daughters. Some died, but many survived.

AT FIRST, THE RULERS THOUGHT THEY WOULD BE ABLE TO RECLAIM THEIR LOST LANDS IN northern China. The most daring commander of the time, Yue Fei, led attacks on the northerners, and openly criticized the way in which other imperial forces were operating. Enemies at court spread rumours about him. His insistence on continuing to fight contradicted the peace party around Emperor Gaozong (r.1127–62). He was imprisoned and poisoned on the orders of the chief counsellor. The emperor's connivance in this act meant that his reputation was sullied forever as Yue became a symbol of military righteousness.

RIGHT *Portrait of the Song emperor, Gaozong, who founded the Southern Song after he fled south when the Jurchens took Kaifeng. Gaozong re-established the dynasty's capital in Hangzhou, which grew to become a prosperous cosmopolitan city.*

Valiant as Yue had been, it became evident that the strength of the Jurchen would prevent the Song from re-establishing control in northern China. The Treaty of Shaoxing in 1141 recognized the reality of foreign rule over all China north of the River Huai. Instead, the Song concentrated on their new domain – only half of what they had previously claimed, but still a vast space which offered opportunities not present in the hardier territories of the north.

Growth of urban centres
The 'temporary capital' of Hangzhou on the east coast grew from a small port to house some 1.5 million people within its walls and in its suburbs. Other urban centres expanded even more – the prefecture of Fuzhou in Fujian province, for

> My hair bristles in my helmet, My breast is filled with violence, My fierce ambition is to feed on the flesh of the Huns, Laughing, I thirst for the blood of the barbarians. Oh, let everything begin anew. Let all our rivers and mountains be recovered, before we pay our respects once more to the emperor.

SONG ATTRIBUTED TO YUE FEI, BUT NOT WRITTEN DOWN UNTIL THE 15TH CENTURY. IT BECAME A PATRIOTIC CHANT, EMPLOYED IN THE RESISTANCE TO THE JAPANESE INVASION IN THE SECOND WORLD WAR

example, reported a population of almost 4 million in 1290. The dynasty, now known as the Southern Song, encouraged urban commercial development and a monetary economy – in part to enable payment of the big indemnities contracted with the Jurchen.

The ruling house quickly adopted the less martial lifestyle of the region where it was now based. The further advance of the northern invaders was checked by the nature of the terrain – the wooded valleys of the Lower Yangzi hampered their cavalry. The canals and ditches dug to water the fields that produced food for the expanding population had the secondary advantage of creating fresh defences.

Maritime links

As the southern ports flourished, the court developed a mounting interest in the sea and in encouraging international trade. Maritime links replaced the old contacts by land across Central Asia. Arabs set up store houses in Hangzhou, Guangzhou (Canton) and other cities, living in districts of their own and being allowed to apply Muslim law. Black slaves were brought from Africa. A new and more open spirit infected officials: a former director of the National Academy chartered ships to explore far-off seas – when his crew tried to halt one journey, he drew his sword and forced them to continue. People began to emigrate to Southeast Asia to escape the pressure caused by rising population levels.

> The people depended on the sea and commerce for their livelihood. They would leave their parents, wives and children without a thought to dwell among the barbarians.
>
> GAZETTEER OF FUJIAN

Drawing on merchant shipping as a source of sailors and skills, a well-armed Chinese navy was built – the first such national force to be established on a permanent basis independent of the army. A president of the Board of Revenue called the sea and the Yangzi 'the new Great Wall', with ships serving as watchtowers. Emperor Xiaozong (r.1163–90) hailed the navy as *'our strong arm, and we cannot afford to neglect it'*.

The largest naval base was located at the mouth of the Yangzi, where a port was developed which would become Shanghai. Well armed, it expanded steadily to number 20 squadrons with 52,000 men by 1237. Half those on its ships were archers, crossbowmen or operators of gunpowder weapons. The navy kept the coast safe for the dynasty, but it remained a defensive force, and proposals that it should extend Chinese influence into the South China Sea were not pursued.

Though they had lost the north, the Song still held the richest half of the country, containing most of the population. Since they could not expand to the west, given the

strength of the rulers in Yunnan and Vietnam, the dynasty concentrated on developing what it had. Its domain, in particular the area around Hangzhou, became extremely prosperous, and the European visitor Marco Polo was highly impressed by it. (See The Southern Song and Marco Polo, pages 152–3.)

Heyday for commerce and culture

The social hierarchy was altered as rich merchants, who were organized into guilds, took their place alongside landowners, military men and senior officials in the élite. Life for the majority of the population in the countryside remained precarious, however, and there was a steady flow of migrants into cities.

People took to specializing in the manufacture of handicraft goods or textiles, giving up the traditional planting of food to feed themselves – they could buy produce at market in return for the money their own products brought. Others concentrated on raising crops to sell for cash. As a result, the network of rural and urban commerce expanded. While the economy grew strongly, the way in which the imperial mint issued coins containing ever smaller amounts of copper undermined the currency. Ten times as many coins were made each year as under the Tang, and the effects were inevitably inflationary and destabilizing. Among other things, this led to the growing use of paper notes among merchants, a practice begun by the traders of Sichuan who needed an easily carried means of exchange to replace cumbersome strings of metal coins.

Culture flourished to the extent that one historian, T.C. Liu, has judged that *'to hypothesize boldly about the evolution of China in the last 800 years, it is the Southern Song that has provided the dominant model'*. But when the final challenge came from the northerners, the remnant empire could not resist. However strong the economic and social advances were, however estimable the cultural achievements of the Song, force still predominated as it had from the days of the First Emperor. The dynasties spun intricate ideological and philosophical patterns. But in the end, brute power determined the outcome.

BELOW With the economic growth of the Southern Song, tradespeople flocked to the cities to sell their wares. This late 18th-century colour engraving shows a Chinese furrier – the strips of fur would be bought by the wealthy to trim winter clothing.

1127 Gaozong becomes first emperor of the Southern Song as Jin forces push the dynasty south from northern China

1129 Northern forces attack Hangzhou and Ningbo

1136 Northerners withdraw from the south

1141 Southern Song acknowledge vassal status to northern Jin in the Treaty of Shaoxing; Southern Song capital is established at Hangzhou

1147 Rise of the Mongols forces Jin to pull back to their northeastern homeland

*c.***1150** Chinese merchants develop seaborne trade with Japan, Korea, Southeast Asia, Malabar and the Persian Gulf

1206 Mongol warrior Genghis Khan is proclaimed Lord of the Oceans

1209–34 Mongol power expands in the north

1213 Mongol forces under Genghis Khan storm Zhongdu

1260 Niccolò and Maffeo Polo set out on the first of two journeys to China

1270 Kublai proclaims a new dynasty, the Yuan, with himself as emperor

1275 Marco Polo enters northern China with his father Niccolò

1276 Hangzhou falls to Mongol forces

1279 The Southern Song are defeated by the Mongols

The Mongol threat

In the 1160s, a boy was born on a hill in the distant steppe of the north with, the chronicles say, a blood clot the size of a knucklebone clasped in his hand. Before the boy was ten years old, his father Yesugai, a Mongol tribal chieftain, had been poisoned and his son, Temujin, whose name means 'iron', was immediately hunted down by the assassins. Though held captive for a while, he escaped and spent many of his early years as a fugitive with his family, hunting and horse-rustling.

He found a patron in a tribal chieftain called To'oril and rose to become a warrior, defeating opponents and seeking supporters until, in 1206, the tribes of the eastern steppe pronounced him Lord of the Oceans, or Genghis (Chinggis) Khan. In 1209, peace envoys arrived from the Uyghurs, who lived to the west.

Genghis had men ready to fight and gathered an army of some 70,000 men to invade China. It was a tiny force given what he faced. His first opponent was the Jurchen Jin dynasty in the north and its capital of Zhongdu, present-day Beijing. The Jin emperor had half a million infantry and 150,000 cavalry, but his advance cavalry of 10,000 men immediately defected – as frontier guards, they were from a tribe that was loyal to Genghis.

Zhongdu was too big to take immediately, and Genghis led his armies away, agreeing a treaty with the Khitans and returning, in 1212–13. He faced a city wall 18 miles (30 km) long and 50 feet (15 m) wide at its base. Once more he veered away, taking 90 towns in a side campaign. Then he laid serious siege to Zhongdu. As his armies cut off the city, cannibalism became common within its walls. After the garrison commander committed suicide, 5000 Mongol troops stormed across the walls, setting off a year of plunder and mass murder; the streets, it was said, were slippery with human fat.

The other northern kingdoms sought help from the Song. They told the dynasty, *'we are to you as the lips are to the teeth. When the lips are gone, the teeth will feel the cold'.* The Song, who had formerly allied with the Mongols against the Jin in another attempt to divide the northerners, now reacted by sending an army north with orders to regain the lost lands of the empire. This brought a lengthy counter-offensive from the Mongols, who adapted their military skills to deal with the southern terrain and developed a navy of their own, using it as an offensive weapon in a way that the Song had not.

LEFT *Illustration showing Genghis Khan (second from right) outside his tent during a military campaign. Genghis first invaded northern China, before turning his attentions to Central Asia and Europe, and it was his grandson Kublai who finally conquered the Southern Song.*

Death throes of the Song

The Song were weakened during this time by several feeble or infant rulers. Once more, it was as if the Mandate of Heaven was being removed from them. Ningzong (r.1195–1224) was dominated by the families of his two wives. His successor, Lizong (r.1225–64), ruled for 39 years, presiding over a period of economic growth, but he gradually withdrew into a life of self-indulgence and paid little attention to the external threats that were shaping up from central and northern China.

Despite this evident danger, the next ruler, Duzong (r.1265–74), a weak man who left state business to court officials, showed little awareness of the scale of the threat from the Mongols. It was as if the Southern Song had become convinced of their invulnerability, forgetting the lesson of what had happened to their predecessors.

After Duzong died in 1274, three of his infant sons came to the throne in quick succession, expiring within the space of four years: Gongzong (r.1275), Duanzong (r.1276–8) and Bing Di (r.1279). In 1276 Hangzhou fell to the Mongol forces. The Song withdrew to the southern coast, where a major naval battle took place – some accounts spoke of the imperial forces chaining 1000 vessels together in a defensive line. But their adversary had developed maritime offensive tactics, and overcame them. A hundred thousand Song troops and sailors were said to have been killed. The dowager empress jumped into the sea to drown and the body of the six-year-old emperor, Bing Di, was washed up on the shore. The Song dynasty was over. The era of the Mongol khans had dawned.

SOUTHERN SONG EMPERORS	
Gaozong	1127–62
Xiaozong	1163–90
Guangzong	1190–4
Ningzong	1195–1224
Lizong	1225–64
Duzong	1265–74
Gongzong	1275
Duanzong	1276–8
Bing Di	1279

THE SOUTHERN SONG AND MARCO POLO

In the late 13th century Hangzhou could claim to be the richest city on earth. Its population was well over a million, and its surroundings were in sharp contrast to the dry and dusty plains around the Yellow River which had been the home of earlier Song rulers.

Unlike the arid northern lands, Hangzhou lay amid fertile rice plantations watered by rivers and canals. The Yangzi Valley was to the north. The seas beyond Hangzhou Bay provided a link with the rest of the world as great Chinese junks plied the seas to Japan, Indochina, Malaya and as far afield as Africa.

The city was vividly described by the Venetian Marco Polo (1254–1324) as a highlight of his fabled journey to the east. It was, he wrote, the greatest city in the world, 'where so many pleasures may be found that one fancies oneself to be in Paradise'. Some recent writers have cast doubt on whether he actually reached China, speculating that he may have put together accounts he gathered from travellers who had made the trip. Even if this is so, these stories attest to the splendour of Hangzhou and the power of China at the time.

In its glory days, Hangzhou reflected the growth in wealth, social mobility and cosmopolitan nature of Song China with its merchants, noblemen, scholars, artists, hospitality, cuisine, mansions and amusements. Its markets were frequented by tens of thousands of people. Its tradesmen formed guilds covering activities from trading in crabs, olives or ginger to bath-house owners who styled themselves 'the companions of fragrant water'. Pleasure grounds were crammed with storytellers, actors, jugglers, acrobats, shadow-play artists and animal trainers. During the great festivals the noise and fun went on day and night. Shops sold everything from false hair to food for caged crickets, decorative fish and fumigating powder to repel mosquitoes. Hangzhou was famed for its jewellery, toys and printed books, its rhinoceros skins, turbans, ivory combs and painted fans.

The man-made West Lake was considered the most beautiful spot of all, 9 miles (14.5 km) in circumference and with two islands on which lavish celebrations were held in large palaces. Hundreds of boats would be on the water at any one time, some carrying up to 100 passengers. Others were waterborne shops selling vegetables and other produce. Small boats owned by rich families were elaborately decorated and powered by blue sails. The emperor's craft, made of cedar wood and adorned with magnificent carvings, were kept in a special area behind a small dyke.

Marco Polo noted that the rich merchants affected 'grave and decorous behaviour'. Though 'very handsome' and with dresses of such magnificence that it was impossible to estimate the cost, their ladies were 'brought up to acquire habits of great timidity and delicacy'. Despite the conspicuous consumption of such wealthy citizens, Hangzhou suffered from food shortages brought on by population pressure, and fires regularly ravaged its closely built houses.

The city was also home to a flock of thieves, beggars and skilful pickpockets, lottery and gambling rings, as well as a large population of prostitutes. Some courtesans moved up the social scale, receiving only upper-class men in their private quarters. One of the most celebrated courtesans had a staff of ten maids and musicians and a luxurious home filled with exquisite gold, silver and jade ornaments; when she died she was buried on a hill reserved for people of high rank.

After it fell to the Mongols in 1276, the take-over of Hangzhou was peaceful, since the dowager empress agreed to surrender on behalf of the nine-year-old emperor Duanzong. The newcomers sent the official seals of Chinese power, books, artworks, maps and imperial treasures to their khan. Hangzhou's time as the richest metropolis in the world was over.

'Like an ancient ruin, the grass grows high: gone are the guards and the gatekeepers.
Fallen towers and crumbling palaces desolate my soul.
Under the eaves of the long-ago hall fly in and out the swallows.
But within: silence. The chatter of cock and hen parrots is heard no more.'

POET ON VISITING HANGZHOU AFTER THE FALL OF THE CITY

An undated illustration depicts Marco Polo's arrival in China in 1275.

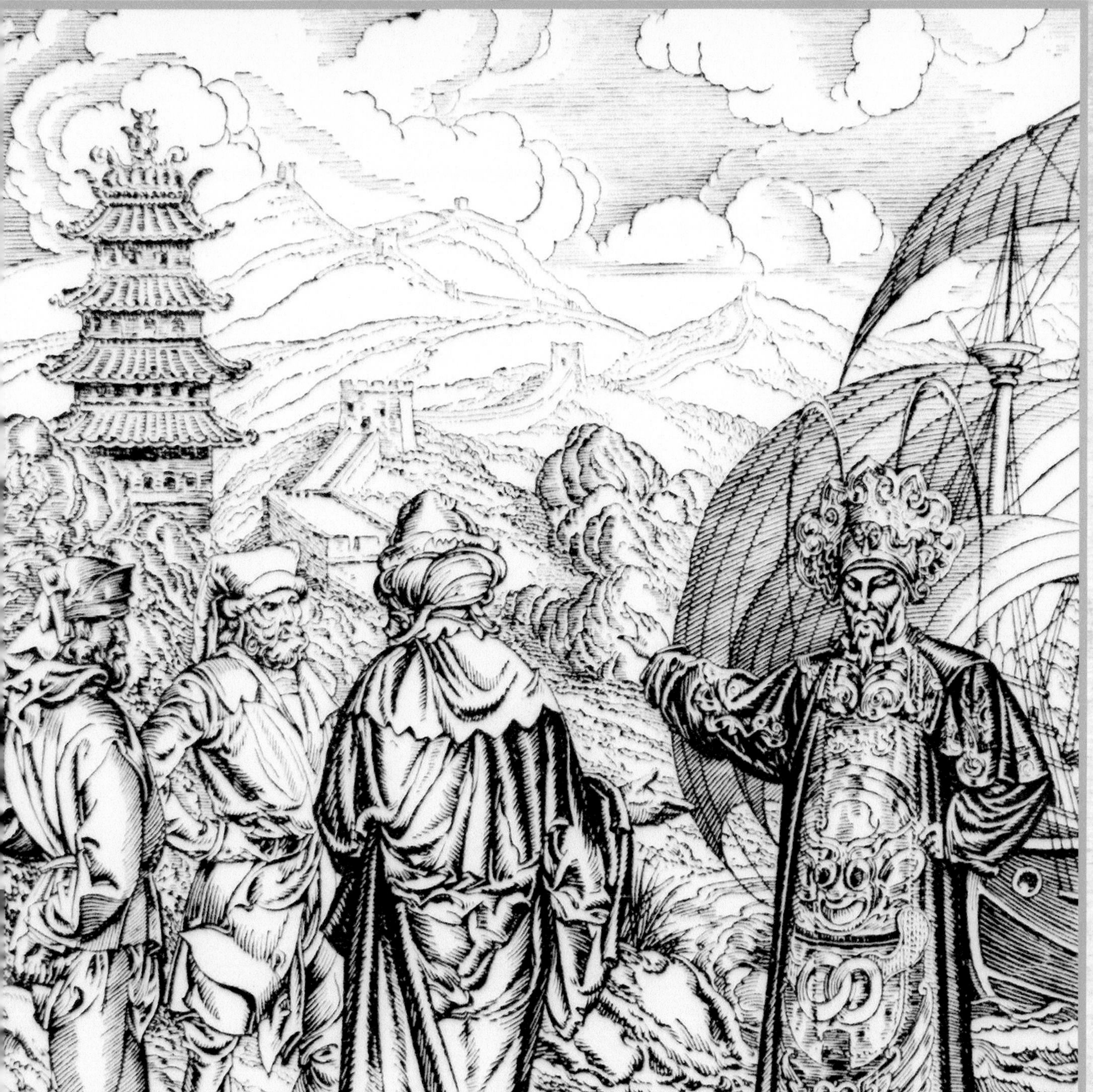

THE YUAN

1279–1368

In 1272 Kublai (Khubilai) Khan, the most sinicized of Mongol rulers yet, read out the edict that named his dynasty the Yuan, a term he took from the Chinese classic of divination, the *Yi Jing*, or 'Book of Changes'. Meaning 'creative force', Qian Yuan asserted the dynasty's legitimacy in Chinese terms, despite its genesis outside China. Kublai was a tribal chieftain, a kha-khan, a Chinese emperor and Buddhist universal ruler, all roles he played adroitly to maintain control of the country and its peoples. This balancing act defined the Yuan dynasty.

THE INITIAL CAPITAL OF SHANGDU, COLERIDGE'S XANADU, WAS COMPLETED IN 1260. This was followed by the khan's 'Great Capital' of Dadu, 200 miles (322 km) to the south. It was finished in 1274, but the Mongol princes did not move for another 11 years. It was a Chinese design and became a northern capital, hence the name we use today, Beijing – *bei* meaning 'north' and *jing*, 'capital'. (See Beijing and the Forbidden City, page 174.) The city Marco Polo wrote of had walls 4 metres (13 ft) thick, and 11 gates. The architect Zi Cong, a monk, based the layout on the god Na-Cha, Buddhism's guardian of the north, with each gate representing a different limb. Kublai himself shot four arrows to determine the perimeter of the city's monumental Wan'an Monastery.

RIGHT *Portrait of Kublai Khan. Unlike his predecessors, Kublai received a Chinese education and was literate. His conquest of the Southern Song resulted in China being reunited again as part of a huge Mongol empire that stretched across much of the Eurasian landmass from eastern Europe to the Yellow Sea.*

❝ The ceiling is adorned so that there is nothing to be seen anywhere but gold and pictures. The hall is so vast and so wide that a meal might well be served there for more than 6000 men. The number of chandeliers is quite bewildering … The roof is all ablaze with scarlet and green and blue and yellow and all the colours that exist, so brilliantly varnished that it glitters like crystal and the sparkle of it can be seen from far away. ❞

MARCO POLO ON THE PALACE AT DADU

The empire carved out by Genghis Khan stretched across 12 million square miles (31 million sq km) from East Asia to the Black Sea. Under his grandsons it was split into three parts; Kublai ruled the Chinese section. Initially, this was restricted to the north of the country, which the newcomers controlled from 1234 onwards. But the south remained beyond their reach, its terrain of fields, waterways, forests and mountains an obstacle to the military power of the Mongol cavalry. Nor were the northerners natural sailors, and many key sectors and cities in the south were on the coast. Kublai staged a long campaign to dominate the whole of the country.

Showdown at sea

The cavalry eventually overcame the difficulties of the terrain and penetrated deep into territory ruled by the Southern Song. They cut off supplies to their adversaries and gradually gained the upper hand. They also built a navy and staged a highly successful land-and-water offensive against the Chinese fleet on the Yangzi in 1273, their horsemen showering the enemy ships with arrows from the banks while the Mongol craft attacked up the river. The Chinese ships were all at anchor because the admiral feared that they would otherwise sail away to escape the enemy; when one caught fire, the blaze spread through the fleet, destroying it and killing thousands of men on board.

LEFT *Having conquered China, Kublai embarked on unsuccessful campaigns against Japan and Indonesia. This illustration by William Henry Blake, following an account by Marco Polo, is of Kublai's fleet passing through the East Indian archipelago.*

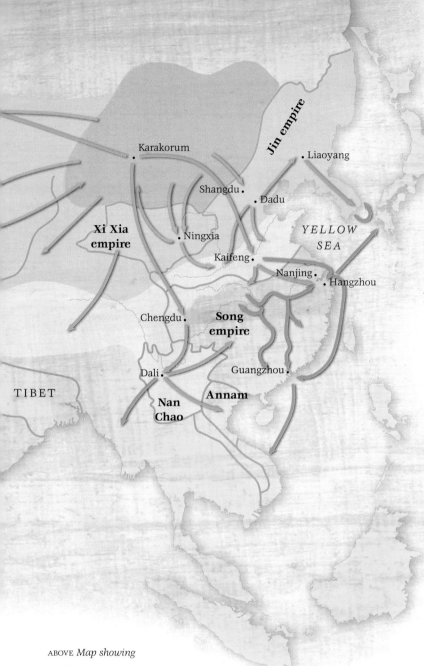

Karakorum

Jin empire

Liaoyang

Shangdu

Dadu

Xi Xia
empire

Ningxia

YELLOW
SEA

Kaifeng

Nanjing

Hangzhou

Chengdu

Song
empire

Dali

Guangzhou

TIBET

Nan
Chao

Annam

ABOVE *Map showing
the Mongol campaigns
of the 13th century. From
the Asian steppes they
swept south and west to
Central Asia and Europe.
Under Kublai Khan they
finally conquered the
Southern Song and,
with it, most of China.*

A final showdown at sea took place off the south coast. With 1000 ships, the Chinese had a numerical superiority of three to one. The nine-year-old Song emperor and his mother were on board one of the ships to watch the encounter. The Mongols used the siege tactics that had won them many cities on land, encircling the Chinese fleet and blocking its supplies for two weeks. With the enemy weakened, they attacked to devastating effect on a morning shrouded in rain and fog. Contemporary accounts put the Chinese death toll at 100,000, among them the young emperor and his mother.

Few achievements won the Yuan more respect than the resulting re-unification of north and south China. With the Mongol acquisition of the Southern Song imperial seals in 1276, the country was a single entity again for the first time since the Jurchen conquest in the 1120s. But it was under foreign rule.

Mongols and Chinese traditions

Returning north after his victory, Kublai claimed overall leadership of the Mongols after the death of one brother, fighting an ultimately victorious war against the other brother. In 1260 he proclaimed himself the Great Khan. The empire he ruled reached – in name, at least – from Korea to southern Russia. The re-opening of the Silk Road linked it with Europe. Merchants and travellers came to China, including, by his own account, the Venetian Marco Polo. (See The Southern Song and Marco Polo, pages 152–3.) But his was a fragmented realm which he failed to subdue entirely. Within his own Chinese state, the administration was bilingual, multi-ethnic and tolerated most religions, such as Nestorian Christianity, the faith of Kublai's mother. The emperor continued to consult shamans. He himself had been designated as a Universal King by a Tibetan lama, who brought Lamaism to the Mongol court.

Although he avoided many traditional ceremonies and duties, Kublai shifted the focus of the Mongol empire to China. While he was growing up, his father had been away at war for most of the time, and the principal influence on him was his mother. She was a woman famed for her intelligence and administrative skills, who taught him that governing China would only be possible if the Mongol ruler adopted the country's traditions.

Kublai left many Chinese institutions in place, while setting up special organizations to cater for the specific concerns of Mongols, such as the Office for Retrieving Lost Animals for their herders. But there was a sharp official division between the Mongols and their subjects; this despite the fact that he recruited more Confucian scholars to his court than any of his forebears as he sought to show his adherence to traditional Chinese ideals – something of far greater importance to the literati than his ethnic background. Under the Yuan, the Tang dynasty became idealized as the apogee of cultural achievement, a perspective that persists today.

Arts, roads and schools

Many Song poets in the south wrote of their sadness at the Mongol conquests, but most later acquiesced to the newcomers' rule. Arts flourished, particularly plays. The great painter and calligrapher Zhao Mengfu exercised his art, and his wife, Guan Daosheng, was China's first recognized woman artist as well as an accomplished poet.

The new dynasty began by developing China's infrastructure. It restored and extended the Grand Canal linking north to south; two and a half million workers laboured on this vital transport route, with a paved highway running 1000 miles (1600 km) along its stone embankments – travelling from one end to the other took 40 days. The ruler had roads built, aided peasant farmers, offered merchants low-interest loans, constructed schools and created a fixed tax rate that did not overburden Chinese subjects. The postal system established by Kublai Khan was unrivalled in the world, with 50,000 horses and nearly 1500 stations. Couriers covered 250 miles (400 km) in a day, ringing bells as they approached a station so that another rider could be ready to take the mail on the next stage of its journey.

The emperor sent an expedition to explore and map the upper reaches of the Yellow River in 1281, and developed commercial contacts with Europe. There would also be a far-off echo of China of this period when Columbus took Marco Polo's *Travels*, which describes Kublai's Shangdu palace, on his voyage across the Atlantic.

The 14-member General Secretariat enforced the emperor's will and recommended official appointments, resolved legal cases involving major crimes and drafted administrative regulations for new laws. One feature of the Yuan was the branch secretariat, which could often behave as though it were

YUAN EMPERORS	
Kublai (Shizu)	1279–94
Temur Oljeitu (Chengzong)	1294–1307
Khaishan (Wuzong)	1308–11
Ayurbarwada (Renzong)	1311–20
Shidebala (Yingzong)	1321–3
Yesun Temur (Taiding)	1323–8
Tugh Temur (Wenzong)	1328, 1329–32
Khoshila (Mingzong)	1329
Toghun Temur (Shundi)	1333–68

governing an external territory or vassal state. Yunnan, Korea and Gansu all enjoyed relative autonomy. The Ming abolished these secretariats in 1376 in a bid to reinstate centralized power.

Feasts and gout

Kublai's court was spendthrift, and persuaded him to lead invasions of Japan, Burma, Vietnam and Java, all of which failed. This spawned inflation, as did the printing of paper money. Though not socially or ideologically prescriptive, Mongol rule stratified society into four classes: Mongol, the 'blue-eyed' (such as Tibetans and Uyghurs), the northern Han and the southern Han. Wisely, Kublai recruited a few southern Han to his court and ordered official histories to be written of the Tang, Jin and Song dynasties. For the last of these, just three of the 23 scholars appointed to compile the work were non-Chinese.

Like all Mongols, Kublai indulged in enormous feasts, showing a particular taste for eating animal organs. But as emperor he could no longer rely on the slimming effects of an arduous life on the steppes, so he turned from the well-proportioned man described by Marco Polo into a hugely overweight figure who had to be carried around by courtiers. His health began to fail; in particular, he was afflicted by severe rheumatism and gout, and special shoes had to be made for him from fish skins. The death of his favourite wife and of their son in 1285 threw him into a depression which he tried to alleviate by embarking on fresh military campaigns abroad. He also had to

ABOVE *The famed Mongol cavalry was instrumental in breaking the Southern Song resistance. Zhao Mengfu, a leading artist and scholar under the Yuan, reflected the prowess of Mongolian horsemen in many of his paintings.*

YUAN MONGOLS

The Mongols who founded the Yuan dynasty in 1279 were archetypal people of the northern steppes. In the late 12th and early 13th centuries, under Genghis Khan, their empire stretched from the East China Sea to the Black Sea and the borders of Hungary, covering 12 million square miles (31 million sq km).

The Mongols perfected tactics of siege warfare and of sending cavalry over huge distances. They were nomadic people who were happiest living in tents and moving about on horseback, a lifestyle that led to the development of their fast-moving, lethal cavalry. All men under the age of 60 were conscripted, so large armies could be raised quickly. Expanding their realm involved wiping out cities that did not submit; the terror this created often resulted in ready surrender by those in their path. Some Mongol commanders chose to fight in winter, when their opponents would be sheltering from the cold, and when their cavalry could ride over frozen lakes and rivers.

Genghis decreed that all male heirs of the ruler could compete for the throne, the decision being made on the basis of military performance and the strength of a claimant's family. This led to feuds, assassinations and the overthrow of sovereigns.

Among his other achievements Genghis, who was illiterate himself, ordered that a written language should be developed, based on the Uyghur script of Central Asia, which was derived from the Aramaic language.

Detail of a hand-scroll painting depicting the Mongol invasion of China. Mongol incursions were usually swift and brutal.

The divide between the mobile Mongols and the sedentary Chinese was enormous – in language, script, food and customs. The Mongols enjoyed enormous feasts, tearing at meat with their sharp knives; traditionally, they worked off the resulting weight with their strenuous horse riding but, as their lifestyle became sedentary in China, they risked growing very fat. Mongol women had a higher status than their Chinese counterparts – for example, the mother of the first Yuan emperor, Kublai Khan, played a major role not only in educating her son but also in teaching him how to be an emperor of the Chinese.

Like Kublai, some other Mongol emperors sought to adopt Confucian ways but the cultural gap was enormous and the Mongol heart always remained in the vast open spaces of the north. Even when in the imperial capital at Beijing, princes often preferred to sleep in tents inside parks planted with grass from the northern steppes.

face a rising by a Mongol rebel. In 1294 he died, aged 79. His body was returned to his homeland and buried in an unknown grave.

Heavy spending and reversion to Mongol ways

After Kublai's death, the Yuan dynasty never again found its feet, and none of Kublai's successors were as adept at using Buddhist and Chinese ideology and symbolism to propel their supremacy. There were recurrent natural disasters, and banditry increased. Power passed to Temur Oljeitu (Emperor Chengzong), after Temur's older brother Kammala had given way. Temur sought to preserve Kublai's politics, with a pro-Confucian but racially balanced administration. However, the bureaucracy had grown too large and corrupt – an investigation in 1303 brought the conviction of 18,473 officials and clerks.

Temur died in 1307. In the following quarter of a century there were seven rulers, and the dynasty became destabilized. Temur's successor, Khaishan, a military commander, was an unsophisticated man from the north who lavished titles and positions on the undeserving, including actors and butchers, and sought to re-create a more Mongolian court at which officials gained excessive power. The emperor borrowed heavily from the monetary reserves to finance the largesse around him. State monopolies were sold off, and paper money was printed recklessly to finance expenditure.

The next emperor, Ayurbarwada, who took power in 1311, reversed these trends, filling the court with Confucians. He revived the civil service examination (his greatest legacy), but made it optional for Mongolians and se-mi (ethnically Inner Asians), and created a racial quota system. His promotion of Confucianism aroused bitter opposition among Mongols at court.

Factionalism grew, and the ruler could not balance imperial finances because of his commitment to Confucian governance theory, which emphasizes low taxes. His successor, Shidebala, who came to the throne at the age of 18, was able to recite Tang poetry by heart and was a good calligrapher. His adherence to Chinese ways was such that his grandmother was said to have exclaimed, 'We should never have raised this boy'. He imposed stricter discipline on the bureaucracy but he alienated the Mongol princes, whose grants were reduced, and he was assassinated in 1323.

> He is good and fair size … He is covered with flesh in a beautiful manner. Not too fat, nor too lean; he is more than well formed in all parts. He has his face white and partly shining red like the colour of a beautiful rose, which makes him appear very pleasing; and he has the eyes black and beautiful; and the nose very beautiful, well made and well set on the face.
>
> MARCO POLO ON KUBLAI KHAN

The family of the elder brother of Temur, Kammala, who had given way to his sibling in 1294, organized the killing. It installed as the new emperor Yesun Temur, a ruler from the northern steppes who reverted to Mongol ways. He barely took the time to govern his empire, leaving most of the work to a Muslim adviser, Dawlat Shah, who filled the administration with Muslims and indulged the Mongolian princes by ignoring their crimes and granting them money.

1279 Kublai founds the Yuan dynasty. Extension of the Grand Canal

1290 Population reduced to 60–80 million by the effects of wars, famine and disease

1294 Kublai dies

Late 13th century Anti-Mongol secret societies develop

1313 Imperial examinations resume

1325 Peasant revolts start

1337 Start of bubonic plague that spreads across Eurasia

1339 Franciscan mission arrives in China for a 14-year stay

1344 Yellow River floods, causing widespread starvation, and fuelling revolt

1352–5 Emergence of peasant leader Zhu Yuanzhang at the head of rebel forces

1356 Rebels take Nanjing

1360s Yuan emperor, Toghun, retreats into semi-retirement

1363 Zhu Yuanzhang defeats another anti-Yuan force in a major battle on a lake

1368 Zhu's forces impel the Yuan emperor to flee from Beijing. Zhu proclaims the Ming dynasty with himself as ruler

In 1328, the year of Yesun's death, a rival faction led by the darkhan (Mongolian prince) El Temur elevated Haishan's son, Tugh Temur, to the Dadu throne. Meanwhile a rival, Ragibagh, was appointed ruler at Shangdu, and Tugh's brother Khoshila led an army from the west to stake his own claim. Tugh abdicated in 1328 in favour of Khoshila but was invited back to Dadu by El Temur the following year. On his way, Tugh met Khoshila for a meal – the latter died four days later, and El Temur was suspected of involvement in his death.

Tugh Temur's reign was dominated by the prince, El Temur, and an adviser named Bayan. Chinese Confucian officials enjoyed little influence. Natural calamities and uprisings by ethnic minority groups added to the emperor's aura of illegitimacy. State coffers suffered too, as the 1323 Shangdu War had cost the government several years' income. Tugh's greatest bequest was the *Grand Compendium for Ruling the World*, housed in the Pavilion of the Star of Literature in Beijing. Rich with symbolism, it might have been a new beginning for Yuan power.

The last Yuan emperor

Instead, Tugh Temur died in 1332 and was succeeded by the seven-year-old Irinchibal, son of Khoshila, who remained emperor for just two months before a year and a half of wrangling placed his 15-year-old brother, Toghun Temur, on the throne in 1333. Officially Toghun was another son of Khoshila and a Turkish woman, but there were rumours that he was really the offspring of a captured Song emperor and a Muslim mother. Lasting until 1368, his reign was the longest of the Yuan, but he was not an effective ruler and brought the dynasty to an end after 89 years.

Toghun was under the wing of authoritarian advisers. The style of government he inherited was not very Chinese, with Confucianism as just one doctrine among a number of others. The functions of state were conducted in four written languages: classical Chinese, clerical Chinese, Mongolian and, probably, Persian. The system was generally well run, and, despite a weighting towards Mongolian candidates, the civil service examination system strengthened unity – the 1333 test was the first to meet full quotas for all ethnicities.

The government received income from land and trade taxes, as well as from its control of salt works and farms. At first, the grain supply was ample, and was carried down the Yangzi before being taken north by the Grand Canal. But after a supply peak in 1329, quantities suffered a sudden, disastrous drop. In the 1330s a particularly virulent form of plague arrived in China. It may have been a form of the Black Death, carried along the Silk Road. However, the timing makes it more likely that it entered China from lowlands near the Himalayas – perhaps brought by fleas in the saddlebags of horsemen – and then to have spread along the great trading route to Europe in 1346. Together with other epidemics, it wiped out two-thirds of the population in some parts of China; 90 per cent of the inhabitants of Hubei province in the centre of the country were reported to have died.

Toghun chose Bayan, the second-ranking adviser of his predecessor Tugh, as his Chancellor of the Right, the supreme post at court. Bayan set himself two chief tasks: to improve the general welfare of the people through such moves as cutting palace expenses and taxes and offering famine relief, and to re-establish what he viewed as the Kublai system of governance by re-imposing ethnic divisions. After decades of intermarriage, this bred anger and discord. Chinese people were not allowed to own horses, iron implements or weapons. Chinese opera was banned. Bayan sidelined the Confucian canon, and was even said to have toyed with the idea of killing all those with the five most common Chinese names. Not surprisingly, rebellions erupted, and the emperor dismissed his chief official in 1340.

Disasters and rebellions

Matters did not improve much, however, as revolts continued and major floods hit various parts of the country, with the Yellow River a particular source of disaster. Fresh epidemics of disease broke out. However, the dynasty's opportunities to re-invent itself were not yet exhausted; Bayan's gifted and youthful nephew Toghto emerged as just the determined and energetic administrator the times required.

To placate the Chinese, he ensured the completion of the Liao, Qin and Song histories. He also undertook a highly ambitious scheme to deal with problems in grain shipments. The Yellow River had repeatedly breached its dykes. So, in 1350 he printed paper currency with which he paid 170,000 troops and civilians to divert the waterway along a more southerly course across China from the sea to the foothills of Shanxi province in the northwest. But, while he was leading a military expedition in 1354 to subdue a rebel city near the Grand Canal, the emperor suddenly dismissed Toghto and had him killed.

Able as he was, even Toghto was unequal to the natural disasters, agricultural downturn and simmering discord that China faced. Once he was gone, Yuan cohesion disintegrated as fresh disasters hit, and armies of forced labourers were put to work rebuilding the Yellow River defences, in terrible conditions that fuelled revolt. In the south, taxation on farmers was increased heavily, and resented. Rebellions were

ABOVE *A Chinese talisman to ward off the plague, from* Eight Texts on Following the Way of Life *(woodblock edition, 1810). After the 1330s, smaller outbreaks of plague continued to occur in China for centuries.*

common in Chinese history, but this time there was the added incentive of attacking foreign rulers.

The Yuan dynasty has sometimes been seen as a parenthesis in Chinese history, with the irruption of northern barbarians into the Celestial Kingdom. This is not entirely fair. The re-establishment of the imperial examination system set a pattern that would persist until the empire finally fell nearly six centuries later. There was progress in the arts. But it was also a time of huge loss of life and recurrent suffering from disasters, disease and warfare under a dynasty rooted in its own, very specific, culture and values. The total population of China has been estimated at 110–120 million when the Mongols arrived, and at 85 million by the end of the dynasty.

Orgies and obsessions

Conditions were ripe for new revolts. In 1351–4 a rising occurred throughout the Huai River valley in eastern China, amid a prophecy that the Yuan would be overthrown by a one-eyed man. Another rising was joined by an upwardly mobile peasant monk, Zhu Yuanzhang, who preached Confucianism. It gained momentum and, in 1356, the rebels overran the city of Nanjing on the Lower Yangzi. The authority of the throne declined seriously as the emperor went into seclusion, indulging in Lamaistic orgies in his palaces and devoting himself to obsessions such as designing an enormous pleasure boat. Dynastic decline was evident.

In 1368 the last Yuan emperor fled the capital. By 1370 the Yuan were back in their heartland in Mongolia, little changed by their Chinese experience. Undone by internal weaknesses, corruption and inconsistency in using Chinese means to govern China, the dynasty was also the victim of a disastrous century. After almost 100 years of foreign rule, China reverted to a Chinese dynasty, one of the greatest: the Ming.

CHINESE INVENTIONS

China was not only the world's longest-lived empire, it also produced a vast array of inventions born both out of the inventive spirit of its people and their practical needs. The development of silk weaving has been traced back to 2000 BC, while the first historical dynasty, the Shang, was associated with the growth of bronze working in the second millennium BC.

Chinese inventions, a few of which were paralleled elsewhere, included paper made from plant pulp (initially used for clothing), and thus paper money, writing, woodblock printing and movable type. Steel and the blast furnace were also invented in China, as were the compass, the crossbow, the horse collar and stirrups, scissors, the abacus, chopsticks, gunpowder, fireworks and porcelain. Wheelbarrows were invented to facilitate the moving of loads; playing cards were made to pass the time; matches were developed to provide fire, and waxed umbrellas to keep off rain and the sun's rays. Europe received its first substantial imports of tea from China, and Chinese cuisine followed.

During the eras before the First Emperor, Chinese physicians pioneered surgery and nutritional care, and the pulse was taken in making a diagnosis. This was followed by the first book on pharmacology and the application of anaesthetic powder in surgery in the second century AD.

Though China was not known as a great maritime nation, its huge treasure ships of the Middle Ages outdid anything seen in Europe at the time. Less spectacularly, the Chinese invented the paddle boat. Some would claim that their invention and use of kites was a precursor to flight.

One of the great questions of history is why the Chinese fell behind the West in manufacturing in late imperial times. The answer seems to be that most inventions were not developed or linked to the broader economy as they were in Europe and North America. Inventors did not become entrepreneurs. Despite advances in mathematics and astronomy, practical science was not much valued in the Confucian system; for some, invention presented a threat to the harmony that man should seek.

The self-sufficient imperial system adopted the new techniques through the centuries, but there was no drive to pursue research, no national marketing or capitalist backing. Some discoveries were only belatedly turned to practical use, for example the compass, which was originally used for *feng shui* divination. As the emperor told a British emissary at the end of the 18th century, China had everything it needed. Given the array of innovations dating back thousands of years, his attitude was understandable. But, before the next century was out, the empire would learn that it could not live on its past.

The compass was a Chinese invention. Early versions like the one below, known as south-pointers, used a carved lodestone to indicate north and south.

THE EARLY MING

1368—1464

Famine, corruption and ethnic tension characterized the dying years of the Yuan dynasty. The impending fragmentation of the country seemed to point to a moral vacuum at the top, as the last of the Mongol rulers continued to over-tax and over-spend. Not just the Yuan, but China itself, was at risk of collapse, with new would-be rulers popping up everywhere under old names such as Xia and Han, and seeking to revive Chinese rule.

INTO THIS DISORDER STEPPED ZHU YUANZHANG, A PEASANT TURNED BUDDHIST MONK, WHO HAD spent three years wandering the roads and mountains of southern China, begging and observing. He had joined the Red Turbans millennial group, which wanted to bring back the lost Confucian moral and political order. Zhu had a much greater clarity of purpose than other pretenders to the throne. He declared that the dynasty he intended to found would be named Ming ('Radiance', or 'Brilliance'), perhaps a reference to the Manichaean king of light and the prophet who would herald the imminent arrival of the Buddha.

After winning control of the Red Turbans, Zhu went to war. His determination, adaptability, wise choice of subordinates and humane treatment of those he defeated all won him respect, just as his military ability won him victories. His army captured Nanjing in 1356 and worked its way north, crossing the Yellow River to take Dadu (today's Beijing) in 1368. Zhu renamed the city Beiping, meaning 'north pacified'

RIGHT *Statue of a warrior on the Sacred Way, leading to the area known as the Ming Tombs, 30 miles (50 km) northwest of Beijing, where 13 Ming emperors are buried, each one at the foot of a different hill.*

I ordered the drug seller Wang Yunjian to swallow one of his own poison pills. Wang held the pill in his hand and his face changed colour. He was upset and hesitated to swallow it. After I made him swallow it, I asked him: "What are these pills made of?" He answered, "Arsenic, Sichuan peas, kneaded into a pill, with cinnabar coating". I asked, "How long after swallowing the pill does a man die?" He said, "Half a day". After he said this, the tears poured down.

FIRST MING EMPEROR

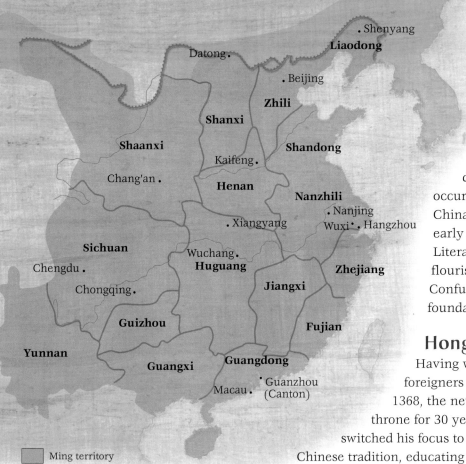

Shenyang
Liaodong
Datong.
.Beijing
Zhili
Shanxi
Shandong
Shaanxi
Kaifeng.
Chang'an.
Henan
Nanzhili
.Nanjing
.Xiangyang
Wuxi•.Hangzhou
Sichuan
Wuchang.
Chengdu.
Huguang
Zhejiang
Chongqing.
Jiangxi
Guizhou
Fujian
Yunnan
Guangdong
Guangxi
• Guanzhou
Macau.
(Canton)

Ming territory

Ming tributary
or buffer state

*ABOVE Map showing
the Ming empire in
c.1590, after its
expansionist years
under the later Ming.*

and gave himself the name of Hongwu ('Great Military Power').

Though serious upsets – including a crushing defeat by the Mongols, natural disasters and dynastic struggles – occurred at the end of the period, China generally prospered under the early Ming. The population grew. Literacy increased. Culture flourished, and a guiding, neo-Confucian ideology provided the foundation for a stable society.

Hongwu's statecraft

Having won power and replaced the foreigners from the northern steppes in 1368, the new ruler, who occupied the throne for 30 years with Nanjing as his capital, switched his focus to statecraft. In this, he looked to Chinese tradition, educating himself in the Confucian annals. He also studied Taoism and, in 1375, wrote his own commentary on the *Dao de Jing* text. He created his calendar and quickly named his successor to try to avoid a power struggle after his death. He set about codifying the 460 articles of the law, based on the Tang code (See Tang Dynasty: the Founders, pages 98–107.)

Turning to the care of the population, Hongwu employed middlemen to ensure successful grain distribution, lowered taxes and carried out an economic census. He built the Palace of Honouring the Ancestors in his capital and performed the public rites appropriate to his position – though he otherwise avoided rituals.

Pursuing Chinese tradition, the first Ming ruler re-introduced the civil service, which grew in importance, although the emperor later reduced the status of officials as they became too bookish for his taste. He tried to train the princes in Confucian ways, and eagerly centralized power, keen to head off the political fragmentation that had characterized late Yuan China. He restructured the military, giving officers farms and hereditary titles. Hongwu also created a National Academy and founded Confucian schools in all prefectures and counties, which grew to accommodate 10,000 students.

Power and paranoia

As he established the new dynasty, the ruler became increasingly power hungry – and paranoid. In 1380 he had his long-time adviser and companion in the conquest of power, Hu Weiyong, tried on charges of plotting rebellion and conspiring with the Koreans and Japanese. Fifteen thousand people were arraigned at the same time. Whether Hu was guilty of anything remains unclear, but he and all the others were executed.

Hongwu then concentrated authority even more tightly in his own hands. He abolished the top administrative body, the Grand Secretariat, and took direct charge of the six ministries of state. A General Direction of the Armies was set up to buttress his control of the military. Surveillance and terror tactics increased, with another round of executions in 1385. At the same time, Hongwu built up the imperial establishment around him: the 3 square miles (8 sq km) surrounding his palace housed 50 service offices and employed 10,000 artisans. His own Embroidered Guard grew from 16,000 to 75,000 men.

Increased corruption

This centralization of power was accompanied by a sharp rise in corruption and the emergence of the eunuchs as an alternative power base in the palace, a problem that persisted throughout the dynasty – the number of eunuchs would later reach 70,000. (See Life at Court, pages 176–7.) Hongwu's heavy-handed treatment of his advisers led many potential candidates among the literati to avoid public service for fear of their lives or because they felt that his rule was illegitimate. The judicial system was especially onerous. It became far easier to bring suspects to trial on flimsy charges, and Hongwu regularly rewrote the laws. In corruption cases the accused were all regarded as guilty at the opening of hearings.

However, the Ming founder's zeal and determination, aided by his rebuilding of the Grand Canal, did end the disunity of the empire. The economy was revived and taxation was rationalized across much of the country. The emperor created self-run agricultural communities to replace the large estates and slavery that had existed

> ❛ The empire is of vast extent; because it almost certainly cannot be governed by my solitary self, it is essential that all the worthy men of the realm now join in bringing order to it … The realm is now at last stabilized and we are eager to discuss and clarify with all learned men the Great Way of governing, to enrich our mind and thereby attain more perfect rule. ❜
>
> PROCLAMATION BY THE FIRST MING EMPEROR, 1368

BELOW *Hongwu's tax reforms improved life for the nation's farmers, and he embarked on ambitious irrigation and drainage projects that increased agricultural productivity. This growth in output supported a steady rise in population – during the Ming years China's population exceeded 100 million, regaining the level of Song times.*

under the Yuan. Farming began to take off, and several million hectares of land were reclaimed for cultivation in the 1370s. Hongwu's most visible flaw, it seems, was his failure to control his own brutality. As a result, he is remembered as a gifted tyrant, whose Confucian mission had its limits – on his death at the age of 70 in 1398, 30 concubines were burned to death with him in Mongol fashion.

Jianwen and Yongle

Hongwu's scholarly successor was determined to civilize Ming rule, and named himself Jianwen (Establishing the Civil) when he took the throne in 1399. The legal system became less punitive, as did land tax. Jianwen was devoted to Confucian social ethics, and chose three distinguished learned men as his most senior advisers; they were even granted executive power.

These three men re-invented the administration in benevolent fashion, focusing on Confucian education. The bureaucracy was pared down, and the extensive land-holdings of Buddhist and Taoist priests reduced; the surplus was distributed among the poor. The prestigious Hanlin Academy (founded under the Tang dynasty) was enlarged, and its top graduates were called on to educate the heir-apparent and the princes.

ABOVE Yongle, the third Ming emperor, was a brilliant general who raised the dynasty to a military peak. However, his decision to move the capital back to Beijing led to his physical removal from China's heart and his increasing isolation within the newly built Forbidden City.

But, as with previous rulers, the princes proved to be Jianwen's Achilles' heel. The emperor waged a campaign to 'reduce the feudatories' (that is, bring the princes to order). But, in 1399, the prince of Yan in Beiping (now Beijing) raised an army to wage civil war. In 1402 he took the capital of Nanjing and named himself emperor as Yongle ('Eternal Happiness'), ending Jianwen's three-year reign.

The new ruler claimed his predecessor had burned to death in the attack on the imperial palace, but many thought Jianwen was still alive. The more Yongle sought to suppress all memories and records of Jianwen, the more legends appeared proclaiming his survival and praising his rule. Yongle was also open to attack because his mother was said to have been a Korean or Mongolian consort of the first Ming emperor and not, as he claimed, the first lady. To this day, his name denotes illegitimacy in Chinese minds.

A military ruler from the start, Yongle was a man of great energy and varied talents as he sought to restore the dynasty to the heights reached under his father. The army grew to a quarter of a million men. A new military nobility with hereditary titles was created. Reinforced border defences were erected along the Great Wall. Yongle, who had spent years as a prince repelling Mongolian incursions, made the northern tribes the focus of his military strategy, launching five campaigns in the 1410s and 1420s against the armies of Arughtai, the Yuan leader, and restructuring the Great Wall. This, together with a doomed attempt to conquer Annam (Vietnam), put a major strain on the imperial purse and also upset the scholar élite.

A move north

The empire's northern focus led to a decision to move the capital from Nanjing to Beiping, which was renamed Beijing (Northern Capital). The new palace compound had more than 8000 rooms and, in 1404, Yongle moved 10,000 households from nine Shanxi prefectures into the city. By 1420 the transfer of the imperial court was complete. But many officials objected, remaining attached to the surviving Song culture of the Yangzi basin. A 'dual capitals' period therefore ensued, but this ended in 1441 when Beijing became first city of East Asia. (See Beijing and the Forbidden City, page 174.)

The move north meant transferring the seat of the empire to a region less dominated by the Han people than the Yangzi area round Nanjing. Yongle's 21-year reign saw China engaging with foreign peoples to an ever greater extent. Diplomatic relations were established with Korea, Japan and Central Asian rulers, though Timur the Lame (Tamerlane), the great conqueror from present-day Uzbekistan, prepared an invasion of China, dying just before he launched it. Yongle recognized the Mongols of Inner Mongolia and split them from the Yuan further north.

The emperor's ambition to assert Ming power abroad led to the seven great voyages under the eunuch Zheng He (1371–1433). A Muslim who had visited Mecca in his youth, Zheng was sent as admiral of the imperial fleet first to Southeast Asia and India. Later missions took him to the Gulf, Arabia and the east coast of Africa. It has been claimed that he also reached America, though scholars deny this. His fleet overawed local rulers, and he returned from his voyages with treasure and acknowledgements of China's superiority. But after Yongle's death, the Ming court turned against these costly maritime expeditions.

ABOVE Illustration from a printed fictional account of the sea voyages of Zheng He, originally published in China in c.1600.

At home, Yongle made important reforms to the grain payment system, introducing currency and silver as means of payment – in 1402 the highest officials still received 60 per cent of their salaries in grain. The grain supply to the north, mainly to feed the new capital, was increased with a new approach that taxed the south in grain and made it pay the transport costs to Beijing. Three hundred thousand labourers were put to work to rebuild the Grand Canal to carry the supplies to the north. Grain tax became a heavy burden on the country, as the state collected around 20 million kilograms (44 million pounds) each year.

The warrior-scholar

Despite his warrior background, the emperor was a scholar, even if his interest in administration was limited. He wrote philosophical essays, practised calligraphy and read history. The *Yongle Dadian*, a 22,938-chapter literary encyclopedia compiled by 2000 scholars over five years and bound in more than 10,000 volumes, was an imperial commission, as was the compilation of the canonical *Five Classics and Four Books*. His concern about his legitimacy may in part explain Yongle's Confucian zeal.

At court he created an inner cabinet, which spawned a more collegiate form of government than the Ming founder had ever allowed. The ruler was good at delegating authority. He laid down separate laws for dynasty and state and revived the Grand Secretariat, which came to dominate his administration. The civil service examinations became the sole means of rising to high officialdom. Stability characterized government ministries. But the eunuchs increased their influence at court, operating spy networks that investigated suspected crimes and carried out sentences themselves. Although Yongle's imperial bodyguard enjoyed similar powers for a time, their excesses led the emperor to depend more exclusively on the eunuchs.

Appropriately for a warrior king, Yongle died while on a military campaign in the north, in 1424. As planned, he had re-made the Ming dynasty and spread China's reputation as never before, yet this achievement left his successors with a complex set of diplomatic relations to manage, a bureaucracy and military that were always in competition and an ill-sited capital city which relied on supplies of southern grain.

Hongxi and Xuande

Yongle's 47-year-old son ascended the throne as Hongxi in 1425. He was a well-read Confucian scholar who had gathered experience running things in Beijing while his father was away on military campaigns. He put general well-being above imperial ambitions, showing an ingrained belief in public service. He took pains to ensure that disaster-hit regions received relief, vagrants were housed and the judiciary was kept in check. He annulled Zheng He's scheduled eighth voyage as part of a fiscal tightening policy, raised the Grand Secretariat from an advisory role to a policy-making body and decided to restore the capital at Nanjing. But he was in bad health and died within the year – ten concubines were buried alive with his body to accompany him into the afterlife.

Xuande, his successor, was an impressive warrior who, at the age of 15, had accompanied Yongle on his second Mongol campaign. Yet Xuande's military achievements were limited to a few battles against the Mongol ruler Arughtai and a well-judged withdrawal from Annam. His attempt to introduce military reforms failed. His reign was most memorable for its cultural and political achievements. Porcelain reached its zenith. Xuande himself wrote passable poetry, composed Imperial Injunctions and Admonitions to Bureaucrats and pursued his passion for calligraphy and animal portraiture as well as for Korean war horses, food and women.

EARLY MING EMPERORS

Hongwu	1368–98
Jianwen	1399–1402
Yongle	1402–24
Hongxi	1425
Xuande	1426–35
Zhengtong /Tianshun	1436–49, 1457–64
Jingtai	1450–7

CHINESE PORCELAIN

Porcelain was first produced in China under the Sui, but its real development was during the eras of the Tang and the Song. It became one of the country's major products, exported around the world, and the Ming were responsible for its arrival in Europe. In the 18th and 19th centuries it would be highly prized in the West. British factories would turn out imitation willow pattern plates and dishes.

Although the very first porcelains came from the north of the country, the art of producing fine ceramics was subsequently developed most fully in southern China, using kaolinitic clay and porcelain stone. Highly fired with increasingly purified clay, the pieces produced could be extremely thin and correspondingly delicate. The aim was to equal the refinement of jade.

The growing popularity of tea drinking produced a fresh market for porcelain vessels. During the Tang , one criterion for judging the excellence of ceramics was the compatibility of their colours with tea. An eighth-century expert prized celadon ware because it complemented the colour of green tea.

An early 15th-century Chinese porcelain jar. The characteristic blue and white decoration associated with the Ming era was achieved by using cobalt imported from Persia.

Under-glaze cobalt painting, developed during the Tang era, is the most common form of decoration.

As well as for use at table, fine porcelain was employed in rituals and for decorative tiles, such as those at the famous Ming period temple at Nanjing.

Exports of porcelain began during the Tang dynasty, bound for Africa, but the trade really took off under the Yuan (1279–1368) and reached Europe through Portugal under the Ming (1368–1644). The method and designs were copied by local manufacturers, and the product became so popular that it was known in English simply by the name of its country of origin: 'china'.

In Beijing, which remained the capital, the Grand Secretariat took on a new role as buffer (or block) between the emperor and the six ministries, and its executive power grew. The ruler turned the over-staffed censorate into a dynamic government institution, and created 'touring' provincial governorships, which lasted for some centuries. Xuande's most enlightened reform was the reduction of taxes, notably land tax for farmers. At the same time, the grain supply to Beijing was improved. His most

BEIJING AND THE FORBIDDEN CITY It was under Yongle
that Beijing became the definitive capital of China. The construction of the Forbidden City
in time for the move in 1421 gave the rulers a fitting centre from which to assert their
special place in the world. Dominating Beijing, the Forbidden City's great walls, chambers,
courtyards, pavilions, red roofs, gleaming pillars and intricate passageways were the
expression of imperial majesty, with more than 9000 rooms covering 10 hectares (250 acres).

Two dozen emperors would preside over China from the Forbidden City, their edicts lowered from the Tiananmen Gate to be taken by messengers across their realm. Outside the vast imperial compound lay a city which was the centre of the empire for its last 500 years. To protect it, tall, thick walls were constructed, described by the French traveller Pierre Loti in the 19th century as being *the colour of mourning … extending without end, in a solitude that was both naked and grey'*.

Beijing was a great trading centre as well as the focus of administration and imperial rituals. Other buildings designed to inspire awe, such as the Temple of Heaven, were constructed for imperial rites. Parks were laid out around lakes. Outside the city, the Summer Palace was built, only to be ravaged by the British and French in 1860, rebuilt and attacked again by the foreigners in 1900.

Even when the empire fell in 1912, the last ruler, the infant Puyi, was allowed to stay on in the Forbidden City until a warlord evicted him in 1924. It then fell into disrepair but, after their victory in 1949, the Communist leadership established itself in an adjoining section of Beijing, Mao Zedong (Mao Tse-tung) installing himself in a hall once used by a Qing emperor and addressing crowds from the top of the Tiananmen Gate. Today, the Forbidden City is one of China's greatest tourist attractions.

The Forbidden City was a symbol of the grandeur of the Ming emperors but it also represented their increasing remoteness from the people they governed.

lasting mistake was to elevate the eunuchs and entrust them with his papers, giving them unprecedented authority over government ministries. He also used them for more personal purposes such as collecting treasures for him and picking Korean virgins to be brought to the harem in Beijing. Xuande's death at the age of 36 in 1435 (followed by the burning of ten concubines) ended a golden age. His successor, Zhengtong, was only nine, and real power lay with the dowager empress and a leading eunuch, Wang Zhen.

Wang Zhen was an authoritarian figure who murdered adversaries and ordered expensive military campaigns into Burma and India. Meanwhile, China was hit by droughts that caused famines, even in usually fertile areas of the Yangzi Valley. The Yellow River burst its banks, forcing many villagers to flee their homes. There were two uprisings in Jiangxi and the southeast.

A foolhardy attack

In the north, the defensive system had been allowed to run down but, at Wang Zhen's urging, Zhengtong launched an offensive in 1449 against the Mongols, who had united under the chief, Esen Khan, undermining the usual 'divide-and-rule' Ming strategy towards the northern tribes. An army of half-a-million men was sent to repel a Mongol advance and chased the enemy forces as they retreated towards the steppes. It was a feint which lured the Ming forces into a fatal ambush. Cavalry attacked the Chinese survivors as they fell back on a fortress. The fortress proved to be another trap. Surrounded, the imperial army was liquidated, and the ruler captured.

Zhengtong's half-brother, Jingtai, took the throne in 1450, re-fortifying the northern defences against the Mongols who held his predecessor. The new emperor wanted to retain the throne, and offered only a low ransom for Zhengtong. But the imperial captive developed a good relationship with Esen, who freed him after two years. When he got back to Beijing, however, he was locked up by Jingtai for six years.

But Jingtai's position was fragile, and he was killed by a coup in 1457. Zhengtong returned to the throne and wreaked revenge on those who had imprisoned him, exiling and beheading officials from Jingtai's reign. His paranoia was such that he also executed some of the leaders of the coup that had brought him back to the throne. Eunuch power increased further. Mongol influences were eradicated – one beneficiary of this was the imperial harem, which saw the end of the killing of concubines to accompany the ruler into the afterlife, a feature of Mongol rule perpetuated by the early Ming rulers.

1368 The first Ming emperor, Hongwu, ascends the throne in Nanjing

1369 Ming forces destroy the Mongol summer capital

1370 Timur the Lane (Tamerlane) begins his rise to dominate Central Asia

1381 Yunnan is integrated into the Chinese empire

1393 Hongwu orders 15,000 officials to be executed for insubordination

1404–5 Tamerlaine marches across the Pamir Mountains to attack China but dies en route

1405 Japan agrees to become a tribute state (but only until 1411)

1420 The Ming capital moves to Beijing

1422 As part of a major expansion of Chinese naval power, the Muslim eunuch Zheng leads naval voyages as far as Africa

1449 A 500,000-strong Chinese offensive against the Mongols ends in disaster

1450 Major rebuilding of the Great Wall begins

LIFE AT COURT
The imperial court was made up of a rich mix of people ranged in careful pecking order below the Son of Heaven: members of the dynastic family, the empress's clan, concubines and eunuchs, followed by officials of differing ranks.

The ruler resided in the Hall of Mental Cultivation within the Forbidden City at the heart of a court which followed a deeply prescribed system of rituals. Everything had its place and its meaning. The traditions had been laid down centuries before the Ming, but they were fully expressed under this dynasty in the city that epitomized imperial China.

Dating from 1406, the Ming-era imperial complex in Beijing covered 2 square miles (5 sq. km) and was enclosed within walls 7 metres (22 ft) high and 9 metres (30 ft) thick. The organization of the city was said to reflect that of the human body. The Tiananmen Gate, to which imperial edicts were carried by richly robed officials and lowered before being borne off across the country by messengers, was the summit from which the ruler bestowed his wisdom on mere mortals. Clothed in imperial yellow, emblazoned with the all-powerful dragon symbol, the ruler went through an endlessly repeated round of ceremonies, prayers to the gods and audiences in the Palace of Heavenly Purity. For the most part, he ate alone, and his meals were tasted by a servant to ensure that they were not poisoned.

For weak or lazy rulers, the elaborate rituals and luxurious isolation could be stultifying and an excuse for inaction. Great rulers knew, on the contrary, how to use their remoteness to bolster their authority. So long as they exercised authority, there was little check on their activity.

Concubines
Concubines rose to become major power players, particularly under weak emperors. At night, one chosen woman was taken to the imperial chamber wrapped in a red covering from which she emerged and crawled up at the foot of the emperor's bed. From that first experience, she could hope to become a power beside the throne. In some cases, the infatuation of rulers for their favourite concubines led them to neglect affairs of state, and allow their partners to advance the interests of their family in ways that disrupted the court.

The only female emperor, Wu Zetian, entered the court as a concubine. (See The Era of Wu Zetian, pages 108–13.) So did her 19th-century emulator, Cixi. (See Cixi, Portrait of a Powerful Concubine, pages 232–3.) Ambitious officials backed concubines who were favoured by the rulers. Parents schemed to get their daughters introduced at court, hoping that they might catch the eye of the ruler. But their existence could be precarious. When their emperor-lover died or was displaced, his concubines were expected to leave court and live a life of seclusion. In the Yuan and early Ming periods, some were even buried alive or burned, to accompany the sovereign into the afterlife

Eunuchs
Eunuchs were thought to pose no threat because their mutilation meant that they could not found family lines of their own which might upset the power structure. But, at crucial periods, as under the late Tang or the Ming, or during dynastic disputes, they came to exercise great power. Often clever and driven by a sense of self-advancement, they numbered thousands and filled senior government and military posts at different periods. But they were always vulnerable and tended to be personally despised. Originally, many came from among prisoners of war. But by the era of the Ming, most were castrated as boys on the instructions of their parents, in the hope that they would rise to positions of importance in the palace.

The first Ming emperor set up a special office for eunuchs in the dynasty's first capital of Nanjing. They took over some household tasks from women, did bureaucratic paperwork and arranged ceremonials. In the power struggle that brought Emperor Yongle to the throne in 1402, the eunuchs backed the winning side and were rewarded with imperial favours. Yongle used them as his private informers at court, sent them on diplomatic missions and appointed one, Zheng He, to head the navy. In 1420, the palace eunuchs were allowed to set up their own jail, the Eastern Depot, where they sentenced their chosen culprits, tortured inmates and carried out executions.

Yongle was able to keep control of the eunuchs, but later rulers were not so forceful. After a defeat in a campaign against the Mongols, the chief eunuch leading the army –

Wang Zhen – disobeyed an imperial order to seek peace and continued the march towards home, precipitating a major disaster that destroyed the Chinese forces and led to the capture of the emperor in 1449.

Some eunuchs became extremely rich; it was said that in the early 16th century one amassed a personal fortune greater than the government's annual budget. At the peak of their power under the Ming, senior eunuchs attended the ruler at all times, arranged court meetings, ran a school for eunuchs, supervised the library and the art collection, were responsible for the upkeep of the imperial tombs and looked after security.

A list of eunuch functions under the Ming showed just how wide-ranging their duties were. They included supervision of

This 16th-century painting depicts a Ming official and his wife. Under the Ming, the role of the high-ranking official in administering the state was restored

workshops, palace maintenance, the imperial seals and regalia, horses, temples and shrines. They were also responsible for the provision of firewood, paper, bells and drums, and for making arms and jewels, for weaving, dyeing, sewing and gardening. They ran an intelligence and spying service and supervised the beating of officials held to have transgressed. They came to be loathed by officials and imperial nobles but repeatedly showed their ability to fight back and maintain their presence at court, too useful to be disposed of by the rulers and unable through their mutilation to found a dynasty or even establish a lineage.

THE LATER MING

1465—1644

In the late 15th century and throughout the 16th, Ming China prospered. Opulent dinner parties, the growing popularity of reading and calligraphy, the diffusion of literacy and the new heights reached in the finer arts (such as painting and the making of porcelain and furniture) all pointed to a civilization once again realizing its potential after years of foreign rule. Despite its faults – such as the absence of a structure to limit the power of the eunuchs – the political system inherited by the emperors of the mid- and late Ming ensured that expert advice was always at hand.

YET THE APPARENT STABILITY OF THESE YEARS SITS ODDLY WITH THE WAY THE COUNTRY WAS ruled. From 1425 to 1521 no Ming emperor reached the age of 40. Many ran courts riven by factionalism and corruption. State revenue and expenditure moved further and further apart. The extreme obsessions and addictions of individual rulers often compromised governance and cost China dear.

After a turbulent childhood, during which his title of Crown Prince was removed at one point, the 17-year-old Zhu Qianshen ascended the throne as Emperor Chenghua in 1465. His own father had questioned whether he was sufficiently intelligent or well suited to become emperor, and throughout his reign Chenghua was taken advantage of by Lady Wan, his favourite palace consort. Chenghua was benign and easily manipulated, although he took high rents from the lands he confiscated and brooked no dissent from advisers. Many eunuchs built shrines and temples, and plundered the richer prefectures of central and southern China. Lady Wan's courtiers sent the emperor pornography, yet his sexual desire hardly needed awakening.

Lady Wan's political influence ensured two major and disastrous policies. Agricultural land was confiscated for imperial estates, turning the farmers into paying tenants. Meanwhile, appointments were made by imperial edicts rather than by the Ministry of Personnel. Moreover, Lady Wan's favoured eunuch, Wang Zhi, became extremely powerful as the head of a new police force, the Western Depot. The Hami region in eastern Turkestan (now Xinjiang) was lost in 1473, and a union among eastern Mongols in the 1470s spawned several wars in the Ordos region.

RIGHT *A Ming-dynasty embroidered silk badge belonging to a court official. The design represents a Chinese unicorn, or dragon (Chi-lin), thought to bring the wearer happiness and good fortune.*

The emperor and Lady Wan died in the same year – 1487 – but the corruption that characterized the Chenghua reign would continue to gnaw away at the foundations of Ming China long after their deaths.

The growing power of the eunuchs

Under the next two rulers, Hongzhi and Zhengde, who ruled from 1488 to 1521, the Grand Secretariat grew in stature but had to compete for power with the eunuchs, now numbering thousands. Both emperors struggled with military challenges throughout their reigns and introduced a reward system to motivate their soldiers, based on the number of enemy heads they collected.

There were plenty of domestic uprisings to overcome in both the north and the south, including one by a matriarchal tribe led by the female warrior Muli. Although these revolts took some years to overcome, the border wars were a worse threat, since the Ming had little intelligence on the Mongols and the measures needed to guard against their attacks were expensive. The Great Wall was extended, in particular far to the west, and the defence system strengthened.

On his accession, the well-intentioned Hongzhi signalled his desire for reform by punishing an official who had sent the former emperor a sex manual. Devoted to Lady Chang, his empress, he seems to have remained faithful to her and to have been a convinced Confucian. He united the contending police forces of the Eastern and Western Depots, culled many court luxuries and uprooted numerous eunuch-run procurement agencies. Despite his determination to achieve the imperial ideal, he could not help but grant costly favours to his wife and to members of her family. Though he appeared to welcome good, critical advice from scholars, he never acted on it. Moreover, his Taoist and Buddhist sympathies resulted in inappropriate appointments at court.

Natural disasters proliferated. The Yellow River burst its banks several times, causing 120,000 labourers to be put to work to divert it south of the Shandong peninsula, a course it held into the 19th century. Although corruption was curtailed initially, the latter stages of the reign saw the return of direct appointments, diversion of salt monopoly funds and bribery of court officials.

Smoke leaves ... When I was young I heard my elders say that in Fujian there were some people who smoked them by inhaling, and that doing this made people drunk. They were called "dry wine". At the end of the Chongzhen reign (1628–44) a man surnamed Peng in the county capital got some seeds from I know not where, and grew them here. He picked the leaves and dried them in the dark. Then those who worked at this business cut them into fine shreds, and they were sold to merchants from places far away.

RECOLLECTION OF MID-17TH CENTURY CHINESE

Troubled times

When the next ruler, Zhengde, came to the throne in 1506 at the age of 14, the country was in a fragile condition. State finances were unbalanced. The northern garrisons were in peril. The eunuchs and officials feuded over policies. Disliking the three senior members of the Grand Secretariat, the ruler looked instead to the eunuchs. Liu Qin, the official appointed to deal with the fiscal shortfall, was a master of self-protection, who was also charged with organizing palace music, dancing, wrestling matches and procuring exotic animals. He insisted on raising taxes through the mines and the salt monopoly, but he also sold military commissions, as well as imposing extra taxes on those he disliked. His tax for the northeast led to a rebellion in 1510; its leader, the prince of Anhua, was captured and suffered death by slicing.

The emperor's most eccentric expenditure derived from his passion for war. Zhengde became close friends with a cavalry officer called Chiang Pin, and moved 3000 border troops to Beijing, installing them just outside the wall of his palace. Inside, he held mock hunts – in one he was so badly mauled by a tiger that he had to spend a month in bed. He began to live in nomadic yurt tents, not only when out on the road but also in the palace. During his much-loved lantern festival, a yurt caught fire, destroying the principal palace buildings. The emperor refused to provide money for rebuilding from his own coffers.

Officials told Zhengde he needed to change his ways, especially as he had all but dispensed with imperial protocol and ritual. Wearied by their criticism, he moved to border areas in 1517, travelling extensively before returning to Beijing. Later that

ABOVE Notwithstanding measures introduced by various reformers to restrict excesses at court, Ming emperors continued to enjoy extravagant pursuits such as the collecting of exotic animals. This painting records the gift of a lion made to the Ming court by an African Swahili merchant.

year, after repelling a Mongol army, he missed the obligatory sacrifice to heaven. He created an imaginary general, giving him the rank of duke and a large annual stipend of grain for going to the borders to inspect the garrisons. This figure was, in fact, the ruler himself, who used the alter ego fiction to allow himself to ignore constant urgings by his advisers not to head to the perilous frontiers.

In 1519 Zhengde finally went south, visiting Nanjing where he drank heavily for eight months. He was said to have ordered the execution of the local prince of Ning, whom he suspected of disloyalty and, having no regard for the economic impact, demanded the slaughter of all pigs in the region because the word for them sounded like the name of the prince. A fishing accident, probably suffered while he was drunk, caused the emperor's death in 1521.

Jiajing's challenges

Zhengde's adopted son, Jiajing, who became emperor in 1522, was hard-working and could recite poetry from an early age. During his four-year reign, China had to cope with Mongols to the north, pirates to the southeast, declining revenues, natural disasters and a bureaucracy that frequently opposed and failed to respect the ruler. But his hardest battle was with his officials over the ancestral rites. He was determined to see his natural father, a son of Emperor Chenghua, fully honoured in the Ancestral Temple, although he had never been emperor – Jiajing wanted legitimacy.

ABOVE *Mongol raids continued to threaten the empire under the Ming. This illustration shows Mongol warriors and horsemen going into battle, complete with a war elephant.*

This and other forms of family memorials met intense opposition from scholars at court, with the neo-Confucian movement now in the ascendant. But the emperor eventually achieved his aim. In the process, he also raised his own profile, refusing to bow to Confucius. He also increased the number of imperial sacrifices to four, for heaven, earth, the sun and the moon – each was given its own temple.

Rebellions began to stir in the north. In 1524 a revolt by the Datong garrison left the governor dead. In 1533 another revolt followed, but the emperor's relative leniency in killing only the ringleaders succeeded in bringing calm for some years. However, in 1542, Mongols under Altan Khan (1507–82) began making regular raids. Insularity precluded the trade agreement sought by the Mongols and encouraged them to continue the attacks. From 1550 to 1568, they raided northern China every year, despite Beijing's upgrading of the capital's garrisons.

In 1542 a group of palace ladies tried to strangle the sleeping emperor with a silk cord as he lay on the bed of his favourite concubine. He became unconscious and spat coagulated blood, but survived. Henceforth he became obsessive in his quest for immortality. He already looked to Taoists for legitimation and fertility prayers (and relied on divination for affairs of state) but he was also advised to fortify his inner and outer *yang*. For the latter, he sent local officials out to find magical plants mentioned in the ancient texts – 1860 specimens were brought to court. For inner

FESTIVALS AND CEREMONIES

For the people of China, the solar–lunar calendar marked out 24 fortnightly periods of the year, each with its distinct name, from 'Spring Begins' in early February to 'Severe Cold' at the end of January.

The three great festivals were those of the lunar New Year, the Duanwu celebration on the fifth day of the fifth lunar month, and the mid-autumn thanks for the harvest on the full moon of the 15th day of the eighth lunar month.

Under the Ming, as under other dynasties, these festivals were the high points of the year for the villagers who made up 90 per cent of the population, living in communities of between ten

Detail from Landscape of the Four Seasons *(c.1619) by the Ming-dynasty painter Shen Shichong. Two of China's major festivals honour the seasons of spring and autumn.*

and 50 households. Special food would be served, and the festivals brought a moment of colour and enjoyment to generally grinding lives, as did ceremonies held by religious groups and sects. In addition, rituals of veneration for the ancestors were held in homes and at family graves.

yang, however, he had been advised to sleep with as many virgins as possible, so as to fortify the 'inner elixir' of immortality – 800 girls aged eight to 14 were selected for him. Meanwhile, he had become addicted to aphrodisiacs, which gradually poisoned him to death.

Floods, refugees and pirates

While the emperor fretted, China suffered repeated flooding of the Huai River. The financial surplus built up in the 1520s had been squandered or lost, and the construction projects of the 1530s had taken their toll on the budget. In 1532 revenues were just half of the value of expenditure, and little could be done for those hit by the floods. Rice doubled in price. A refugee exodus from the region hit Beijing, where the dead were soon to be seen rotting in the street.

BELOW Piracy has long been a feature of the coasts of Asia. From 1520 there was a particular upsurge in bandit activity along the southern coast of China. This illustration is of a fully manned Chinese pirate boat of the type found at Canton in the mid-19th century.

In Zhejiang and Guangdong piracy was on the rise. Again, the neo-Confucian temper of the times was an impediment to doing business with outside powers, so illegal trade prospered in southern regions. Trading rights extended to the Japanese were withdrawn. The court tried repeatedly to crack down on piracy, sometimes working with pro-Ming traders to control the region. But the years 1553 and 1554 saw a stream of imperial defeats in the south, and the loss of some 20 administrative towns and garrisons to illegal trade groups – by 1554 the garrisons of the raiders held 24,000 men.

In 1556 the tide turned as the Ming defeated forces led by the pirate Xu Hai, who had attacked Zhejiang. Wang Zhi, the other leading regional threat, was caught and executed in 1559. Eight years later the southeast was finally opened to trade, which triumphed over neo-Confucian hostility. Ships from Spain and the Americas began to purchase Chinese goods in earnest, bringing new risks.

The insomniac emperor Jiajing died in 1567. He worked incessantly in his later years but failed to reverse the trend of declining revenues, as land disappeared from the register and private individuals began to build up their wealth with what had once been imperial resources. Having been impossible to ban, commerce now proved impossible to tax.

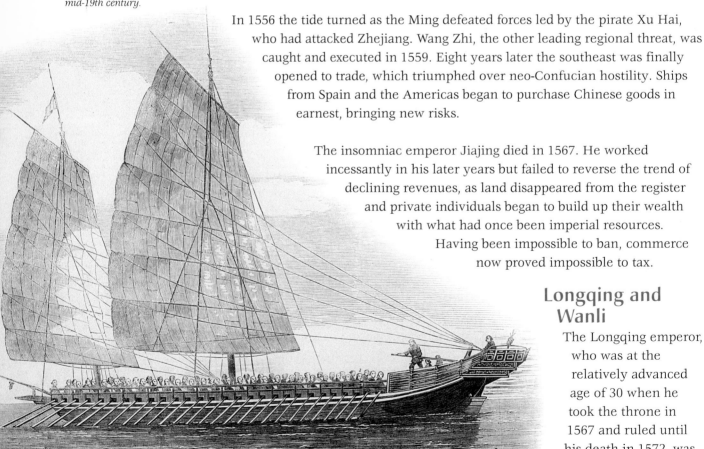

Longqing and Wanli

The Longqing emperor, who was at the relatively advanced age of 30 when he took the throne in 1567 and ruled until his death in 1572, was frugal, generous and

REBELS AGAINST THE MING
The recurrent revolts that faced the Ming emperors showed the difficulty of ruling a country as large and varied as China. Most of the risings were localized, often instigated by bandits who might be former soldiers, sometimes in cahoots with corrupt local officials.

An unusual and spectacular episode of banditry that showed the weakness of the imperial ability to maintain order came in 1555 when a group of Chinese and Japanese pirates landed near Hangzhou. They probably numbered only about 60 men, but they rampaged through Zhejiang, Anhui and the Lower Yangzi to reach the suburbs of Nanjing. Too few to enter the city, they forged on to the city of Wuxi before being surrounded by imperial forces and wiped out. Their raid had lasted for three months, during which time they looted at will and killed an estimated 5000 civilians.

Historians have interpreted this brutal uprising in one of two ways – either as evidence of the weakness of the Ming forces or as a sign that the region attacked was so peaceful that no defences were considered necessary.

liberal. China's foreign trade was allowed to increase and the southeastern garrisons were fortified, but the emperor himself was unskilled in statecraft. His passive rule sparked an unhealthy factionalism in the Grand Secretariat.

His nine-year-old son Zhu Yijun, who succeeded him as Emperor Wanli, ruled from 1573 to 1620. For the first decade of his reign, China prospered under the effective rule of the statesman Zhang Juzheng, who filled the granaries with a nine-year supply of grain and enriched the imperial coffers. Zhang adroitly used his influence (through letters to his main lieutenants, in particular) to extend his political reach beyond his formal powers. His 'single whip' fiscal rationalization was a key improvement after the tax disorder of previous years. Zhang pared down local government bureaucracy, hounded corrupt officials and sued for peace with Altan Khan to the north. He also pushed budgets down and attacked vested interests.

The bureaucracy began to operate more smoothly. Material prosperity grew. But Zhang's example died with him in 1582. Criticized for missing the 27-month mourning period following his father's death, he was posthumously denounced and his family's lands confiscated. He was the Ming's last great statesman.

Zhang's death allowed Wanli to exert his own influence on the court and country. Many Zhang policies were reversed, and Wanli's involvement in bureaucratic affairs robbed him of respect. In his early years, Wanli had been disciplined for drinking and for excessive practice of calligraphy, among other pursuits. As a ruler he was intelligent, unusually lenient – or indecisive – in choosing punishments and greedy in hoarding

LATER MING EMPERORS

Chenghua	1465–87
Hongzhi	1488–1505
Zhengde	1506–21
Jiajing	1522–67
Longqing	1567–72
Wanli	1573–1620
Taichang	1620
Tianqi	1621–7
Chongzhen	1628–44

goods. Living an increasingly cloistered existence, he sought to paralyze the bureaucracy, or simply to ignore its advice.

Opposition from neo-Confucians

This, and the ruler's growing disdain for statecraft, slowed down the machinery of government. The neo-Confucians were unimpressed, and many flocked to the Donglin Academy, which was founded in 1111 but had fallen into disuse before being revived as a centre for teaching Confucian principles. The scholar-officials trained there had a strong public service ethos, believing that their life's work was to nurture their morality. They played an important role in court factional politics, seeking to reduce the power invested in the Grand Secretariat and to structure government more loosely.

The balance between emperor and officialdom that had held under the Ming relied on a degree of shared determination to govern, but there was now major disagreement between the emperor and the Donglin Academy scholars. In 1605 Wanli used a personnel evaluation to sack or sideline 280 officials in Beijing and Nanjing. In reaction, senior civil servants began to quit their posts without authorization, and the emperor increasingly left senior offices vacant. Moreover, his appointment of eunuchs to the powerful tax and mining commissions (which led to much exploitation), combined with his ambition for the succession (which defied the primogeniture approach favoured by most officials), further cut him off from his bureaucracy. He lost interest in policy and hoarded revenues. The state approached paralysis.

Foreign contacts

Events in Southeast Asia would have an enduring impact for China. In 1567 the emperor had lifted the ban on foreign trade and even allowed the people of Fujian province to go to sea – the result was a new wave of Chinese communities throughout Southeast Asia. A Spanish colony set up in Manila in 1570 acted as a magnet for migrants from China. But, when the newcomers were searched for weapons, they prepared to defend themselves. In 1603 a massacre resulted, in which 15,000–20,000 Chinese were killed. There were also more peaceful contacts with the Europeans, including Jesuit missionaries from Europe who hoped for millions of converts. (See Jesuit Missionaries in China, pages 192–3.)

Internal and external threats

By now the Ming faced threats from almost all directions, while the court was split by feuds between the ruler and senior

1465 Emperor Chenghua ascends the throne

1517–21 Portuguese ships enter Chinese waters for the first time, while Pacific trade grows after Magellan lands in the Philippines. China imports new crops, including sweet potatoes, peanuts and tobacco

1524 Datong garrison revolt, followed by recurrent rebellions over the following decades

1542 Imperial concubines try to strangle Jaijing in his bedchamber. Mongols start raids into China

1557 Portuguese colony is established at Macau, which becomes a base for Jesuit missionaries

1560 Japanese pirates land in Fujian and loot cities

1567 Ban on foreign trade lifted

1600 Population passes 150 million

1605 Emperor Wanli starts a feud with Confucian officials

1616 Manchu leader Nurhaci declares a new dynasty, the Jin, later renamed the Qing

1620s Fresh rebellions and disasters, including Yellow River bursting its banks

1642 Manchus expand in the northeast

1644 Manchus march into China as Ming rule implodes in the face of revolts. Manchu strongman, Dorgon, puts his six-year-old nephew on the throne as the first emperor of the Qing dynasty

officials and blighted by faction fighting over the
imperial succession.

To the southwest, Yang Yinglung, whose family had held
on to much of the area since the Tang dynasty, rebelled
and caused trouble for a decade, before a battle lasting
104 days ended with his suicide. Japan's two invasions of
Korea posed another threat. Initially the Chinese armies
crossed the Yalu River, only to make a four-year truce in
1593, but Beijing's ensuing offer of vassal status to the
Japanese emperor Toyotomi Hideyoshi failed to impress.
China invaded a second time, Hideyoshi died, and Japan's
armies left the peninsula.

China was slow to confront another threat from the
northeast, the Manchus under their leader, Nurhaci, a
tactical genius who was uniting the clans of what would
become Manchuria. He was allowed to become a rallying
point for the tribes as he developed a large army. By the
time the empire did turn its attention to the menace, its
coffers were badly depleted by spending elsewhere, and
its army was in poor condition.

As a result, imperial forces failed to make an impression
against Nurhaci, thanks in part to the 'madman general'
Tu Sung, who led his men into two ambushes. As news of
the defeats reached Beijing, food prices there soared, and
army desertions ran into thousands. It was in this climate
that Wanli, now all but cut off from his bureaucracy and
his country, finally died in 1620 after one of the longest
imperial reigns. His death may have been hastened by his
extreme obesity and a weakness for opium.

Decline sets in

The next three emperors, ruling from 1620 to 1644, presided over the final decline
and fall of the Ming. During this time, China was plagued by floods, droughts, crop
failures and other natural disasters. Several mutinies and rebellions broke out in
different parts of the country. An influx of silver from trade with Spanish merchants
had destabilizing effects on Chinese society; while at court, factionalism took hold,
and a struggle for power ensued between the eunuchs and the more Confucian-
minded scholars, who mostly had strong links to the Donglin Academy.

China was not without hope, however. Its merchant class grew richer from export of
its goods – silks, cottons and porcelain – and the establishment of the ports of Manila
and Nagasaki in the 1570s allowed these goods to begin to appear in Kyoto, Lima,
Mexico and London. 'Blue China', the seafaring country which sold its goods to the
rest of the world, developed fast in this period.

ABOVE *A facsimile of
the 1781 edition of the
Manzhou shilu, an
illustrated description
of the life of Nurhaci,
whose descendants
completed the conquest
of China and established
the Qing dynasty.*

WANG AND 'RADICAL IDEALISM' Wang Yangming

(1472–1529), the most famed Confucian thinker under the Ming, taught that everybody was capable of becoming a sage. *'Everyone, from the infant in swaddling clothes to the old, is in full possession of innate knowledge'*, he wrote.

Applying what has been dubbed 'radical idealism', Wang taught that the main thing was to look into one's own being to improve oneself. In contrast to the traditional scholarly approach, he believed that thought and action should be combined. Learning came best through experience, not through 'ivory tower' contemplation.

Wang's thinking may have been prompted in part by events in his own life. After passing the imperial examination and entering the civil service, he defended officials who had advised the emperor to punish a favoured eunuch. Wang was sentenced to 40 strokes of the bamboo cane and exiled to wild Guizhou in the southwest. While there, he developed his philosophy, and returned to become a prominent general for the Ming, defeating a leading rebel, Fan Wang.

Portrait of Confucius, whose teachings influenced scholars of the Ming court, including Wang Yangming.

'Magnificent Prosperity'

The next ruler, Emperor Taichang, the son of a girl serving on the staff of Wanli's mother, had had a turbulent boyhood in a succession struggle between Confucian officials, who supported him, and his father, who preferred a younger son, born to his favourite concubine, Lady Zheng. Taichang's reign name meant 'Magnificent Prosperity' and the very first days of his rule were promising. Orders were issued to reverse Wanli's worst legacies by releasing silver from the imperial coffers for the protection of the north, and by naming officials to many posts that had been left vacant. But the day before his 18th birthday, the ruler fell so seriously ill that the celebrations were cancelled. The rumour mill had it that he had been weakened by sexual activity after he was presented with eight beautiful maidens by Lady Zheng.

A eunuch then advised the ruler to take a laxative, which induced extreme diarrhoea. A red pill, made by a court official and apothecary, was administered to deal with this complaint. The emperor said he felt better and took a second pill. The next morning he was found dead. Argument raged over what do with the apothecary; some considered that he should be rewarded for causing Taichang's death. Eventually he was exiled to the northern border on the instructions of the eunuch Wei Zhongxian, who became the main power behind the throne under the next ruler, Tianqi.

Terror at court

Instead of asserting control and establishing order after the scandal of his predecessor's death, Tianqi, who became emperor at the age of 15 and ruled from 1621 to 1627, retreated into his imperial apartments and practised carpentry, at which he was especially skilled. The autocratic eunuch Wei Zhongxian began to take over the running of the country from his government stronghold, the directorate. He and Madame Ke, who had been the ruler's wet nurse, terrorized the court and launched a palace purge in 1621 following a strong critique of Wei delivered by the censorate.

Although several more public service-minded Donglin officials took senior positions in the 1620s, some of them soon resigned. In 1623 a new censor began a corruption purge, which upset the eunuchs. Wei organized an attack on the Donglin Academy faction at court, all the while amassing wealth for his family.

Disorder in the country

Disorder around the throne was matched elsewhere in the country. In the northeast, defections from the regime became a serious problem and Shenyang was taken by the Manchu forces in 1621 – soon the Manchus controlled all territory claimed by the Ming east of the Liao River. But then a prominent general, Yuan Chonghuan, led an offensive which turned back the Manchus and showed that they were not invincible.

In Sichuan in the southwest, a chieftain from the Lolo minority launched a big rebellion and took Chongqing before attacking Chengdu. Further rebellions were sparked in Guizhou and Yunnan. All of these events hit the grain supply, and further economic strain was caused by a decline in Sino–Spanish trade, fires in several cities, an earthquake that killed 120,000 and the Yellow River bursting its dykes in 1623. The last of these disasters provoked peasant uprisings, troop mutinies and pirate raids.

> I beg you to ... select with all speed crack troops who can press strongly forward with the force under my command so that our combined force will be able to strike all the way to the gates of the capital, exterminate the roving bandits who are in the very palace precincts, in that way to make a show of great righteousness in China. Then my country's reward to your northern state will not merely be in the form of wealth and valuables, but it is certain to lead to a grant of territory as well ... The gold and treasure accumulated by the bandits are beyond calculation. As soon as your righteous troops arrive it will all be theirs.

APPEAL TO THE MANCHUS TO COME TO THE AID OF THE DYNASTY BY MING GENERAL WU SANGUI

Manchu raids

In 1628 the next ruler, Tianqi's brother, Emperor Chongzhen, ascended to the throne and instantly demoted the eunuch Wei Zhongxian, who later committed suicide. The new ruler made several senior appointments from among Donglin Academy scholars, but these were not sufficient in number to outweigh other court factions. As a result, there were Donglin resignations, and the eunuchs rose to power once again.

Piracy came under control and Sino–Spanish trade enjoyed a rebirth, centred on Manila. But drought in the northwest brought desperation and cannibalism. The Manchus, now under a new leader, penetrated the Great Wall in 1629 to raid the Beijing region before returning north and taking Dalinghe. Rebels in Shaanxi spread east and southeast, towards Beijing and into Henan; before long their control had spread to Jiangxi and parts of the south. Peasants became easy recruits for such movements. In 1639 drought, floods and locust plagues sparked fresh disaster – infanticide and mass starvation plagued the worst-hit regions.

> Weak and of scant virtue, I have offended Heaven. Because I allowed my ministers to mislead me, rebels have taken my capital. I die too ashamed to meet my ancestors. My head-dress removed, my hair hanging over my face, the rebels may quarter my body. Yet I pray no harm befalls my people.
>
> FINAL WORDS OF THE LAST MING EMPEROR CHONGZHEN WRITTEN ON HIS SLEEVE, 1644

Foundation of the Qing dynasty

In 1636 Abahai, the Manchu leader, declared the foundation of the Qing dynasty in the northeast, while back at court the years 1634–8 saw 19 different Grand Secretaries. The emperor had made the crucial mistake of ordering the execution of Yuan Chonghuan, the last commander who might have held the Manchus at bay, after falling for invented allegations that he was conspiring with the enemy. The general, who suffered death by 1000 cuts, went down in Chinese history as a heroic figure undone by court intrigue.

Nonetheless, there were brighter spots, for a time at least. In the northwest the Ming enjoyed success in achieving stability, thanks in part to its appointment of a rebel leader as regional commander of Gucheng. Yet as one threat was plugged, another emerged – notably in the form of a new Manchu attack on the Beijing region and Shandong. Then, to the south, a rebel leader crossed the Yangzi to attack eastern Sichuan before moving into the Hukuang region north and south of the middle Yangzi in present-day Hunan and Hubei; the Ming commander there committed suicide.

The rebels captured the cities of Wuchang and Changsha, while other insurgents seized Kaifeng and Xiangyang in central China. By 1642 the Ming's northern defences were down and the Manchu leader, Abahai, sent his brother Abatai on a seven-month campaign through eastern China – 94 towns and cities were reportedly conquered during this period.

In April 1644 the last emperor of the Ming walked to a hill north of his palace and entered the pavilion that housed the Imperial Hat and Girdle Department. With the aid of a eunuch, he hanged himself, a victim of problems that had troubled the dynasty since its inception three centuries before. The Ming had broken the spell of foreign rule in China. Their demise meant that the country would have to wait another 270 years until the Chinese once more ruled their own nation.

TOMBS OF THE EMPERORS

Thirty miles (50 km) northwest of Beijing, 13 Ming rulers were laid to rest in a site carefully selected for its good *feng shui* below an arc of hills that had the prized attributes of quiet water and dark earth. The building of the Ming Tombs began in 1409 and continued until the fall of the dynasty.

Each tomb was set at the foot of a separate hill in an area covering some 15 square miles (39 sq. km), surrounded by a wall 25 miles (40 km) long. The tombs were linked by a wide avenue known as the Sacred Way which began with a high, wide, red archway decorated with carvings of clouds, waves and divine animals. Along the Way stood figures of animals, real and mythical, making up an extraordinary collection of 15th-century sculpture.

The Sacred Way is the avenue leading to the tomb of Emperor Yongle, the third Ming emperor. He was the first emperor to be buried at the site.

The tombs are a major tourist attraction, but only three have been excavated. Though the gallery in one shows the finery of the Ming, no excavation work has been done since 1989, so most of what the Ming rulers took to their graves remains hidden.

JESUIT MISSIONARIES IN CHINA
Three centuries after Marco Polo's travels, another celebrated European visitor arrived in China. But, whereas the Polo family had travelled east for trade, Matteo Ricci went to the Ming court to try to convert the Chinese to Christianity.

Matteo Ricci (1552–1610), who was born in the papal states of Italy, was the best known of a wave of Jesuits who set out to convert the most heavily populated state on earth. There had been Nestorian Christians and a Catholic mission in China under the Mongols, but they lost their position after the fall of the Yuan dynasty. By 1663, under the newly installed Qing dynasty, the number of converts reached 10,500, expanding to 200,000 by the end of the 17th century.

The Jesuits calculated that, to win over the Chinese, their missionaries would have to speak and read the language and be able to reason in ways that resonated with the Chinese. As a result, their emissaries underwent rigorous training, and China was seen as the fulfilment of their vocation.

The enclave established by the Portuguese in Macau in 1557, where the Jesuits built a fine cathedral, was their launch pad. Once in the Middle Kingdom, they busied themselves with practical matters that enabled them to make links with local people. Their skill in mathematics and astronomy was attractive to educated Chinese, particularly at court, where they also introduced artistic refinements such as perspective in painting. As a result, they were allowed to proselytize for their religion.

But the Jesuits had a problem over some basic issues, such as how to express their idea of God clearly in Chinese. Attempted definitions were complicated by the terms used for divinities in the native language. The scope accorded by the Jesuits to their Father in Heaven ran up against the Chinese notion of heavenly power, which bestowed on their emperors the mandate to rule. In 1627, a conference held in the Yangzi Delta unsuccessfully tried to grapple with the problem of terminology.

Though the missionaries across China provided the essential grass-roots operation, the outstanding Jesuit in the early

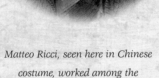

Matteo Ricci, seen here in Chinese costume, worked among the Chinese people for almost 30 years.

decades of activity in China was Ricci, who became well known back in Europe through the publication of a memoir he wrote of his life in China.

Ricci's phenomenal memory was said to enable him to read 500 Chinese characters and be able to recall them all instantly. Having learned Chinese, he set up a mission in southern China in 1583. While there, he drew the first map of the world in Chinese. In 1601, after two years in Nanjing, he was allowed to move to the Ming dynasty capital of Beijing, where he cut an unusual figure with his blue eyes and curly hair. Having presented a chiming clock to the court, he was allowed into the Forbidden City. He did not meet the emperor, but he instructed court eunuchs on European ways and gave them lessons in Western music. He translated Confucian texts into Latin and the works of Euclid and Western mathematicians into Chinese. He took the garb of a Chinese scholar and lived in Beijing until his death in 1610.

The Jesuit expansion in China continued after his death. The towering, fair-haired German missionary, Adam Schall von Bell (1591-1669), who was knowledgeable about artillery as well as astronomy and mathematics, won an eminent position at the Manchu court, enjoying the favour of the second Qing emperor. At the same time, another missionary worked with the Ming court in exile. Whatever the outcome of the struggle between the Qing and the Ming, the Church wanted to make sure it was represented in each camp.

The Ming never regained power, and Schall became the most important Catholic in China and a favoured figure at the court in Beijing, where his direct way of speaking cut through the circumlocutions endemic in Chinese official language. But, after the death of his protector on the throne, Schall's position weakened. It was not his religion that his enemies objected to but his success at court, where his skill and the accuracy of his scientific readings had led to his being appointed to the key position of director of the imperial astronomy.

The first Catholic missions in China were established in the prosperous Portuguese settlement of Macau. This undated engraving shows crowds lining up to worship at the Jesuit cathedral in Macau.

In 1664 Schall suffered a stroke, at the age of 72. His enemies turned on him. He was accused of using Catholic spells to harm the imperial family. His voice now only a broken mumble, the Jesuit was reduced in rank as one charge after another was levelled against him. He was imprisoned and then sentenced to be decapitated. But, as the date of the execution approached, a comet appeared over Beijing, followed by an earthquake that knocked down one wall of his prison. The portents were clear, and the German also had the support of the young emperor's grandmother. He was freed, and died peacefully the following year.

In the early Qing era, the Jesuit operation in China became distinctly over-extended. Twenty separate missionary stations were established but there were not enough priests to manage them efficiently. New missionaries did not necessarily have the linguistic skills and cultural understanding that lay at the heart of the enterprise – some missionaries had to use interpreters to hear confessions, or were reduced to showing booklets in which sins were listed in Chinese characters so that converts could point to those they had committed. The absence of skilled manpower meant that converts were increasingly left to their own devices.

Most serious of all, however, the fundamental dichotomy between the claims the Jesuits made for their God and the status the emperor assumed as the Son of Heaven. These proved insurmountable in the long run. In 1724, the once tolerant Qing dynasty declared Christianity to be 'heterodox'. The dream was over.

THE EARLY AND HIGH QING

1644–1799

The Qing expanded China's land area **hugely** and presided over a multi-cultural court that produced some of the greatest examples of Chinese art. At the height of its rule, the empire may have accounted for one-third of the world's wealth. But the dynasty ended in a fight for survival against mass revolts, repeated humiliations at the hands of Europeans and Japanese and, finally, the abdication of the infant Last Emperor, bringing the empire to a close after 2133 years.

THE FINAL RULERS OF IMPERIAL CHINA CAME FROM MANCHURIA, NORTHEAST OF THE GREAT Wall, where their predecessors had founded a dynasty under the Chinese name of the 'Great Qing' – the second word meaning 'pure'. The Manchus rode south into the power vacuum created by the collapse of the Ming dynasty in 1644, and took Beijing from peasant rebels. While they were successful militarily, the Qing faced the problem that had confronted the Mongols when they founded the Yuan dynasty in the 13th century. They constituted a tiny minority of the population – by most estimates never more than 2 per cent.

Unlike the Yuan, they resolved this over time by adopting traditional Chinese ways and forms of government. The new dynasty could count on the allegiance of Ming turncoats who rallied to its flag and kept the system of government running under the overall dominance of the Manchu emperors, princes and clans grouped beneath the distinctive banners they bore with them into battle. The Qing emperors adopted Confucian philosophy and carried out traditional Chinese rituals. The new dynasty made much of the excesses of the late Ming, and played on its role as avenger while using adherence to traditional values to buttress its claim to the throne.

Thus successive rulers forged a multi-cultural, multi-ethnic realm in due course as the empire reached its zenith before declining to disaster. Yet if the old Confucian ways remained in place, there was considerable social dynamism. A doubling of the

RIGHT *A 19th-century engraving representing the life of the Chinese emperors. Like that of many earlier dynasties, the Qing court had a strict hierarchy; the emperor and the imperial family were surrounded by courtiers and officials, all of whom enjoyed prosperity and privilege, but who owed their position to his favour.*

population led to a major expansion in land given over to arable farming, the emergence of a large labour force and a strong demand for goods. The first decades of Qing rule were marked by constant wars against internal rebels and external foes, but internal peace set in over much of the country at the end of the 17th century. Still, the rulers remained foreigners, and nostalgia for the Ming would linger on, particularly in rural areas and among secret societies, erupting into major revolts two centuries after the dynasty had ascended the throne.

The Qing sought to have the best of two worlds – to adopt Confucianism and classical Chinese patterns as foundations for their rule, but also to remain as a dynasty apart, which alone represented the whole of a colonial empire that came to embrace Muslims, Mongols and Tibetans as well as minority populations within China proper. But they had nothing new to offer, no new rallying point for their people beyond their military power and membership of a growing colonial empire. At the height of their glory in the late 18th century, the model they gave their citizens was a static one, seeking as it did to draw on the past but lacking a clear vision of the future, despite a rapidly evolving society as the population and the nation's wealth both boomed.

Pigtails and privileges

For all their adoption of Chinese traditions, the Manchus never left their new subjects in any doubt as to who was master – the Han were made to shave the front of their skulls and wear pigtails as a sign of submission. Intermarriage between Manchus and their subjects was forbidden. Though the prohibition had little effect, foot-binding was officially outlawed. Chinese were not permitted to emigrate to Manchuria. Only Manchus were allowed to live in the Forbidden City and the surrounding area. Manchu nobles grabbed land and privileges. The new dynasty might adopt Chinese methods when they were useful, but it never lost sight of its origins. Manchu rituals were celebrated in the Forbidden City, and food laid out for the magpies from whom the rulers believed they were descended. '*We who bear the name of Manchus should be true to the way of the Manchus*', wrote the second emperor.

The new dynasty was fortunate in the 17th and 18th centuries in having able rulers. While there was no lack of intrigue and back-stabbing at court, the young conquerors who had ridden in from the north in 1644 maintained a disciplined, united front towards their subjects. Their many military units were roughly equal in strength, so none was tempted to fight the others in an attempt to dominate; they also had a solid economic base in the estates held by the various banner forces. Their unity was

ABOVE *The successful military campaigns launched by the invading Manchus on urban centres across China generally resulted in the massacre of any Chinese who refused to surrender.*

MANCHU BANNERMEN
While fighting as a unified force owing allegiance to the ruler, the Manchu army which defeated the Ming to conquer China was organized under a system of units known by their banners.

There were 24 different banners involved in the conquest of China. In all, some 170,000 men took part in the attack from the northeast. The Banner troops continued to spearhead Qing expansion into China after the new dynasty took Beijing. They were tough and often ruthless fighters. They were rewarded with estates and posted to garrison towns to maintain order. But, once the Qing controlled China, the need for their services declined. They became increasingly parasitic, contributing little to the economy and living off the land, keeping apart from the Han population. The sedentary life of China was appealing but ultimately destructive to their reason for existence – fighting. Alongside them, the Chinese soldiers who served the dynasty, known as the Green Standard troops, were even worse. The end result was to significantly weaken the Qing when it faced major threats from domestic foes in the 19th century.

These replica bannermen guard the Old Zhonghua Gate in southern Nanjing.

particularly important at the start of the dynasty since the Manchu chief, Hung Taiji, son of the Qing founder Nurhaci, had died suddenly on the eve of conquering China.

The rule of Dorgon
Hung Taiji's death left one of the conquering leaders – his brother, Prince Dorgon – as the dominant figure. It was said that when the elders of Beijing went outside the city walls to welcome the newcomers he dismounted from his horse, stepped into the waiting imperial carriage and announced, '*I am the Prince Regent. The crown prince will arrive in a while. Will you allow me to be the ruler?*' The crowd replied affirmatively. As the most competent of the princes, it was proposed that Dorgon should take the throne, but other leading Manchus wanted one of Hung Taiji's sons to succeed. This led to factional jousting that ended with a compromise choice – the late leader's sixth son, six-year-old Shunzhi, as emperor, with Dorgon and another prince as regents.

As the main figure at court, Dorgon co-opted senior Ming officials into the regime, exempting them from the head-shaving order. He cut taxes and outlawed rape and the owning of slaves by Manchu soldiers. Ming officials who rallied to Manchus were given an amnesty and allowed to retain their jobs.

Banner armies (see Manchu Bannermen, page 197) of some 80,000 troops, allied with Chinese mercenaries, took the provinces of Zhili around Beijing, Shanxi to the west and Shandong to the east, before capturing the ancient imperial capital of Xi'an (formerly Chang'an) in Shaanxi province. Such successes consolidated the Qing position in the north, but central and southern China presented a major challenge, since an array of Ming armies and entrenched regional forces had established themselves there in the declining decades of the fallen dynasty. Apart from their military prowess, the Manchus had another advantage in the divisions that existed between their opponents, as provincial barons preferred to fight on behalf of their own territory and armies rather than combining forces against the invaders.

Dodo's pacification campaign

Dorgon's brother, Dodo, led an extraordinarily swift and effective campaign south to Yangzi at the head of banner forces and soldiers from northern China. He captured 138,000 Ming troops, who joined him in attacking the key city of Yangzhou on the road to the early Ming capital of Nanjing. After fierce resistance, Yangzhou was taken and subjected to an orgy of murder and rape by the Chinese troops who had defected. On 8 June, 1645, one year after Dorgon had entered Beijing, Nanjing surrendered to Dodo without a fight, and another 100,000 Chinese soldiers joined the Manchu ranks. The campaign had starkly illustrated the choice faced by Ming loyalists: in Yangzhou they had put up a fight and been massacred; at Nanjing they had surrendered and had been left in peace. Still, there was stiff resistance as the Manchus advanced through the Yangzi Delta, where the head-shaving decree aroused armed protests. But, by the late autumn of 1645, Dodo completed his pacification campaign and returned to Beijing. In his wake he left a legacy of brutality that would long be remembered by opponents of the new dynasty. In addition, the violence imposed by the northern Chinese soldiers on the richer, more sophisticated urban inhabitants of the Yangzi, would further deepen divisions within the nation.

Notwithstanding Dodo's victories, southern China and the biggest province of Sichuan remained outside Manchu authority, and there were recurrent revolts in the Yangzi Delta. The southwest was not brought under Beijing's control until 1659. Despite a successful offensive into the southeast in 1646, fighting went on there involving the Qing, local warlords and Ming loyalists. There were revolts by Muslims in the north and in some of the dynasty's own garrisons. Taiwan remained under the control of the Ming admiral, Coxinga. Fighting went on in one region or another for a further 35 years before the Manchus established full authority over all of China.

At one point Dorgon, who had asserted his power by suppressing a plot to depose the boy emperor in favour of another prince, insisted on leading a successful campaign against the rebels in the northwest. He seems to have grown tired of administration and the task of balancing the Manchu clans. At the end of 1650 he set off on a hunting expedition on the steppes near the Manchu imperial city of Jehol beyond the Great Wall. Apparently over-exerting himself, he died on 31 December, at the age of 38.

ABOVE *During the stability that was established after the Qing conquests, commerce and international trade grew. The élite demanded more consumer goods, and merchant classes benefited from the increased trade. This trader is setting out his stall of hand-crafted purses and handkerchiefs.*

THE SOUTHERN RESISTANCE
After the Manchus replaced the Ming as emperors, resistance formed in southern China on behalf of the ousted dynasty. One of the movement's key figures was a 41-year-old merchant and smuggler, Zheng Zhilong, who had risen to become an admiral in the imperial fleet and who now headed a large band of pirates and privateers. Zheng was known also by the name given to him by Christian missionaries: Nicholas Iquan.

For two years Zheng fought against the Qing before betraying the Ming cause and rallying to the new regime. He went to Beijing, where he was fêted by the Manchus and given the post of Great Mandarin. However, his son, Coxinga, continued the struggle at the head of the forces his father left behind in the south, in particular the navy.

Coxinga met with initial success from his stronghold at Xiamen on the east coast, but when he sought to expand to Canton on the Pearl River Delta, he was forced by an imperial army to withdraw, and his troops suffered heavy losses. But he hit back by attacking other southeastern towns, besieging one for six months and reducing its inhabitants to cannibalism.

Coxinga's resistance efforts made him a Chinese national hero; this portrait is from a triptych commemorating a play about his life.

coast, and the inhabitants were moved inland. In Beijing, a death sentence was delivered on Coxinga's father in an attempt to cow the son. It had no such effect and, in 1661, the execution was carried out: first two of Zheng's other sons were sliced to death; then Zheng himself was killed in the same manner.

Coxinga was not intimidated, but his health began to fail. A year after Zheng's execution, the last heir to the Ming – who had fled into Burma before returning to China – was captured by a southwestern warlord who had rallied to the Qing. The heir and his son were strangled with a bowstring. Learning of this, the last Ming's wife smashed a porcelain bowl and used a fragment to slash her throat.

The Qing offered him a deal, invoking the example of his father, but he declined, saying *'there is a greater duty than mere loyalty to one's family'*. Although battered by a huge storm that sank dozens of ships with the loss of 8000 men, his navy remained the dominant maritime force in the region, and Coxinga felt strong enough to launch another land expedition in 1659 – against Nanjing. This proved to be a campaign too far. Defeated by imperial forces, he sailed with his remaining troops to Taiwan, where he defeated the Dutch who had settled there, forcing them to leave. His victory made him a hero to the Chinese, both at the time and for centuries to come, for having defeated the Westerners in battle.

The island of Taiwan remained Coxinga's haven as the Ming cause withered on the mainland. To prevent communication between the rebel and the people of his former domain, a deep exclusion zone was traced along the southeast China

Tradition tells that, when the news reached Taiwan, Coxinga, ill with fever, walked to the family tomb while a storm was beating outside. He lifted a Ming memorial but the effort was too much for him and he fell to the ground. *'How can I meet my emperor in heaven with my mission unfulfilled?'*, he called out. He bowed forward, covered his face with his hands and died, the memorial clasped to his breast. He was 39.

Soon afterwards, a Ming admiral who had gone over to the Qing led a successful attack on Taiwan. The surviving 40,000 troops of the resistance army and navy were sent to live deep in the interior of China. A small group of Ming loyalists sailed to Southeast Asia, and anti-Manchu sects would stage periodic revolts in the hope of a restoration. But the rule of the foreign Qing was being firmly established and would last until the end of the empire.

The emperor Shunzhi

The serious, studious, physically fragile first Qing emperor, Shunzhi, took full power after his uncle's death. Aged 13 when he ascended the throne, he learned Chinese, promoted Chinese officials and converted to Buddhism. He also held lengthy conversations with a long-bearded German astronomer-mathematician and Jesuit missionary, Johann Adam Schall von Bell – astronomy was particularly important given the significance attached by the court to the ritual calendar. Bell was raised to the rank of mandarin and allowed to open churches which were said to have made half a million Christian converts. (See Jesuit Missionaries in China, pages 192–3.)

Around him, princely factions jostled for power. Dorgon's clan was not strong enough to claim his inheritance, and his regency came to be vilified as a dictatorship, with its main supporters persecuted and deprived of their positions by rival groups. The feuding enabled the young ruler to assert his authority in the absence of a Dorgon-like figure, buoyed by fresh military success in the south and southwest, and the extension of imperial rule in central China under a Han governor who repaid the emperor's trust.

Shunzhi, depicted in an 18th-century portrait as a full-faced man with a curved moustache and spade-shaped beard, showed considerable independence of mind. He rejected two imperial brides suggested by his mother, and preferred to spend personal time with a Mongol concubine. During his reign, fiscal reforms were introduced and tax evaders pursued. The emperor attacked corruption among leading scholar-officials, including one major scandal in which imperial examiners in the Beijing region were found to have taken large bribes in return for giving degrees – some were executed.

Religious leanings and wild rages

At the same time, however, the emperor sought to encourage civilian government by the same official class he was trying to purge, including scholars from the south who joined the prestigious imperial élite school in the capital, the Hanlin Academy. This provoked hostility among Manchu nobles who found the ruler too soft, too intellectual and too apt to adopt Chinese ways. The spectre of the late, ineffectual Ming emperors was a warning of where that could lead. For Shunzhi the incessant factionalism among court functionaries and the opposition to reform from the Manchu old guard may have caused him to look favourably on the ideas propagated by Schall and the Buddhist priests he consulted and whose ranks he spoke of joining.

ABOVE *An engraving of the influential German Jesuit astronomer Johann Adam Schall von Bell (1591–1666), working in his observatory in Peking (Beijing).*

In September 1660 his favourite concubine died. This provoked in the emperor a mixture of deep depression and wild rages. He was said to have spat blood and tried to hack at his own throne with a sword. (One side effect of his doomed love affair was that, thereafter, no concubine was permitted to spend a whole night with the emperor, to ensure that none could obtain such a hold on the ruler's emotions.)

On 2 February, 1661, Shunzhi contracted smallpox. He summoned two secretaries to his bedside and dictated his will, naming his third son as heir. The boy was chosen both because he had survived an attack of smallpox and because he was the son of a senior concubine from an important clan; he was therefore considered preferable to his brothers born to Chinese concubines or members of disgraced or minor families.

The emperor died three days later. There were rumours that he had not really passed away but had retreated into seclusion in a Buddhist monastery, either out of grief or because nobles who felt threatened by his policies had forced him from the throne. The fact that a senior officer in his bodyguard and the highest-ranking concubine committed suicide so that they could serve their master in the afterlife argues against such tales – unless, that is, both were either duped or killed themselves to add credence to the death story.

The High Qing

Like his father, the new emperor, Kangxi – whose reign marked the beginning of the period known as the High Qing – came to the throne in 1661 as a minor; he was seven years old. He sat on the throne for 61 years, the longest period of any imperial rule, coinciding with Louis XIV of France and Peter the Great of Russia. Ushering in the greatest period of Qing glory, that of the 'Three Emperors', he was an acute politician with a sense of imperial destiny – for himself, the dynasty and the nation.

The early years of his reign were, however, a disturbed time. After being dictated to the secretaries on his deathbed, Shunzhi's will had been taken away for a fair copy to be made. It was returned to the ruler and then to his mother, with whom he was on bad terms, and to a group of princes and senior officials. The next day, what purported to be this will was read out. It consisted of a list of self-criticisms: laziness, extravagance, a failure to heed the advice of his mother or of Manchus, neglect of the army and excessive bias towards Han officials and court eunuchs. In other words, it was a *mea culpa* designed to bolster the position of the Manchu veterans. It was almost certainly a forgery conjured up after the real will had fallen into the hands of the dowager empress. The only genuine element was the naming of Kangxi as the heir.

The rise of Kangxi

Four Manchu barons took control as regents. They moved swiftly to dismantle Shunzhi's administrative measures, executed some of his civilian staff, elevated bodies that represented the conquering élite, downgraded Chinese civil administration and proclaimed the supremacy of the military. Harsh measures

ABOVE *Unlike Chinese men, women did not have to change their dress under the Qing. Foot-binding was outlawed (though in practice it continued).*

201

were taken against the Han. Schall and his European astronomer colleagues were removed from their posts and thrown into prison, accused of treason and incompetence. The boy emperor remained powerless, looked after by staff and nurses who allowed him to smoke tobacco.

The death of one of the regents in 1667 precipitated a crisis. One of the other three, Oboi, was growing ever more powerful, threatening to become a second Dorgon, backed by his army and a network of supportive officials. On 21 August, at a lengthy meeting with his mother and the regents, Kangxi said the dead regent had wanted

202

him to take over full power. He added that he felt he was still too young to do this; the dowager agreed. Showing the required deference to the emperor, the regents said he should take power but they would be happy to go on helping him.

The dowager suggested that the Ministry of Rites identify an auspicious date for Kangxi to exert personal rule. This appeared to be an ideal solution, since it was assumed by regents and mother alike that the date would be far in the future. Instead, the ministry selected the coming 25 August – the emperor later rewarded its head by appointing him Grand Secretary, Minister of Revenue and Minister of the Civil Office.

Having staged his first coup at the age of 13, Kangxi moved ahead with determination and speed. He ordered an investigation into one of the regents, who had asked to be allowed to retire. The investigation found him guilty of 24 offences. The imperial council sentenced him and one of his sons to be sliced to death, while two other sons, a grandson and a nephew were to be beheaded together with a number of officers found guilty of having plotted against the emperor. All their relatives were to be enslaved. Kangxi agreed to the verdict with one modification – the regent was to be strangled, not sliced.

Step by step, the teenage ruler built up his own strength. He shuffled senior officials, reversed a forced relocation of Han people in the south that had been ordered by the regents, and restored the European astronomers to favour. He lulled Oboi and the other regent into a sense of security by making them dukes of the first rank and by taking the daughter of one as a concubine – he would marry her later, after the death of his first wife.

THE SACRED EDICTS In 1670 Kangxi issued the Sacred Edicts, which outlined 16 maxims based on Confucian teachings. Through these maxims, Kangxi instructed ordinary people on how to behave for the greater moral good.

1. Strengthen filial piety and brotherly affection to emphasize human relations.
2. Strengthen clan relations to illustrate harmony.
3. Pacify relations between local groups to put an end to quarrels and litigation.
4. Stress agriculture and sericulture so that there may be sufficient food and clothing.
5. Prize frugality so as to make careful use of wealth.
6. Promote education to improve the habits of scholars.
7. Extirpate heresy to exalt orthodoxy.
8. Speak of the law to give warning to the stupid and stubborn.
9. Clarify rites and manners to improve customs.
10. Let each work at his own occupation so that the people's minds will be settled.
11. Instruct young people to prevent them from doing wrong.
12. Prevent false accusations to shield the law-abiding.
13. Prohibit sheltering of runaways to avoid being implicated in their crime.
14. Pay taxes to avoid being pressed for payment.
15. Unite the baojia system to eliminate theft and armed robbery.
16. Resolve hatred and quarrels to respect life.

In June 1669 Kangxi was ready for his next move. An imperial edict denounced Oboi for fixing bureaucratic appointments, blocking access to petitioners to the throne, insulting behaviour and heading a 14-man clique which discussed government business in secret. The other regent was accused of colluding with Oboi. All 15 were arrested, tried and sentenced to death, in some cases along with their families. Kangxi spared the lives of five, including the two regents, and Oboi was sent to jail, where he died. At the age of 15, Kangxi was now his own master. Three years later, he set out to expand his domain to establish the frontiers that would become those of the empire in its last 240 years.

Consolidation and control of information

While boldly extending and consolidating the empire, Kangxi was a cautious man. His notations on memorials in imperial vermilion ink vaunted the pursuit of harmony and advised officials not to risk stirring up trouble by unconsidered initiatives. He went out of his way to win over the Chinese. His Sacred Edicts, which were read out twice a month, stressed Confucian values. (See The Sacred Edicts, page 203.) He halted the confiscation of land by Manchus and cut taxes. Official salaries were raised to placate civil servants.

In an artful move, he called an examination to identify the best scholars in the country. Many of those who were summoned to it were still not reconciled to Qing rule. But the prize Kangxi offered to the top 50 examinees squared the circle – they were asked to compile a massive history of the Ming. This was not something they could reject, particularly since the job came with official positions and integration into court.

Seeking to encourage national unity, Kangxi instituted a geographical quota system at the Hanlin Academy in Beijing so that official students from poor, distant provinces could be assured of places. To bolster the administration, he developed a system of 'palace memorials', consisting of confidential reports to the throne that circumvented official bureaucratic channels and so gave the ruler an independent source of information. For Kangxi, secrecy and complete control of the flow of information were paramount.

Though personally frugal, he inaugurated an era of extraordinary artistic achievement. His motives were not only for the sake of art itself but also to proclaim the majesty of the Qing through the creation of jewels, ornately decorated silk robes and objects in jade, gold and silver. Paintings of the emperors on their provincial tours

RUSSIAN RAPPROCHEMENT

Fearing that Russia might ally with its opponents in the Mongol empire of Galdan, Kangxi decided to try to conclude the first Chinese treaty with a European power.

In 1689, he sent emissaries to meet the Russians at Nerchinsk in Siberia. Riding with a large guard force, the Manchu prince entrusted with the mission was advised by a Portuguese and a French Catholic missionary from Beijing. A treaty was concluded, and recorded in five languages: Manchu, Russian, Chinese, Mongol and Latin. Not being the language of any of the interested parties, the Latin version was accepted as the authoritative one.

The treaty settled territorial disputes and provided the basis for trade between China and Russia. A hostel was established in Beijing for Russian diplomats and merchants. Other treaties followed between the two countries. The emperor was now free to concentrate on destroying the Galdan realm of Mongolia. This took eight years, ending with the Mongol's suicide and Manchu supremacy in the northwest. (See Kangxi, Qianlong and the Expansion of the Empire, pages 218–19.)

portray them surrounded by their subjects – be they northern nomadic princes gathered outside a yurt tent on the traditional Manchu hunting grounds or southern farmers and townspeople. The Forbidden City became a hive of activity as Kangxi established imperial workshops to turn out porcelain, carvings, furniture and elaborate handicrafts.

As shown in his exploitation of the arts and his grand tours of China, Kangxi set great store by the assertion of dynastic power and prerogative. Everything was designed to strengthen the throne and its occupant, who identified himself with the country. The primacy of the dynastic principle was a hallmark of Manchu rule, an assertion of omnipotence and ultimate wisdom. Anything which challenged authority was anathema; when the Vatican insisted on the universal nature of the papacy, Kangxi turned violently against the Jesuits and banned their activities. The same applied in Tibet, where he moved to check the independent authority of the Dalai Lama.

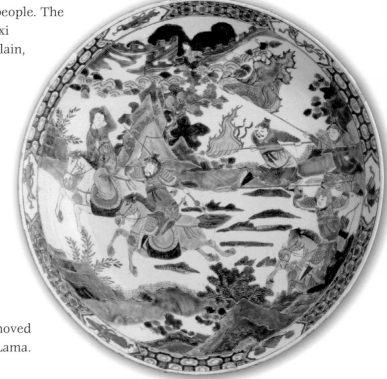

ABOVE *A porcelain plate depicting Kangxi leading his cavalry into battle. As well as being a great warrior, the emperor encouraged the development of traditional Chinese arts.*

Economic depression

Kangxi's rule had firmly established the dynasty, and the emperor had broadened its base. But despite his valedictory observations (see quotation, page 206), he sought sympathy from his officials and complained of lameness, giddiness and memory loss. Frequent wars, compounded by the inefficiency of tax collection and by corruption, stretched imperial finances. At the end of his rule, the treasury reserves amounted to just one-quarter of the annual tax take. Stocks in granaries were low.

Though the economy was improving and the population was growing again, China was hit by a period of depression at the end of the 17th century, leading a scholar to reflect, '*the empire grows poorer every day. Farmers are destitute, artisans are destitute, merchants are destitute, and officials, too, are destitute. Grain is cheap, yet it is hard to eat one's fill. Cloth is cheap, yet it is hard to cover one's skin'*.

Kangxi depended increasingly on his authoritarian machine of favoured court figures, guards and eunuchs, using the system of secret memorials to gather information on the factions that surrounded him. He appointed special commissioners to handle specific issues. Favoured officials became fabulously rich, owning great houses and estates and starting businesses from trading in salt to textiles and pawn shops.

The emperor's final years were clouded by the succession issue. Kangxi had 56 children, the first born when he was 13. Among them were 38 boys, but only his second son, Yinreng, was born to an empress. As heir apparent, Yinreng was entrusted with the conduct of day-to-day affairs while his father was away from Beijing fighting rebels in the northwest in 1696. But he was dissolute and probably mentally unstable. There was a scandal about the procuring of young boys for him. Kangxi removed his designation as heir apparent and put him under house arrest in 1708, releasing him the following year and then shutting him up again in 1712.

The ageing ruler could not make up his mind who to name instead – the Manchus did not practise primogeniture. Yinreng's supporters still formed a powerful lobby. When Kangxi died in 1722, he had not announced his decision. But his fourth son, Yongzheng, claimed that his father had chosen him on his deathbed, and mounted the throne at the age of 45.

EARLY AND HIGH QING EMPERORS

Shunzhi	1644–61
Kangxi	1661–1722
Yongzheng	1723–35
Qianlong	1736–95

Succession claims and counter-claims

Yongzheng's claim to the throne was immediately disputed by some of his brothers, notably one who had been away fighting in Tibet at the time of their father's death. The new emperor was accused of having poisoned Kangxi and of having altered the will's reference to the heir, changing it from the 14th son (the commander in Tibet) to the fourth – himself. Yongzheng faced down these challenges, sidelined or killed his siblings and removed power from princes who might dispute his right to rule. In a pattern that repeats itself through Chinese history, he had the account of the previous reign edited to remove any doubts about his own claims to the Mandate of Heaven.

Yongzheng was the first Qing to come to the throne as an adult experienced in administration. He had stood in for his father on a number of occasions and had clear ideas about how the empire should operate. While well versed in Confucianism, he distrusted the scholar-officials who had assumed the right to continue to administer the regime. Nor did he have any time for their assumptions that provincial dignitaries would be allowed decentralized power from far-away Beijing.

A diligent ruler

The impression we have of Yongzheng is of a highly determined, highly intelligent ruler, an extremely hard worker who liked to fashion his vision of the empire on his own, or through a small group of trusted associates. '*I am determined to be the first in*

'I have enjoyed the veneration of my country, and the riches of the world. There is no object I do not have, nothing I have not experienced. But now that I have reached old age, I cannot rest easy for a moment. Therefore, I regard the whole country as a worn-out sandal, and all the riches as mud and sand. If I can die without there being an outbreak of trouble, my desires will be fulfilled ... I have revealed my entrails and shown my guts. There is nothing left for me to reveal. I will say no more.'

KANGXI'S VALEDICTORY, WRITTEN THREE YEARS BEFORE HIS DEATH IN 1722

the empire in diligence', he wrote. He had plenty to do; for all his father's achievements in asserting the rule of the new dynasty, the empire was riddled with inefficiency and corruption – the important province of Shandong, for example, was more than ten years behind in passing tax revenues to Beijing.

During the day, his court duties meant he had no peace. So he preferred '*working at night when I can operate as I please*'. Among his priorities was to select officials who would help him to dominate the provincial élites. To find them, he pored through the records of the Board of War and the Board of the Civil Office. Again, this was a nocturnal affair. '*Often, I go without sleep all night*', he said. '*I must get the right man*

ABOVE *As the country prospered under the Qing, the disparity in wealth and lifestyle between the élite (typified by this nobleman and his wife) and the ordinary people became more evident.*

before I can relax'. To encourage probity among officials and to fight corruption, he instituted supplementary salaries for deserving bureaucrats, known as 'nourishment of virtue' payments.

Yongzheng's central thrust was to increase state power, elevating the public sector above the private interests of the élite gentry, with their local perks and powers to collect taxes on behalf of the central state, which gave them the opportunity to purloin funds for themselves. The emperor, he believed, should deal as directly as possible with his subjects, without intermediate layers of regional functionaries. A determined activist, he brought in a major reform of the tax system to try to eliminate loss of revenue to the treasury through embezzlement by provincial administrations, and to decrease the imposition of fees by local governments.

ABOVE *Drawing from an album depicting the cultivation and production of rice, originally published in China in c.1750. The figures in the foreground of this scene are worshipping at a shrine.*

Insisting on adherence to Confucianism, the emperor had no time for Taoism, which he dismissed as heretical. He was scathing about Buddhism. In an amplification of one of Kangxi's maxims about exalting orthodoxy, he observed, *'Just think about it, who has ever seen a Buddha? What is a Buddha? ... All this talk about fasts, processions, building temples and making idols is invented by idle and lazy Buddhist monks and Taoist priests as a plan for swindling you. Rather, to be perfectly loyal to the ruler and to fulfil filial duty to the utmost is the whole duty of man and the means of obtaining the blessing of Heaven'.*

Expansion and racial equality

Shown in a portrait as a man with his father's long face and somewhat sad eyes, Yongzheng insisted that there should be no distinction between the Manchus and the country they now ruled, and denied any place for racial differences. The Han, he argued, came from separate 'native places' across the country; the Qing happened to have their 'native place' in Manchuria, but that did not mean they were disbarred from occupying the throne. Nor did he refrain from strengthening China's position in the northwest, embarking on a long war against Mongols there. He also waged war in the southwest, where land was reclaimed for crops in mountainous areas and the empire fought to bring minority groups under its control. As their realm expanded, the emperor and his advisers constructed the idea of a domain containing people of different ethnic groups who would all become children of the dynastic empire. The ruler prized trust, efficiency and devotion to the public interest as he defined it. He was ready to back to the hilt those who served him well. When one favoured servant came under attack, he reassured him, *'If you are fair and loyal, what have you to fear? If you had even a tiny bit of self-interest in this, you could not fool me. You are one of those who really understands my wishes, and I trust you to do your best'.*

The isolated authoritarian

Yongzheng greatly expanded the system of private memorials to the throne initiated by his father. On average, he received ten a day; sometimes the number shot up to 50 or 60. At the start of his reign, the emperor urged officials to contact him, he read all they sent him and wrote personal replies. Later, he shared the work with a few close associates, including one of his brothers. The memorials covered everything from water control to fighting bandits, and reported on the shortcomings of civil servants.

It was an authoritarian, denunciatory system, but it was the most effective way for a reformist emperor isolated in the Forbidden City to operate. In keeping with his tough-minded approach to life and ruling, he had this advice to his people: *'If you do not seek happiness which is not your lot in life and do not meddle in matters that do not concern you but simply mind your own business, you will enjoy the protection of the gods'.*

Fearing court intrigues if he named his successor, Yongzheng kept the name of his heir sealed in a box lodged behind a sacred tablet. When it was opened after his death in 1735, it revealed that he had picked his fourth son, Qianlong, who would rule for almost 60 years and represent the peak of Qing glory.

Qianlong and a return to old values

Born in 1711, Qianlong was 25 when he ascended the throne, which he occupied until 1795. He had been Kangxi's favourite grandson, and he made his grandfather his model, retiring after 60 years in order to avoid reigning longer than him.

A strong, vital man who walked erectly into his 80s, who could read without spectacles until his death and who hunted until the age of 86, Qianlong was the most open-minded of the 18th-century Qing emperors. He was, however, also one who wanted to preserve and, if possible, increase the despotic power of the throne. He was in the habit of meting out harsh punishments, including the executions of three Grand Secretaries and two imperial commissioners.

Shown in a portrait of 1736 as a man with a smooth, clean-shaven face and penetrating eyes, he was devoted to his first wife; after her death and that of a son, he was described as acting like a 'crazed lion' – more than 100 senior officials were punished for failing to display the requisite degree of sorrow at the deaths. But he had his second spouse declared mad when she tonsured her hair to become a nun.

ABOVE *These pottery figures represent a mandarin and a lady. Both have tasselled hats that are typical of early Qing official dress. The man wears a short robe and cloth high boots, while the woman is dressed in long robes and holds a tablet.*

He was both extremely self-confident and aware of the potential cracks in the regime. In an announcement in 1778 that he would step down from the throne 17 years later, he explained that he was not naming a successor because of the long history of feuding among princes at court and of the way in which the 'masses' would 'secretly watch' any designated heir to take advantage of him. The implication was that the emperor had to keep all power to himself and that secrecy formed an essential plank of imperial majesty.

Conquests and statecraft

This intelligent ruler combined the Manchu focus on the military with a firm grasp of Chinese statecraft. The first was shown by his conquests and by the way in which he exaggerated both rewards and punishments to his commanders, handing out lavish gifts to the successful and having some generals and Mongol princes executed after their defeats in ill-judged campaigns; one commander was beheaded in front of his troops.

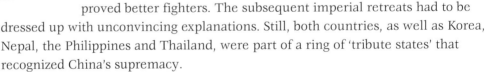

Under Qianlong the nation experienced its greatest territorial expansion, which confirmed it as the richest nation on earth, stretching over 4.5 million square miles (11.7 million sq km). Tibet was brought under Chinese control by armed intervention in 1751. In 1756–7 Chinese forces conquered the huge expanse of Central Asian desert as far as the Pamir Mountains – what was known at the time as the 'New Territories' and later became Xinjiang, bringing its Muslim inhabitants into the realm. Outer Mongolia and border regions with Russia followed.

Not all the foreign forays were successful; attempts to invade Burma and Vietnam flopped – in the first case the jungle made the imperial cavalry useless and in the second the Vietnamese proved better fighters. The subsequent imperial retreats had to be dressed up with unconvincing explanations. Still, both countries, as well as Korea, Nepal, the Philippines and Thailand, were part of a ring of 'tribute states' that recognized China's supremacy.

ABOVE *Under the Qianlong emperor, strict guidelines were introduced concerning requirements for official dress. He also reinstated the 12 imperial dragon symbols used by the First Qin Emperor. These can be seen on this lavishly embroidered silk robe dating from the Qianlong period.*

Golden Stream and White Lotus

If most of the country was at peace, there were recurrent revolts on its edges. Ethnic minorities staged a series of risings in the far southwest in defence of their homelands and customs and against the exactions of Chinese moving in to exploit their lands and treat them as virtual slaves. In the wild country of Sichuan, imperial forces faced similar lengthy opposition from Tibetans known as the Golden Stream people. They lived there under a legendary leader, Solobun, whose grandson was caught and decapitated, his head being taken to Beijing to be presented to Qianlong.

Closer to Beijing, the dynasty faced a rising in 1774 in Shandong by a sect leader whose beliefs were linked to the White Lotus Buddhists who called on the support of an 'Eternal Venerable Mother'. The revolt had some success before it was put down, its leader sitting immobile and cross-legged in a burning room as his clothes and

beard caught fire. In the following decade Muslims revolted in Gansu province in the northwest, while Triad secret societies in Taiwan led a rebellion which was suppressed by a force of 60,000 troops.

Though the empire eventually came out on top, such resistance and the flops in Vietnam and Burma undermined the reputation of the bannermen forces. Their numbers had risen to 200,000. Chinese troops recruited in Green Standard units were increased to 600,000 to fight imperial campaigns, but they would become infamous for their lack of discipline and lawlessness.

海上
迎山
雄晉
表不
空魁
首免
詩斗
克安
平
秦
岳山

ABOVE *Qianlong won
ten significant military
victories during his reign
and awarded himself the
title 'Old Man of the Ten
Completed Great
Campaigns'. This
engraving entitled*
Victories at War of the
Chinese Emperor
Qianlong *dates from
the 1790s.*

Mass appeal

Despite its drawbacks, the Qianlong rule saw the multi-ethnic realm brought to its peak, and its ruler showed different faces to appeal to the various peoples of his vast colonial domain. Thus, while following Han traditions in building the Chinese state, he also declared himself to be the reincarnation of the Buddha's intellect, which made him an object of veneration in Tibet and Mongolia. Portraits showed him as a hunter – to appeal to the people of the northern steppes – and as a scholar – to appeal to the Han élite. He pursued the traditional course of setting himself up as the defender of the poor, offering charity and soup kitchens to the impoverished and expressing his faith in the good sense of the peasantry. But he also protected rich merchants against officials who wanted to regulate their trade, and against smugglers who undercut their rate for monopoly products, notably salt.

Like any colonial ruler, he had to assure the position and authority of the imperial class, the Manchus, while also seeking to placate the far larger population they had colonized – the Han, Mongols and Muslims. His problem was that the Han majority formed the backbone of the administration; he depended on them to run the country but, as a foreigner, he could not assume their loyalty to him. Rather, they owed allegiance to their own traditions, their own scholarly class and their ancestors, while other Han felt their prime connections with their localities, their lineage clans and their local gods instead of with the remote sovereign.

Mounting tensions

Social divisions also exacerbated the threat to national cohesion. Among both the Manchus and the Han, wealth disparities grew as the country became richer. The leading nobles and Chinese merchants and senior officials drew ever further away from the poor – not just the peasants but also many Manchus, whose combination of profligacy and unreadiness to undertake productive work was proving a fatal flaw. In the mid-century one-fifth of the direct members of the imperial house lacked a regular livelihood. Half the lands granted to banner families around Beijing in the 17th century had been sold secretly to Chinese.

In the south, the poverty of the bannermen was such that they had to be forbidden from pawning or selling their weapons, armour and flags. Rising rice prices in the later part of the 18th century made things even worse for the poor. Resentment rose against corruption that went beyond the norm. After Qianlong did away with the 'nourishment of virtue' bonuses instituted by his father to lessen the need for officials to take bribes, graft increased, sometimes involving rings of officials; in one case a group of 56 bureaucrats was executed for having run a racket to embezzle military funds and famine relief money.

The emperor faced continual Han criticism, even if it was only expressed with the utmost care. Some of the scholarly class were not convinced by the territorial expansion, both because of the way in which it diluted the position of the Han by the absorption of other races and because they perceived it as a pretext for Qianlong to expand his despotic authority.

Many Han were also unhappy at what they perceived as the appointment of too many Manchus to senior provincial posts: '*Manchus on the inside, Chinese on the outside*', as the saying went. In fact, the number of Manchu officials did not grow much, except in the Far West, and the emperor seems to have tacitly acquiesced in Han efforts to block such a development.

> The emperor sent us several dishes from his own table, together with some liquors, which the Chinese call wine; not, however, pressed from the grape, but distilled or extracted from rice, herbs, and honey. In about half an hour he sent for Sir George Staunton (the British Minister Plenipotentary) ... The order and regularity in serving and removing the dinner was wonderfully exact, and every function of the ceremony performed with such silence and solemnity as in some measure to resemble the celebration of a religious mystery.

JOHN BARROW, MEMBER OF THE BRITISH MACARTNEY MISSION TO CHINA IN 1793

But the swelling population meant that more and more Chinese were chasing the fixed number of imperial posts, and their resentment rose accordingly. Even worse was the effect of the large number of graduates of the imperial examinations for whom there were no jobs, since appointments remained fixed. Around 5000 students passed the top level of the examination each decade, but the ranks of the magistrature, which was their main source of employment, only numbered 1285. As a result, Qianlong calculated, graduates would have to wait an average of 30 years before obtaining a post. This produced a lot of bright, highly educated but discontented men, to whom had to be added the half-million graduates at lower levels who saw the value of their study vitiated by the growing practice of selling off minor degrees to rich individuals.

1644 The Manchus take Beijing. The first Qing emperor, Shunzhi, is enthroned; power is held by the regent Dorgon

1645 Ming supporters in Nanjing, led by Coxinga, surrender; Coxinga retreats to Taiwan

1659 Southwest China is finally brought under Qing control

1670 Kangxi's Sacred Edicts

1681 Manchu control of mainland China complete

1689 Treaty with Russia

1751–60 Imperial control of Tibet and Xinjiang

1770 English merchants begin to trade opium from India and Afghanistan for tea, silk and other commodities

1774 'White Lotus' rising in Shandong

1793 Macartney mission to China

1799 Qianlong dies and Heshen commits suicide

Population and trade boom

Still, peace and prosperity boosted the economy, and the élite fuelled a growing demand for consumer goods and luxuries. A Manchu prince described the main feature of Qianlong's rule as the number of rich people in the country – not just nobles but merchants, whose homes were often larger and more opulent than those of the nobility, and whose taxes contributed a fast-growing slice of imperial revenue. Some scholars worried that their contemporaries were consuming so much that there would not be enough left for future generations. The introduction of new crops such as multi-harvest rice, sorghum and sweet potatoes encouraged a population boom. During Qianlong's reign, the number of his subjects doubled. Land reclamation policies were pursued and minority populations were driven back into the wilds of the southwestern highlands so that their territory could be taken over by the Han.

China's trade expanded greatly. Merchants went to Indochina and further afield in Southeast Asia. Exports of porcelain, paper, cotton, tea and manufactured handicrafts created a sizeable surplus and a strong flow of silver in payments from the West to the empire. In a bid to balance this, the British began to import opium from India to the only Chinese port where foreigners were allowed, Canton.

Palaces and scholars

Qianlong devoted much attention to scholarship and the arts, seeking to place himself among the ranks of the great rulers of the imperial tradition. A talented calligrapher and painter, he is also thought to be the author of more than 42,000 poems. He sponsored publication of the *Four Treasures* – 3500 classical texts of history, philosophy and fine writing that were gathered together and copied by 15,000 scholars to make 36,000 volumes. The aim was not primarily scholarly, however, but political: the compilation of a body of accepted orthodoxy on which the empire could rest.

Like his predecessors, the emperor valued secrecy and tightly controlled the flow of information, often starving officials of news. He had provincial libraries combed for the slightest sign of dissident thought. Some 3000 separate 'evil books' were taken to Beijing to be burned between 1772 and 1793. The persecution of suspect scholars was extreme and provided the occasion for local score-settling. In one case, an imperial degree-holder was accused by his enemies of having compiled a dictionary that was critical of another work associated with the Kangxi emperor; the scholar was executed and his sons and grandson condemned to become slaves.

A string of opulent palaces was built, including a reproduction of the Tibetan Potala at the imperial summer resort of Jehol. The emperor re-established contact with the

Jesuit missionaries, which had been broken by his father and grandfather, and asked them to work on plans for a summer palace outside Beijing *'in the manner of European barbarians in the midst of multitudes of fountains'*. He renewed Kangxi's provincial tours, making six trips that were commemorated by grand paintings.

Despite his intelligence and strength, age took its toll on the emperor in the last decades of the 18th century. He became a great self-publicist, proclaiming himself the 'Old Man of the Ten Completed Great Campaigns' (which included the failures in Burma and Vietnam). On his 80th birthday he declared that his reign had brought China to a condition of 'small tranquillity' – a stage before the full golden age dawned.

He also fell under the influence of a handsome palace guard called Heshen, who rose to the post of Grand Secretary amid rumours of a sexual relationship between the

ABOVE *Detail of a 17th-century lacquer screen depicting the exploits of the Portuguese in China. Portuguese explorers opened the way for lucrative trading in porcelain, tea, silk and other commodities between China and the West.*

ageing emperor and the young man. For 20 years Heshen was able to use his position to enrich himself through enormous corruption and to promote friends and family (See The Influential Heshen, opposite).

The combination of Heshen's depredations, the accumulated cost of foreign wars, the swelling of the armed forces and high spending at court posed a challenge for imperial finances. The expenditure on individual campaigns and one-off glory projects could be absorbed. The danger was that the state would get into a pattern of higher outlays as a regular matter, and that it would then be exposed by an economic downturn. With tax revenues buoyant, things would be all right so long as conditions remained bullish. The test would come when the wind went out of the dynasty's sails.

> The empire of China is an old, crazy, first-rate Man of War, which a fortunate succession of able and vigilant officers have contrived to keep afloat for these hundred and fifty years past, and to over-awe their neighbours merely by her bulk and appearance. But, whenever an insufficient man happens to have command on deck, adieu to the discipline and safety of the ship. She may, perhaps, not sink outright; she may drift some time as a wreck, and will then be dashed to pieces on the shore; but she can never be rebuilt on the old bottom.

LORD MACARTNEY IN 1794 AFTER HIS ABORTIVE MISSION TO CHINA ON BEHALF OF KING GEORGE III

Rejecting the British

For all his magnificent display and public self-congratulation, Qianlong had one of his recurrent onsets of pessimism in 1793 when he surveyed the country's economy and rapidly reproducing population; he concluded that, unless the Chinese learned frugality, the Qing empire faced disaster. The trouble was that the whole system he had built beneath him pointed in the other direction – towards military glory, encouragement of conspicuous consumption and toleration of corruption at the highest level.

As he congratulated himself on his victories and received kow-towing delegations from neighbouring countries, the 'Old Man of the Ten Completed Great Campaigns' found it hard to be modest about himself or his realm. When King George III sent a British mission to Beijing in 1793 to seek an expansion of trading opportunities, the emperor contemptuously waved aside the 600 packages of gifts it brought. Receiving the mission on his 83rd birthday, Qianlong told its leader, Lord Macartney: '*I set no value on strange or ingenious objects and have no use for your country's manufactures*'. The envoy's refusal to kow-tow in the required manner ensured that the mission failed.

For the Chinese the episode was of no importance. They were not hostile to foreigners, who were allowed to work in China. Rather, the 'barbarians' were regarded as inconsequential, though the cautious Kangxi had foreseen trouble. But the non-meeting of minds came to take on enormous historical significance, reflecting the lack of imperial interest in modern technology and the world far beyond its borders. This complacency, together with the self-sustaining nature of the predominantly agricultural economy and the tight corset of the political and intellectual system, meant that, just as it appeared to be at its zenith, the empire was on the brink of the decline that would lead to its eventual extinction.

THE INFLUENTIAL HESHEN

The lively, intelligent young bannerman, Heshen, was noticed by the Qianlong emperor when the palace guard was 25 years old and the ruler 65.

Heshen was a handsome young man with very light skin and full red lips. A Korean diplomat wrote of the young Heshen as being *'elegant in looks, sprucely handsome in a dandified way that suggested a lack of virtue'.*

Lord Macartney, the leader of the British mission to Beijing of 1793, found him *'quick and fluent'*, though Heshen advised the emperor against having anything to do with the visitors.

The story was that Heshen owed his spectacular rise to a decision by Qianlong that he was a reincarnation of a concubine with whom the ruler had either been infatuated or whose death he had caused unwittingly as a boy. Rumours of a homosexual affair spread.

Whatever the truth about their relationship, the emperor showered Heshen with official posts. Enjoying his ruler's complete trust, he became chief minister and accreted even more power when Qianlong formally stepped down from the throne in 1796.

Under Qianlong, some court officials amassed great wealth and power. This Qing-era portrait shows a dapper young man in his finest clothes.

He and his relatives and cronies looted the military treasury, gouged the peasantry, grabbed high positions and extorted fees for their services. His fortune was estimated at $1.5 billion in today's money. His brother became imperial pro-consul in Tibet and governor-general of Sichuan as well as running the lucrative Ministry of Works.

The death of Qianlong in 1799 spelled the end of Heshen's career. He was arrested and sentenced to death by slicing. However, the new ruler allowed him to commit suicide instead.

An inventory of his possessions after his death recorded mansions containing 3000 rooms, 117 banks or pawnbrokers, hoards of precious metals and stones, jade, silk and furs, 100,000 fine porcelain vessels, 460 European clocks and 24 solid gold beds. Twenty-six thousand ounces of gold were reported to have been found behind a false wall in his main residence; one million ounces of silver were buried in the cellar. He employed 600 servants and had as many women in his harem.

KANGXI, QIANLONG AND THE EXPANSION OF THE EMPIRE
Two Qing rulers, Kangxi in the 17th century and Qianlong in the 18th, took the empire to its territorial zenith, enlarging China to the size it is today.

When the adolescent emperor Kangxi set out to expand his empire in the 1670s, he began by trying to transfer three southern barons who had established virtually autonomous rule after being rewarded with extensive territorial holdings for having joined the Qing against the Ming. They reacted badly, as Kangxi may well have expected. In 1674, they staged a revolt which lasted for seven years. At first the southerners were successful, inflicting a series of defeats on the imperial forces. Some generals who had been considered loyal to the central government changed sides. Kangxi offered the main rebel chieftain an amnesty; he refused it.

The threat to the dynasty was magnified for a time by a simultaneous rising of Mongols who took the Manchurian capital of Mukden (now Shenyang). This was, however, put down through military force and the intervention of the emperor's Mongol grandmother, to whom he was close.

But the Qing did worse and worse in the south, where the rebels occupied part or all of ten provinces stretching from Yunnan and Fujian. The emperor recalled later how he had not been able to hide his despair as posters criticizing him went up outside the capital. Justifiably, he turned against his Manchu commanders and entrusted greater responsibility to Han Chinese generals.

In 1677, the dynasty rallied and began to gain the upper hand on the back of improved generalship, superior resources and divisions among the rebels. One of their commanders surrendered. The main leader died after murdering the third because he was suspected of being about to give up. Province after province gave way. A southern warlord who went to Beijing to yield was sliced to death, and his head put on public display.

By 1681, the Qing were victorious, though the south would remain a seedbed of hostility to the dynasty, which was kept alive by pro-Ming secret societies and which broke out into a massive revolt in the mid-19th century. The abiding fear among the Manchus of the old dynasty was shown when an inoffensive Ming descendant who was found living as a scholar in an east coast province was summarily executed.

Mongol threat

When Taiwan was won back by a fleet of 300 vessels in 1683, the empire was re-united. Kangxi reached agreement with Russia on the Siberian frontier and sent a military expedition to Tibet. (See Russian Rapprochement, page 204.) His main aim was to subdue a tribal federation in the northwest led by a brilliant commander, Galdan, who had been trained as a lama in Lhasa and so enjoyed considerable spiritual authority. Coming from the north themselves, and mindful of how they and the Mongols before them had swept down on Beijing, the Manchus were particularly anxious to eliminate this source of danger as Galdan planned to re-establish a Mongol empire.

In 1696, Galdan advanced into Jehol province just north of the Great Wall and threatened the capital. Two imperial armies forced the attackers to retreat, but could not defeat them. In 1696, Kangxi personally led an offensive across the Gobi Desert against the northwesterners. In a letter to his favourite eunuch, he wrote of *'journeys across deserts, combed by wind and barbed with rain, eating every other day'*.

The emperor and his soldiers tracked the enemy by their hoof prints, and Kangxi wrote of riding through deserted camps where the bodies of the dead lay among abandoned saddles, drinking pouches, Buddhist scriptures and fishing nets. At a big battle by a river, Galdan's army was defeated; his wife was killed, but he escaped into the fastness of the Altai Mountains on the Siberian–Mongolian border.

The following year, the emperor set out once more to pursue his foe. Local rebel forces surrendered and, in June, Kangxi received news that after another defeat Galdan had killed himself. This capped a string of successes since the nadir at the hands of the southern rebels in the mid-1670s. *'Heaven and earth have protected me and brought me this achievement'*, he wrote to the eunuch. *'As for my own life, one can say it is happy. One can say it is fulfilled'*.

*Map showing the growth of
the Qing empire during the
period of expansion under the
Kangxi and Qianlong
emperors.*

Between 1756 and 1757 Chinese armies
swept through Central Asia, bringing the
entire area from Dunhuang to the Pamir
Mountains under their control and
incorporating the 'New Territories', modern
Xinjiang, into the empire. By 1759 the
empire covered nearly 4.5 million sq
miles (11. 7 million sq km), including
Outer Mongolia and parts of
Russia, while Korea, Nepal,
Burma, Thailand, Vietnam and
the Philippines recognized
Chinese dominance.

In the later part of his 60-year rule,
Qianlong felt the urge for more
foreign offensives to try to
extend China's reach even
further. He launched abortive
attacks in Burma (1766–9) and
Tongking (Vietnam; 1788). Then
he sent expeditions to Nepal
(1788–92) and Tibet to ward off
possible Russian, French and British infiltration.

Qianlong's costly campaigns

Under Qianlong, a series of campaigns
doubled the size of the empire. Tibet was brought
under Chinese control by a display of military strength in
1751, accompanied by favours for the lama religious
authorities. Since the end of the 17th century Beijing had been
the centre for publishing Tibetan and Mongolian works and
Qianlong encouraged the translation of lama texts into
Manchu and Mongolian.

China was thus constantly flexing its territorial muscles, but
this helped to drain imperial finances and meant that, at the
end of Qianlong's reign – which marked the end of the High
Qing period – the dynasty was faced with money troubles as
well as a country that had had its fill of the expansionism
launched by Kangxi more than a century earlier.

THE DECLINE OF THE QING

1799~1874

The fifth Qing ruler in China, Jiajing (1796–1820), was proclaimed emperor in 1796 after his father undertook his promised retirement in order to show devotion to his grandfather Kangxi by not occupying the throne for longer than he had. Qianlong and his favourite, Heshen, still dominated the court, however, and it was not until the old man's death in 1799 that his fifth son came into his own.

JIAJING IMMEDIATELY MOVED IN A DETERMINED FASHION TO UNSEAT HESHEN, ACCUSING HIM of a long list of crimes. These included abuse of office, dereliction of duty and lese-majesty, causing the campaign against the White Lotus rebels to be delayed, having shown no sorrow at Qianlong's illness and amassing huge wealth. He was also criticized for having broken a court taboo by prematurely revealing the identity of the heir and of having had the effrontery to be carried into the Forbidden City through a gate barred to anybody except the emperor. The outcome was inevitable: Heshen was forced to commit suicide.

Jiajing was an intelligent, conscientious ruler, but conditions in China were far from ideal. The heavy spending by his father was having its effect on the treasury. Though the economy was still strong and self-sufficient, costs and the price of rice were rising. Hunger was a common problem. Soil erosion was reducing the amount of arable land and there was serious flooding on the Yellow River. Piracy increased. The Manchus were no longer the force they once were, and the Han scholar class remained semi-detached from the dynasty.

Qianlong's reaction to the 1793 British mission led by Macartney had shown how closed China was to new ideas, at a time when the West was powering on with its industrial revolution. The Heshen experience had alienated many people from the throne and, when the new emperor made public an inventory of the favourite's colossal possessions, it only served to underline how indulgent his father had been.

RIGHT *Before the 1842 Treaty of Nanjing, foreign traders had to deal exclusively with certain Chinese merchants, known as Hong merchants, who were licensed by the Chinese government. This portrait shows an elegantly dressed Hong merchant.*

Fraying rule

The revolts that took place during the later part of Qianlong's rule in the west, in Taiwan and in Shandong reflected the depth and breadth of latent anti-dynastic sentiment. In 1813 rebels reached Beijing and the emperor narrowly escaped assassination before they were repulsed – the attackers were said to have enlisted the help of eunuchs in the Forbidden City.

The fabric of imperial rule was fraying, and social tension was aggravated by the wealth collected and flaunted by favoured merchants and monopolists. Zong Zizhen, a prominent scholar, recalled that there had been a time when everybody shared the contents of their bowl of soup, those of high social status using big spoons and those below using smaller ones. Now the two sets of spoons were attacking one another, as '*the wealthy vie with each other in splendour and display while the poor squeeze each other to death*'. This, he warned, would stoke hatred and lead to '*the most perverse and curious customs*' which would '*fill the space between heaven and earth with darkness*'.

Jiajing thought he could lead by setting an example of morality and frugality. But his spending cuts only alienated officials and Manchu clans, and encouraged increased corruption. In 1820 the emperor died from a stroke while in the imperial hunting preserve in Jehol. Scholars lamented the state of the nation. All the signs pointed to the inevitable dynastic decline after the long era of success. What was in many ways surprising was that the Qing held on for almost another century.

A dynasty in trouble

No dynasty in Chinese history, perhaps no ruling group in global history, faced such a concentrated array of shocks as the Qing in the middle of the 19th century – and survived. It was beset by huge internal revolts, confrontation with technologically superior foreigners, dynastic in-fighting and natural disasters on an enormous scale. And behind the dynasty's troubles lurked the inevitable question of whether it was all a sign that the Qing had forfeited the Mandate of Heaven.

The throne was for the most part unwilling to change. Whatever the evidence to the contrary, it assumed that its powers remained intact. For the time being it was preserved by a variety of factors, above all the absence of a new dynasty waiting in the wings, as the Manchus had been in 1644. The foreigners were not going to take over China. The mid-century rebels wielded great power at times but were not a new dynasty. The most potent force in the country, the gentry-scholars, was a conservative force. So the Qing held on. But the image of 'Unchanging, Eternal China' that was spread around the world was largely false, for the mid-century produced deep-seated changes which fundamentally affected both the nature of power inside the country and its place in the world.

As the Daoguang emperor ascended the throne in 1821, life went on as usual for most people in most parts of the nation. Farmers followed the rhythm of the seasons (see Farming and Rural Life, page 242); imperial officials tried to administer huge districts

ABOVE *Copy of a Chinese drawing from 1853 of Emperor Daoguang.*

and extracted what they could in 'squeeze'; communications were poor and the emperor was far away; Manchu bannermen and Green Standard Chinese troops kept to their old-fashioned ways; scholars defended the tenets of Confucianism; and anti-Manchu secret societies plotted. But the first challenge was sailing in on the South China Sea.

The Opium Wars

The British had sought to make up for their large-scale imports from China, particularly of tea, by exporting opium from their empire in India to the one Chinese port open to them, Canton. In its rejection of the Macartney mission, the empire had made it evident that it did not want British manufactured goods, so the drug filled the gap, and met with an ever-growing demand both for its narcotic effect and as a medical remedy. The East India Company and, through it, the British government did extremely well out of the trade as exports soared to 900 tons a year by 1820 and then to 1400 tons by 1838.

The throne reacted by re-affirming an existing ban on opium. Little notice was taken either by the British or Chinese merchants, and the imperial authorities lacked the means to impose their will in the faraway south. The British, meanwhile, sought talks with Beijing to open up China for general trade, but got nowhere. Trying to make its policy take effect, the throne introduced the death penalty for Chinese narcotics merchants. But the court came to realize that the only way to get results would be to send an envoy with full powers to Canton to check the traffic.

An upright commissioner, Lin Zexu, was despatched to the south in March 1839. He imposed a ban. The British traders in Canton refused to submit at first, but they were in a weak position, a handful of foreigners against the Qing. Merchants who did not deal in opium were unwilling to see their activities put at risk by drug traffickers.

BELOW A lithograph, c.1860, showing a view of Canton from the river. The Chinese government's attempts to stamp out the illegal opium trade in Canton sparked a series of wars with Britain.

> ❝ Opium is a poison, undermining our good customs and morality. Its use is prohibited by law ... As to Guangdong and Fujian, the provinces from which opium comes, we order their viceroys, governors and superintendents of the maritime customs to conduct a thorough search for opium, and cut off its supply. ❞
>
> IMPERIAL EDICT OF 1793

BELOW This statue of Lin Zexu, the commissioner charged with imposing the ban on opium trading in Canton, stands in Shenzhen city, Guangdong province.

So the British superintendent, Charles Elliott, ordered the drug traders to hand all their supplies to him. He passed 20,000 chests each containing 120 pounds of opium to the commissioner, who destroyed the drug by mixing it with water, lime and salt and dumping it in the Pearl River. Lin Zexu also wrote to Queen Victoria asking why her government banned opium at home but made large sums out of selling it in China. He insisted that the British merchants sign a bond promising to keep out of the drugs business.

Matters were aggravated in July 1839, when British sailors destroyed a temple at the mouth of the Pearl River in the delta south of Canton and killed a Chinese man. The British resisted a demand by the Chinese that they hand over six men for trial. Elliott also refused to agree to the bond proposal. Taking a tougher line, he instructed the British in Canton to evacuate the city and cut off trade. The opium merchants then staged a counter-offensive. They accused Lin of destroying their private property to the tune of £3 million. Lobbied by Scottish merchant houses which were making big profits from the drugs trade, the government in London backed them. The right to free trade was evoked as the moral justification for sending in the Royal Navy to punish the Chinese.

In August the British seized the rocky island of Hong Kong. The Foreign Secretary, Lord Palmerston, greeted the news with disdain – the small island was far from what he sought for Britain in the Far East. But it served a broader purpose as the base from which to launch an attack up the Pearl River, which was blockaded. Royal Navy ships and troops from India sailed in.

The first humiliation

The first Opium War broke out in June 1840. The technical superiority of the British warships was immediately evident. With their rifles and cannons, the Indian soldiers made mincemeat of Chinese forces. The British gained control of Canton and the forts commanding the Pearl River. They also advanced at the mouth of the Yangzi, capturing barges that collected taxes on river traffic and thereby cutting imperial revenue.

By 1842 the court felt obliged to seek a peace. The resulting Treaty of Nanjing – the first of a series of 'unequal treaties' forced upon the empire by foreigners over the ensuing six decades – was concluded on a British warship moored in the Yangzi on 29 August. Britain was given Hong Kong and some smaller nearby islands, and China agreed that, as well as Canton, it would open for low-duty trade the ports of Amoy (now Xiamen), Foochow (now Fuzhou), Ningpo (now Ninbo) and Shanghai. Britain was compensated for the loss of the opium that had been destroyed by the commissioner, and its citizens were granted immunity from Chinese law; transgressions by foreigners

would be dealt with by their own courts. British missionaries would be allowed in to China. The opium trade was to continue.

ABOVE *The East India Company's steamer,* Nemesis, *together with rowing boats of her companion ships, launches an attack on Chinese war junks during the first Opium War, c.1841.*

Still, the emperor was not worried. He was advised that the foreigners were no more important than '*dogs or horses*', and he told a mandarin they were '*not worth attending to*'. The Qing mind-set was in the north, far from the coasts where the British had arrived. Neither side could understand the other. For the Europeans, the Chinese way of thinking and acting was impenetrable. For the Chinese, the barbarians were a temporary nuisance that would sooner or later evaporate.

But they did not disappear. The foreign concessions in China were part of a much wider exercise in 19th-century imperialism that spread across much of the globe. Secure in their port concessions, exempt from Chinese law and with the growing presence of missionaries adding a moral element to their presence, the Europeans, led by the British, became an established feature of coastal China. A clash of civilizations was shaping up, which the dynasty only dimly recognized. For the Qing, the much greater challenge was closer to home.

The Daoguang emperor was well-meaning, but he lacked political clout and resolve. When financial shortages hit the imperial treasury, he responded by wearing old clothes and stopping his visits to the imperial hunting estate. Reductions in official salaries were, as in the past, not only ineffective but counter-productive in encouraging corruption. He made the inhabitants of the coastal region pay the indemnity to the British, and his reaction to problems on the Grand Canal caused by poor maintenance was to order shipments of rice to Beijing to go by sea instead, causing heavy unemployment along the waterway.

The Taiping rebellion

In the middle of the 19th century, China needed strong leadership. Banditry was rising, spurred in part by natural disasters which deprived the farmers of their livelihood. There was fresh unrest in border regions including Tibet and Xianjiang, where Muslims took over desert settlements. Anti-Manchu sects, such as the White Lotus groups, were active. In southern China, pirates and members of the Triad self-help movement proliferated, and a young teacher called Hong Xiuquan fell into a deep depression after failing the imperial examination. Taking to his bed in an isolated country village, he had a vision of ascending to the sky where he encountered a tall, imposing man with a long golden beard who denounced 'demon devils' plaguing the world. Jumping up, Hong declared himself to be an emperor, writing the title Heavenly King, Lord of the Kingly Way in red ink on a sheet of paper.

> Those with millions owe us their money.
> Those who are half poor, half rich can till their fields.
> Those with ambitions but no cash should go with us.
> Broke or hungry, Heaven will keep you well.
>
> SONG OF THE TAIPING REBELS

At first he did not know what to make of his vision. But after reading some Christian tracts given to him by a missionary in Canton, he decided that the tall man had been the Christian God, and that he was the Son of God and the brother of Jesus Christ. The 'demon devils' who had to be eradicated were the Qing. Confucianism was to be destroyed and a Heavenly Kingdom of the Taiping (Great Peace) created.

Preaching this, along with a doctrine of millennial egalitarianism that prohibited killing, stealing, witchcraft, gambling and opium, Hong gathered a band of followers at the start of the 1850s in the wild country of the south occupied by Triads and the Hakka people. The latter had come to Guangdong and Guangxi provinces from other parts of China and were now an oppressed minority. Starting by destroying temples, the rebel alliance built up their armed strength and scored a victory over imperial forces. Emboldened, Hong and his followers marched north into Hunan province and, despite a serious reverse in a river battle, swept on to the Yangzi, attracting peasant support with their offer of a life free from oppression.

While the Taiping under Hong were gathering strength, other revolts challenged the dynasty. One group of rebels attacked Canton. Another defeated imperial forces on the border of Fujian and Zhejiang provinces in the east. In the southwest, Muslims established the Kingdom of Pacified Souls in the lakeside city of Dali in Yunnan.

SHANGHAI – GATEWAY TO THE WORLD

In the last 70 years of the empire, Shanghai grew to become China's most modern city, home to foreign businessmen and adventurers as well as to a swelling Chinese population.

Lying on the Huangpu River by the mouth of the Yangzi, Shanghai was ideally placed to act as a bridge between China and the rest of the world – a role it fulfilled to spectacular effect after the fall of the Qing, when it became a world metropolis in the 1920s and 1930s – and is doing so again today.

Under the 1842 Treaty of Nanjing following China's defeat in the Opium Wars, the township of Shanghai became one of five ports in which foreign states were granted concessions and their citizens could live outside Chinese law. Its settlements were divided into the international sector, run by the British and Americans, and the French Concession. In 1864, the city was threatened by the Taiping rebels but was saved by a combination of freezing winter weather and the formation of the Ever Victorious Army under American and British mercenaries. (See The Ever Victorious Army, page 230.)

The foreigners brought with them Western ways of life and of doing business, along with amenities such as electricity, sewerage and, in the last days of the empire, motor cars. They set up trading houses and built factories. British businessmen built homes reminiscent of those they had left behind. After their army defeated China in the war of 1894–5, the Japanese moved in as well. In time, the city would become a magnet for refugees, including White Russians after the Bolshevik Revolution and Jews fleeing persecution in Europe.

During the 19th century Shanghai grew from a small township to a large, strategically important international trading centre; to some, it was a symbol of China's humiliation at the hands of foreign powers..

The settlements also attracted many Chinese, who found them preferable to the Chinese city that lay beside the French Concession. By 1872, 70,000 Chinese had moved in. Some, known as *comparadors*, acted as go-betweens for the foreigners with the local merchants, becoming rich in the process. Bankers and tradespeople flocked from other parts of China. Entrepreneurs built railways and silk and cotton mills.

At the same time, the legal status of the settlements attracted dissidents plotting against the Qing. In the autumn of 1911, revolutionaries took Shanghai with the support of the modernizing businessmen and the underworld secret societies. At Christmas that year, the leading revolutionary, Sun Yat-sen, returned from a trip to the US and Europe and was made China's first president a week later.

For Chinese nationalists, Shanghai was living proof of the humiliation of their country by the foreigners in the last decades of the Qing. But at the same time, it introduced a Western model to China, an experiment set apart from an empire which refused to accept how the rest of the world was changing.

1796 Jiajing ascends the throne

1800 Population reaches 300 million

1840–2 Opium Wars with the British; the Treaty of Nanjing gives the British Hong Kong island as well as concessions in Shanghai and other ports

1850 Taiping revolt starts in the south and spreads to Yangzi. Major rebellions then break out in eastern, southwestern and western China

1853 Taiping rebels take Nanjing; their leader, Hong, is proclaimed king

1860 Anglo-French force attacks Beijing for alleged Chinese failure to keep to treaty terms. The Summer Palace is looted; the court flees, and the emperor dies on his hunting estate. American mercenary Ward forms what will later become known as the Ever Victorious Army, to defend Shanghai against the Taiping

1862 The concubine Cixi emerges as the major power at court following the accession of her infant son to the throne

1864 Collapse of Taiping, followed by gradual suppression of other revolts. Hong dies

Triads of the Short Sword Society held the Chinese city of Shanghai for 40 days. A major rising in Xianjiang gathered pace as its leader, Yakub Beg, declared himself ruler in the great trading city of Kashgar. White Lotus sects were active and, in Shandong, fast-riding outlaws called the Nien staged a huge uprising under a chief who nurtured imperial ambitions.

Amid all this, Daoguang died in 1850 and was succeeded by his fourth son, Xianfeng, who was no more effective than his father. Despairing of bringing the country under control, he preferred to spend as much time as possible at the Summer Palace outside Beijing. While the emperor prevaricated, his armies did poorly against the rebels.

As it entered the second half of the 19th century, China was thus a deeply divided country behind the screen of imperial unity. The biggest rebel movement, the Taiping, took the former Ming capital of Nanjing, slaughtered 20,000 Manchus there and, in March 1853, proclaimed it their holy city. Hong was enthroned as the heavenly king after being carried through the streets on a gold palanquin. One of his highly effective young military commanders led an army that got to within 100 miles (160 km) of Beijing. Other Taiping forces took the large Yangzi city of Wuhan and forged through provinces across southern-central China.

The gentry fights back

The death toll, devastation and destruction of imperial credibility were all enormous. But the Qing were saved by four factors: the rebels never co-ordinated their efforts; despite the dreams of the Nien leader, they had no credible new emperor to propose – Hong was set on destroying the imperial system, not inheriting it; after their initial successes, the Taiping lost momentum; and finally, the threat to the Confucian order was such that major gentry figures in the provinces took matters into their own hands. They expanded local militias into well-organized, well-led armies that could make up for the weakness of the imperial forces. Bit by bit, year by year, these gentry generals chipped away at the rebellions. They were scholars who were fighting for the preservation of their society. The conflicts were extremely bitter. No mercy was shown on either side. The casualty toll will never be known, but has been estimated at 30 million.

As the gentry came to the salvation of the dynasty, the foreigners staged a fresh incursion. After clashes in Canton, the British and French decided that the Chinese were not living up to the terms of the Treaty of Nanjing. A joint expedition under Lord Elgin marched on Beijing. The emperor and his court fled to the hunting estate at Jehol beyond the Great Wall. The emperor's brother, Prince Gong, stayed behind to negotiate as best he could while the foreigners sacked the Summer Place and temples.

In Jehol, the emperor fell ill and came close to death. He had not chosen a successor. A group of powerful court officials, headed by the chief censor, got him to appoint them as a regency council. As the ruler weakened, the concubine mother of his only son ran into his bedroom with their five-year-old boy, asking what was to become of him. If the regents took control without an heir having been selected, they could choose whoever they wished. Xianfeng said he wanted the boy to succeed him. Then, or so the story goes, he turned over and expired.

Dynastic power struggle

This created a power struggle between the regents and the concubine, who was joined by Prince Gong and the imperial widow. They ambushed the regents as they returned to Beijing with Xianfeng's corpse, accused them of terrible crimes and had them executed – the concubine was said to have wanted the chief censor to be sliced to death, but this was commuted to a public beheading. Two Manchu princes who had sided with him were allowed to hang themselves. Five others were disgraced.

The coup left China with an infant ruler and a government in the hands of the trio consisting of Gong, the widow and the concubine. The widow was the weakest of the three. Gong was competent, and got on with the foreigners, with whom he had reached an agreement that they should withdraw from the capital in return for a large indemnity and further port concessions.

But the dominant figure in the group was the concubine, Cixi. Then aged 26, she would come to play the major role in court politics until

BELOW *British and French troops storm Beijing in 1860. The emperor fled the fighting and died on his hunting estate, having failed to name a successor. This would set the stage for a series of power struggles as the dynasty entered its final years.*

THE EVER VICTORIOUS ARMY

Gentry leaders called in foreigners to defend Shanghai against the Taiping revolt. The initiative came from a wanderer from Salem, Massachusetts, in the United States – Frederick Townsend Ward (1831–62) – who persuaded Chinese merchants to pay for him to raise an army to defend them.

Charles Gordon leading the Ever Victorious Army in November 1863 in an assault on the fortified wall at Soochow, a city close to Shanghai.

Ward's force was made up mainly of drifters, deserters and drunks. Long-haired and seemingly fearless, Ward went into battle bearing no weapons, smoking a cheroot and carrying a riding crop. Having achieved little with his force of foreign mercenaries, he went on to form a small army of 3000 Chinese which, with mortars and artillery, scored several successes around Shanghai. Ward profited considerably from the pickings of war, married the daughter of a local banker and took Chinese nationality. The emperor awarded him the Order of the Peacock Feather and gave his troops the name of the Ever Victorious Army. Fighting outside Shanghai in September 1862, Ward was mortally wounded. He was accorded full Chinese honours at his funeral.

Ward was succeeded by another American, Henry Burgevine, who was considered unsatisfactory by the local governor and went over to the Taiping rebels. The new commander of the Ever Victorious Army was Charles Gordon, the British officer who had taken part in the pillaging of the Summer Palace in Beijing. Gordon's first impression of his army was rough. But he improved it through tough discipline, and his soldiers played an effective role in the fight against the rebels along the Lower Yangzi. Gordon went into battle carrying only a small rattan cane, though he kept a revolver hidden under his tunic. He was appalled by the massacres of the Taiping, who eventually surrendered, and he kept the head of one under his bed to wave at Chinese officials. Initially he refused imperial honours, but later accepted. 'Chinese Gordon' was killed fighting in the Sudan in 1885 and became one of the icons of Victorian imperialism.

her death in 1908 as the dowager empress. (See Cixi – Portrait of a Powerful Concubine, pages 232–3.)

While Cixi was rising to power in Beijing, the Taiping were losing momentum on the Yangzi. Their forces were dispersed, and they failed to deliver on their promises. Staging so many campaigns at the same time was too much even for a Heavenly Kingdom. Their leaders fell out and embarked on bloody in-fighting which caused their best general to leave for a long campaign in the west of China. He was lured into surrender by imperial forces and executed by slow dismemberment while his army was slaughtered. The promised re-distribution of land was patchy, and the Taiping did not put down roots in the territories they conquered. Their love of lavish clothes and jewels made a mockery of their professed egalitarian vision. Hong was a non-ruler, enjoying the company of 60 wives as he listened to the music from an organ taken from a Christian church.

The gentry armies grew in size and fighting ability. The principal gentry leader, Zeng Guofan from Hunan, set the pattern. He started by recruiting only peasants who had a direct interest in defending their villages and fields from the rebels. Eventually, his army grew to 120,000 men. He made sure they were properly paid, trained and disciplined – rape was punished with death. By stressing the link between the army and the rural communities, he deprived the rebels of grass-roots support.

End of the great revolt

The Taiping staged a last major campaign against Shanghai. Zeng's leading subordinate, Li Hongzhang, organized the city's defence, recruiting American and European mercenaries to help, and constituting what came to be known as the Ever Victorious Army. In a once-in-a-lifetime event, snow fell as the rebels advanced by land and through the waterways. Their soldiers froze and their boats were unable to advance. There were mass killings of Taiping in nearby cities. Up the Yangzi, Nanjing was besieged by a gentry army. Hong said manna from heaven would keep his flock alive. But he died on 1 June, 1864, possibly from eating poisoned weeds.

A month and a half later, the pro-imperial forces blasted a hole in the Nanjing city walls from a tunnel dug beneath it. The Taiping defenders were massacred. Hong's 14-year-old son, who had been proclaimed his heir, fled but was later caught and killed. This revolt was over. Li Hongzhang waged a long and ultimately successful offensive against the Nien outlaw-rebels in the east. Another gentry figure, the methodical, much-respected Zuo Zongtang, re-conquered the Far West from the Muslims in a decade-long campaign that ended in the suicide of the rebel leader.

The dynasty was saved, but only thanks to the intervention of the gentry generals and their armies. These men were loyal to the traditional ways and would work within the system. But longer term the gentry, who had come to the rescue of the Qing, would exact their price and present the dynasty with a new set of challenges.

19TH-CENTURY QING EMPERORS	
Jiajing	1796–1820
Daoguang	1821–50
Xianfeng	1851–61
Tongzhi	1862–74

CIXI – PORTRAIT OF A POWERFUL CONCUBINE

The petite and beautiful concubine Cixi dominated the last stage of China's imperial history. She would be accused of being a sexual predator and blamed for ruthless scheming in the corridors of power, including the murder of rivals.

After the death of her son Tongzhi in 1874, in contravention of time-honoured procedures, Cixi installed a young nephew on the throne. This act above all others was a sign of her great determination – and nerve. But, if there was one person widely blamed for the failure of the empire to adapt to modern times, it was Cixi – though her defenders say she did the best with a bad hand, surrounded as she was by reactionary Manchus and unrealistic reformers.

Daughter of a minor Manchu family, the concubine Cixi (1835–1908) entered the imperial court at the age of 16. *'Prepossessing in person, she was so kindly in manner and suave of disposition that she won every heart, persuaded every hearer, disarmed envy and hatred'*, a Western observer wrote. A mere 1.5 metres (5 ft) tall, she was noted for her sweet voice, her high-heeled shoes, her heavy make-up and her refusal to adopt the subordinate role reserved for women in China.

Ten years after entering the court, she took part in a coup that elevated her to a leading position in the regime. Within a few years, she got the better of her two associates, the widow of the late emperor and Prince Gong. Though Gong remained on the scene for decades, Cixi rose to become the dominant figure in the Qing empire in the second half of the 19th century and until her death.

After Empress Wu – China's only female emperor – Cixi was the outstanding female figure in Chinese imperial history. (See The Era of Wu Zetian, pages 108–13.) Revisionists have tried to paint her as a conservative lady who simply tried to achieve balance between Manchu factions. Like Wu, she was accused posthumously of sexual depravity and many crimes: poisoning rivals, having a concubine thrown down a well, even causing the death of emperors.

Events show that she was a formidable and, at times, ferocious power player, who knew how to use the majesty and mystery of the dynastic principle to utmost advantage. It was said that, before the emperor slept with her and fathered their child, she had an affair with a Manchu general. But when he was discovered making love to another concubine, she had him sent into temporary exile.

As she aged, Cixi identified herself with a Buddhist goddess and was photographed wearing robes that evoked this deity. Like Wu before her, she had to draw on all the resources at her command to exert her authority in a male-dominated world. For most of her time in power, she operated from behind the throne, through emperors she dominated. Whether she dreamed of ascending the throne, as Wu had done, is not known. But throughout, she made a determined attempt to make the best of a failing dynasty.

However, she had no grand plan. She tended towards conservative consensus and, in this, held China back from true modernization. She maximized the perks the system offered her, for example, diverting naval funds to build a marble boat at her beloved Summer Palace.

Late in life, she made a catastrophic mistake in backing the peasant rebels known as the Boxers, who were protesting about the presence of foreigners in China. (See The Boxer Movement, page 239.) In a swift volte face she then took on the persona of a nice old lady who gave tea parties for foreigners and entertained the idea of reform.

The latter image has caused some historians to paint her in a kindly light. The other, more popular portrait sees her as a woman who exercised power with great ruthlessness – even if some of the stories of sexual rapacity spread after her death appear to have been exaggerated. Still, throughout the four decades from her amazing rise to power in the 1860s, she epitomized the outdatedness, ignorance, uncertainty and fumbling of the last tenants of the Chinese empire. As such, Cixi was a fitting symbol for its end.

Cixi as a young woman. She, in effect, ruled China as empress and then as dowager empress from 1861 until her death in 1908. The empire ended four years later.

THE EMPIRE ENDS

1874–1912
The failure to modernize politically, economically and militarily sealed the fate of the empire when it faced growing discontent from its own people and challenges from abroad at the end of the 19th century. The fact that it lasted until 1912 was final proof of the endurance of the system established by the First Emperor more than two millennia before.

CHINA IN THE LATER 19TH CENTURY WAS NOT THE 'UNCHANGING' COUNTRY DEPICTED BY MANY foreigners. True, most of the country and most of the population remained rooted in the countryside. Agriculture dominated the economy, and life was ruled by the rhythm of the seasons. (See Farming and Rural Life, page 242.) But there were attempts at rejuvenation, with the introduction of Western technology by entrepreneurs who used their official positions and contacts to set up factories, build railways and make modern weapons. These 'Self-Strengtheners' were, in their way, minor precursors of the explosive growth China would experience a century later. New armies were organized. Gentry figures in the provinces pressed for more local power. An energetic Ulsterman, Robert Hart, made the imperial customs into an efficient source of revenue, and a telegraph service was inaugurated.

International influences

The concessions granted to the British, French and others in coastal cities and along the Yangzi brought in modern city infrastructures and business methods. They also attracted a sizeable number of Chinese, particularly to the international settlement and the French Concession in Shanghai. The impact of the foreigners on China as a whole was quite limited, but, for nationalists with growing doubts about the dynasty, they were both models and targets – targets because they insulted China's sovereignty, but also examples of modernization and liberty. The Westerners did not bother themselves with such paradoxes. For most of them, life was simply sweet and lucrative.

Despite such unsettling influences, for most of China life went on as it had for centuries. The chaos of the mid-century rebellions abated and economic recovery set in, punctuated by natural disasters such as a famine in the north that was estimated to have killed 15–20 million people. While a foreign ministry was established under

RIGHT *Portrait of the dowager empress Cixi, painted by a Chinese artist of the naive school, from a photograph taken in 1903, five years before her death. Cixi rose from relatively humble origins to rule over all China.*

大清國當今聖母皇太后萬歲萬歲萬萬歲

one of the victors of the dynastic coup of 1861, Prince Gong, the dynasty found it hard to come to terms with the changing world around it. Mandarins at court still rejected foreign influences. The Confucian mind-set predominated. The dowager empress Cixi held sway at court. Her son, the emperor Tongzhi, turned out to be a depraved young man, a bisexual who visited brothels, drank heavily and contracted venereal disease. Even so, he married and, under the influence of his bride, seems to have gained some independence from his mother.

Cixi exerts her authority

In 1874 the emperor caught smallpox. He appeared to recover, but died suddenly at the age of 18; there were rumours that his mother, fearing he would insist on taking up his full duties again, had done away with him. Cixi installed her four-year-old nephew as the Guangxu emperor, and continued to rule in his name. Her daughter-in-law committed suicide.

The choice of new ruler was deeply controversial. He was not the son of his predecessor as tradition demanded. Equally problematic, he was of the same generation as Tongzhi, so could not go through the necessary rites of filial piety towards him. One court official was so shocked that he committed suicide during the enthronement. But Cixi used her skills and influence to get her way. While she exerted her authority again, she had always to balance the various factions at court and make sure that she did not arouse the opposition of the Manchu nobles. They had become increasingly reactionary and predatory, stoking the hostility felt by Han Chinese towards their rulers from beyond the Great Wall.

The foreigners continued to press their claims, with the French staking out a position in the south to link up with their colonies in Indochina, the Russians moving into northeastern China and the Germans joining the game by grabbing concessions in the eastern province of Shandong. Despite having been forced to flee Beijing in 1860, Cixi and her entourage showed no more concern about this than their predecessors had. But the end of the decade brought disasters that even the most self-confident rulers could not ignore.

War with Japan

Japan, which had adopted foreign methods in a way that China had not, pressed its claims in Korea, which the Qing regarded as their tribute state. This led to full-scale war in 1894. The Japanese scored a series of resounding victories on land and at sea, advancing into Manchuria and threatening Beijing. A peace agreement was reached which was so draconian that Western powers intervened to force the Japanese to give up some of the territory they had acquired.

The outside world took a disdainful view of the empire. *The New York Times* called it '*a standing menace to the peace of the world ... an anachronism, and a filthy one*'. Japan's Foreign Minister spoke of '*a bigoted and ignorant colossus of conservatism*'. The reaction in China was one of outrage at the

ABOVE *Yuan Shikai, president of the Chinese Republic from 1912–16. Yuan was a high-ranking military official under the Qing; but instead of saving the dynasty, he turned against it, securing power for himself after the resignation of the revolutionary leader Sun Yat-sen.*

THE LAST QING EMPERORS

Guangxu	1875–1908
Puyi	1909–12

national humiliation. The emperor Guangxu, a slight man with large, sad eyes who was constantly in bad health, had been terrified of Cixi as a boy. But in 1898 he gathered up his strength and oversaw a programme of reforms, drawing on the support of students, reforming intellectuals and a few officials. The administration was to be modernized and education improved; China was to enter the wider world and Manchu privileges were to be curtailed. The emperor consulted with advocates of change from southern China and with a visiting Japanese statesman. Some of his associates tried to gain the support of a leading young general, Yuan Shikai, for a military coup against the reactionaries. Yuan betrayed the reformers by informing his Manchu superior. Cixi was told. She rallied the conservatives. The emperor was despatched to live in confinement at the Summer Palace. Reaction triumphed.

Within two years there was a fresh convulsion when the Boxers swept out of Shandong in 1900, proclaiming undying support for the dynasty and hatred for the foreigners. (See The Boxer Movement, page 239.) They claimed that the Westerners

ABOVE *This woodblock print by Japanese artist Mizuno Toshikata depicts a battle in July 1894, showing the assault on Songhwan during the Sino-Japanese war.*

had brought down China and destroyed its ancient traditions through their missionary teachings and innovations such as railways. As the Boxers reached Beijing, Cixi made the fatal decision to ally with them, egged on by a document said to come from the foreigners, which set down impossible demands – in fact, it was faked by a reactionary prince.

The Boxer siege

China declared war on the foreigners – though it did not take the trouble to inform them. The decline of imperial authority was demonstrated when major provincial governors refused to join the war party and reached local agreements with the Westerners. Still, tens of thousands of Chinese Christians were killed, together with 150 foreigners. The worst massacre of Westerners was in Shanxi province in the northwest, where the governor invited 45 Christian priests, missionaries and their families to his capital and had them beheaded.

> If we fold our arms and yield to them, I will have no face before my ancestors when I die. Rather than waiting for death, is it not better to die fighting?
>
> THE DOWAGER EMPRESS AS CHINA DECLARED WAR ON THE FOREIGNERS, 1900

The foreign legation quarters in the capital were put under siege, though it does not seem to have been pursued very energetically by imperial troops. Western and Japanese soldiers marched across from Tianjin but were stopped by the Boxers. A second attempt by a 20,000-man multinational force in August 1900 was more successful, and the siege was lifted after 55 days and the deaths of 65 foreigners in the legation area.

The foreign troops killed and pillaged at will in what the correspondent of *The Times* described as '*systematic denudation*'. Cixi and the emperor had already left, travelling to safety in carriages and carts along the Great Wall to the old imperial capital of Xi'an. Before she left Beijing, the dowager was said to have had the emperor's favourite concubine, whom she saw as a rival, thrown down a well to her death. '*I cannot tell you how fatigued I was*', Cixi said later of the journey westwards. '*So long as I live, I cannot forget it*'.

Behind her, senior officials who had stayed in Beijing, including the aged Self-Strengthener and hammer of the mid-century rebels, Li Hongzhang, reached an agreement with the foreigners. It provided for the punishment of some of those who had backed the Boxers and a heavy indemnity that was to be paid off in instalments lasting to 1940 – Russia was allocated 29 per cent of the total, Germany 20 per cent, France 15.75 per cent and Britain 11.25 per cent.

Return to Beijing and attempts at reform

Cixi and the emperor returned to Beijing in early 1902, the dowager covering the last part of the journey by train in a special compartment fitted with opium-smoking paraphernalia. She now went out of her way to ingratiate herself with the Westerners: '*The court is overdoing it in civility*', the customs chief, Robert Hart, remarked.

A programme of reform was launched, including the abolition of the imperial examination system, which only alienated those who had studied long and hard for

THE BOXER MOVEMENT
A succession of natural disasters and the incursions of the foreigners had created a widespread sense of doom in Shandong province in eastern China and surrounding area in the 1890s.

Shamans foretold the end of the world if the people did not rise against the cause of their ills – Westerners and their religion. Peasants took up arms against the missionaries, who exacerbated the situation with the arrogance of imperial Christianity and the protection they offered to converts.

The region was the home of 'spirit boxers' who claimed that their rituals gave them invulnerability. They ate magic charms and staged ceremonies which, they claimed, meant they could withstand bullets. Under the slogan 'Support the Qing, Destroy the Foreign', they used their martial arts shows to recruit young men. Gathering growing support in the countryside, where oppressive gentry were also attacked, their members stormed churches and killed Chinese Christians. Unrest spread to Beijing and Tianjin. A wall poster summed it up:

An illustration of Boxers destroying the railway line between Beijing and Hong Kong, from a French newspaper of 1900, Le Petit Parisien.

> *Rip up the railroad tracks!*
> *Pull down the telegraph lines!*
> *Quickly! Hurry up! Smash them …*
> *When at last all the Foreign Devils*
> *Are expelled to the very last man,*
> *The Great Qing, united, together,*
> *Will bring peace to our land.*

By 1900 they were ready to break out of their home regions and advance on Beijing to preserve the dynasty – a poor, peasant movement that had no idea of the disaster it would leave in its wake.

1875 Cixi installs her four-year-old nephew on the throne as the Guangxu emperor

1878 The first modern cotton mill opens in Shanghai as Self-Strengtheners press for China to adopt foreign technology

1894–5 China is heavily defeated by Japan, and signs a punitive peace treaty

1897 Germany occupies Qingdao in Shandong province

1898 Guangxu initiates sweeping reforms, which are reversed after 100 days by conservatives and Cixi. The emperor is detained in the Summer Palace

1899–1901 Boxer rising leads to the siege of the foreign legation quarters in Beijing; foreign troops take the capital, while the court flees; China signs a punitive peace treaty

1908 The emperor and Cixi die within a day of one another. Two-year-old Puyi is placed on the throne

1911 October revolution spreads across the country from Wuhan

1912 (January 1) Republic of China is proclaimed in Nanjing with Sun Yat-sen as the first president. Leading imperial general Yuan Shikai backs regime change. (February 12) Cixi submits the abdication edict on behalf of the last emperor

their degrees. Other changes were generally poorly co-ordinated. Promises of a parliament were delayed. But provincial assemblies, which did come into being, provided a convenient forum for anti-dynasty gentry who agitated to be given more decentralized power. That ran counter to the basic thrust of court policy, which was to hold on to as much authority as possible.

Revolution looms

The centre was further weakened by Cixi's death in November 1908, a day after the emperor died – there were rumours that she had had him poisoned to ensure he did not rule once she was gone. Her choice as successor, her great-nephew Puyi, ascended to the throne aged two. The new regent exiled his long-time enemy, the powerful general and provincial governor Yuan Shikai, and tried to assert central control.

The tug-of-war between the court and the gentry continued, with fights over the rights to railways – Beijing wanted to grant the rights to foreigners in return for loans, but the provinces wanted to have them for themselves. The urbanization of the more modern-minded members of the gentry brought them together in provincial assemblies and emboldened them to put pressure on the court for political reform to give them greater power. Revolutionary societies plotted risings; though they flopped, they represented another sign of the mounting opposition to the regime. Officers in the new army corps founded by the dynasty to strengthen China became increasingly alienated. Han resentment of the Qing rulers soared, especially after the regent named a government consisting almost entirely of Manchus.

Then, on 9 October, 1911, a bomb went off by mistake in the headquarters of a revolutionary group in a foreign concession in the Yangzi city of Wuchang, part of a three-city complex known as Wuhan. When police arrived and seized the list of members of the group, the revolutionaries were forced into action. On 10 October revolutionary army officers and local gentry took over Wuchang, followed by the other two adjoining cities.

The revolution quickly spread across central and southern China. To try to save itself, the court recalled Yuan Shikai. He demanded sweeping powers. These were agreed. The regent resigned. Imperial troops won victories in savage fighting in the Middle Yangzi. But Yuan was after a bigger prize. He reached an agreement with the commander in Wuhan and told

THE LAST EMPEROR

The son of a Manchu prince, Puyi was enthroned in December 1908, at the age of two years, 10 months, in the absence of a direct heir to his predecessor. Just over three years later, in February 1912, his mother – the dowager – submitted the abdication edict that ended the empire.

The boy was allowed to stay in the Forbidden City, where he was taught by an English tutor, Reginald Johnson, and learned to ride a bicycle and play tennis. A brief attempt by a reactionary general to restore the empire in 1917 quickly collapsed, but Puyi stayed on in the palace until 1924, when a warlord expelled him. He sought refuge in the Japanese concession in the port city of Tianjin.

In 1932 Puyi, a slight, bespectacled figure, reappeared as the nominal ruler of the Japanese colony of Manchukuo, in his dynasty's homeland of northeast China. Though he was proclaimed emperor of Manchukuo in 1934, he was a puppet ruler. In 1945 he was captured by Soviet forces which invaded Manchuria, and was taken to the USSR as a prisoner. Handed back to China after the Communist victory of 1949, he underwent 'thought reform' and was finally released to become a gardener in the palace in Beijing where he had once sat on the throne. He died at the age of 61 in 1967 during the Cultural Revolution.

Puyi, the last emperor of China; as the first emperor of Manchukuo, he was a puppet monarch for the Japanese.

the court that the regime had to change and that China would be declared a republic. On 12 February, 1912, the dowager empress agreed on behalf of the infant Puyi.

Dynasty's end

The empire was over, though Puyi was allowed to stay in the Forbidden City. (See The Last Emperor, above.) The revolution that had overthrown the last dynasty was the work of the provincial gentry and the new armies. The main revolutionary leader, Sun Yat-sen, was fund-raising in America when it took place. Though he became the first president of republican China on 1 January, 1912, he handed power to Yuan Shikai after three months. China was now set for nearly 40 years of internal discord, invasion and civil war until the Communist Party took power in 1949. The empire had gone, but its traces remain to this day.

FARMING AND RURAL LIFE

As the population of China soared under the Qing, most people still lived in the countryside. While cities grew in the United States and Europe, China remained a predominantly rural society. Landlords and imperial officials were at the top of the social scale. Below them were hundreds of millions of peasants.

Most lived a precarious existence, piling up debts in bad years and struggling to pay the interest. As a sociologist would put it later, China's small farmers were like a man standing in water up to his neck – any ripple could drown him, be it a bad harvest, illness or a natural disaster. And, in the words of a folk song after a string of calamities in the east of the country:

> This year famine, Next year flood,
> Grass, roots, tree bark gone for food.
> Deep in debt, When the debt comes due:
> One picul [unit of weight] is repaid as two.

Rice, wheat and sorghum were the staple foods. Meat was reserved for special occasions. The imperial monopoly meant that salt was a luxury. Men did heavy field labour, carrying loads on their backs, since animals were too expensive for them to buy. Lighter agricultural work was done by children and women, who spun, sewed, washed and cleaned.

Peasant clothes were made of cotton. Their houses were usually constructed of mud and earth. Clean water might be a rarity, and there was no modern health care – traditional remedies were used, along with the spells of travelling soothsayers. Epidemics were frequent, and disease was spread by the wide use of human and animal waste as fertilizer. Sects, secret societies and outlaw gangs proliferated. Outside the harvest and planting seasons young male agricultural workers drifted in and out of bandit units.

Chinese peasant farmers irrigating their rice fields with paddles worked by foot – a gruelling, often unproductive process, in marked contrast to the life of the gentry.

China after the Qing

The fall of the empire in 1912 did not mean the end of traditions reaching back to 221 BC. The revolution changed the political regime, but the social structure stayed the same. The gentry still acted according to their interpretation of Confucian principles. Having become president of the new republic, Yuan Shikai went on to declare himself emperor in 1915, but opposition at home and abroad forced him to step down just before he died in 1916. After Yuan's attempt to assume the Mandate of Heaven failed, a reactionary general – a former stable boy who had been noticed by the dowager empress Cixi – staged a short-lived bid to restore the Qing. As China descended into the anarchy of a decade of warlords fighting for control, strands of the old China remained.

The Yangzi general, Wu Peifu, regretted the fact that wars were no longer fought according to ancient principles. Jiang Jieshi (Chiang Kai-shek), the salt-seller's son who led his army out of the south to reaffirm national unity in 1926–8, aspired to what has been called 'Confucian Fascism'. In the puppet Japanese state of Manchukuo in the northeast, the last emperor, Puyi, became a pathetic figure, enthroned by the Japanese but completely dominated by them in the final humiliation of the Qing.

When the Communists defeated Chiang's Nationalists in 1949, Mao Zedong (Mao Tse-tung) made his victory proclamation of the People's Republic from the walls of the Forbidden City. Later he would identify himself with the First Emperor while his wife evoked the memory of Wu Zetian. Most recently, the 'harmonious society' proclaimed by Hu Jintao, China's president and Communist Party leader, contains striking similarities with the themes espoused under the empire.

In the 21st century, much of urban China looks extraordinarily modern as skyscrapers sprout up in hundreds of cities. The economic figures are astounding. But the way the country operates – good and bad – harks back to an earlier time. Most people still live in the countryside. The dynasties are gone but not forgotten as new rulers grapple with the age-old problem of holding together such a huge and disparate country, and trying to propel it to fulfil the destiny envisioned by the early emperors for the Middle Kingdom.

ABOVE *Mao Zedong (Mao Tse-tung) and Zhang Guotao (Chang Kuo-t'ao), photographed in the courtyard of the Supreme Communist headquarters in China in 1938. Shortly afterwards Zhang, who was a founding member of the Communist Party, defected to the Chinese Nationalists.*

GLOSSARY

Words in SMALL CAPITALS can be looked up elsewhere in the Glossary.

alchemy an early form of science which combined the disciplines of chemistry, physics, medicine, spiritualism and astrology in an attempt to arrive at an understanding of the world. Among the original goals of alchemists was the transformation of base metals into gold or silver and the creation of an elixir that would cure all known diseases and prolong life indefinitely.

ancestor worship a religious practice based on a belief of the continued existence of the deceased. Ancestors are venerated and their well-being ensured by means of prayers and offerings, in the hope that they will intercede in the spirit world on behalf of the living and bring them good fortune. *See also* ORACLE BONES.

Bronze Age the period in the development of human civilization when the most advanced metal technology was bronze. As a technological development it has no set dates, occurring in different parts of the world at different times, but broadly between the Stone Age and the Iron Age. In China, the Bronze Age refers to the period between *c.*1800 and 770 BC when bronze was produced on a massive scale for making weapons and ritual objects used by the ruling élite.

bronze-working the manufacture of artefacts and tools using bronze – an alloy of copper and tin.

citadel a heavily guarded defensive structure, such as a fortress, usually built in a commanding position overlooking a city or other strategic place; often used as a place of refuge during times of war or conflict.

concubine a woman kept as a wife by a king, emperor or other man of high status, without being formally married. Generally concubines had few legal rights and low social status, although some rose to prominence and were highly influential at court. The offspring of such unions were widely acknowledged as being the man's children but had lower status than the children of the official wife.

Daoism *See* TAOISM.

divination ascertaining information about the future through the interpretation of omens or other signs, usually on behalf of a third party (often an emperor). Methods widely used in ancient China included the roasting of animal bones (known as ORACLE BONES) or tortoise shells and observing the cracks that appeared on the surface.

dowager empress a widow (or CONCUBINE) who holds a title derived from the deceased emperor.

eunuch a castrated man placed in charge of a harem or acting as another type of court functionary. The appointment of eunuchs to oversee the wives and CONCUBINES of an emperor meant that the women did not come into contact with other men who could impregnate them, thus ensuring that any offspring were genuine heirs of the emperor. In imperial China, eunuchs often took advantage of weak or young rulers to wield considerable power.

feng shui an ancient TAOIST system that studies the flow of energy through the landscape and defines rules for the arrangement and orientation of objects within a given space; the favourable or unfavourable effects are taken into account when designing or siting buildings, tombs or graves.

foot-binding the practice of binding the feet of young girls to stunt their growth for aesthetic reasons. Thought to have originated under the Tang, it was carried out in some parts of China for many centuries and only discontinued in the early 20th century. The feet were tightly bandaged from about the age of six, resulting in deformity and severe pain; some women ended up as virtual cripples.

funerary pits collective burial chambers, often containing items such as weapons, jewellery and clothing thought to be of use to the occupants as they made their journey into the afterlife. Human sacrifices were sometimes buried in the grave to act as companions to the deceased in the next life.

geomancy a form of DIVINATION involving observing lines and geographical features in the natural landscape in order to identify favourable sites for a specific purpose. It also concerns the study of the hidden force of energy (*qi*) at work in the landscape, as practised by followers of FENG SHUI.

lacquer work the production of artefacts coated with black and red lacquer, a natural varnish made from the sap of a tree. In the finest examples of lacquerware, very thin layers of lacquer are applied one on top of the other to the surface of a decorated object. Once exposed to air, the laquer forms a 'plastic' coat that is resistant to water and corrosion, and is highly durable. The technique was traditionally used only on precious objects, such as the doors and shutters of temples and palaces, or on furniture in which valuable textiles and holy books were stored.

lodestone a piece of the mineral magnetite, which has magnetic properties.

loess grainy, wind-blown soil, made up of clay or silt particles, found in the middle reaches of the Yellow River Valley. It originates in Central Asia, from where it is blown across northern China and settles in the Yellow River, giving the water the characteristic colour to which the river owes its name.

mandarin an official or nobleman in imperial China.

memorial a written request, or petition, submitted to the emperor by one of his subjects.

memorialist A person who draws up or presents a MEMORIAL.

Mongol a nomadic people originating on the steppes of Asia.

Mughal empire the dynasty founded by descendants of the MONGOL empire living in Turkestan in the 15th century. It was an important imperial power in the Indian subcontinent and parts of present-day Afghanistan from the 16th to mid-19th centuries.

necropolis a large cemetery, often an extensive and elaborate burial site associated with an ancient city.

oracle bones animal bones bearing inscriptions made by diviners who used the bones to foretell future events. The inscriptions are among the earliest examples of Chinese writing. *See also* DIVINATION.

physiognomy the practice of judging a person's character by the study of his or her facial features.

pictogram a symbol used to represent an object or an idea; the earliest form of written communication, a precursor to writing.

Red Turbans peasant rebels who rose against the MONGOL Yuan dynasty in the mid-14th century, in part inspired by the messianic views of the WHITE LOTUS sect. *See also* YUAN.

reformist a person who espouses a movement for political or social reform.

sancai-glazed pottery also known as three-coloured ware, sancai was popular under the Tang dynasty. Artists began to experiment with multi-coloured glazes – yellow, green and blue – to decorate their pottery, rather than the single colours used under earlier dynasties.

shaman a priest or priestess who acts as a medium between the human world and an invisible spirit world; one who may use magic for the purposes of healing or DIVINATION.

Silk Road trade route stretching from western China through Afghanistan and Uzbekistan to Iran and the Middle East.

sinicization the adoption of Chinese ways.

sinification *See* SINICIZATION.

Sixteen (16) Kingdoms a collection of short-lived sovereign states prevailing from AD 304 to 439 in parts of China and adjoining areas during the Period of Disunion.

stupa a Buddhist religious monument, originally only a simple mound made up of mud or clay (or a cairn in barren areas) to cover supposed relics of the Buddha.

sutra a Buddhist scripture.

Taoisom (or Daoism) a religion derived from the philosophical doctrines of the sage Laozi, based on the notion of the unity of humankind, nature and the universe. Taoism developed into a popular religion devoted to the worship of China's ancient gods.

vassal a person who works land owned by a feudal lord, and in return vows homage and allegiance to him.

White Lotus a banned religious group which emerged in the latter years of the MONGOL Yuan dynasty. Its ideas were drawn from both Buddhism and TAOISM, and it promised the return of a Messiah-like figure, the Maitreya. *See also* YUAN.

Xiongnu nomadic people originating in the Mongolian steppes who fought a long series of border wars with the Chinese during the Han dynasty and who invaded northern China after its collapse.

Yellow Turbans peasant rebel groups who, inspired by TAOIST religious ideals, rose against the Han in its declining years. The name derived from their distinctive yellow headgear. Although the rebellion was eventually put down, it ultimately contributed to the downfall of the Han by enabling the generals commissioned to suppress the rebellion to set up as semi-independent warlords.

yang *See* YIN.

yin *yin* and *yang* are the two fundamental principles of Chinese philosophy involved in the concept of *qi* – energy or the life force which exists in all living things and in the earth itself. *Yin* represents the female principle and is associated with passivity, cold, darkness and the earth; *yang* is linked to male attributes, such as activity, light, heat and the heavens.

Yuan the MONGOL dynasty which conquered and re-united China, ruling from 1279–1368 before being supplanted by the Ming.

INDEX

Page numbers in **bold** refer to the main treatment of a subject; page numbers in *italics* indicate illustrations; numbers in brackets, e.g. (17), locate information within a feature box.

A

Abahai 190
Abaoji 139
Abatai 190
agriculture 10, *169*, 178
  development of **(75)**
  self-run communities 169–70
  taxes 118
  under Han rule *52*
  Zhou period 23, 24
Aguda 145
Aidi, Later Tang emperor 123
Aidi, Western Han emperor 58
Altan Khan 182, 185
Amoy (Xiamen) 224
Analects (28)
ancestor worship (17), 23
ancestral spirits 16–17
Andi, Eastern Han emperor 73
animal collection *181*
An Lushan **(124–5)**
  rebellion 118, 119, (124), *125*
Annals of Lü Buwei, The (38)
Annam (Vietnam), Ming attempt to conquer 171, 172
Anyang (Yin) *19*, 20
Arab store houses 148
archaeological discoveries 12, 16, *19*
'armies of demons' 83
arts 130
  Later Tang dynasty 117
  Qing dynasty 204–5, 214
  Song era 135, **(138)**
  Yuan dynasty 158
Art of War, The **(26)**, 27
Arughtai 171, 172
assassination attempts on Zheng 34, **(34)**
astronomy 17, 135, 200

August Emperors 34, 38
Auspicious Bronzes of the State (17)
Ayurbarwada (Renzong), Yuan emperor 161

B

banditry (185), 226
bannermen, Manchu *197*, **(197)**, 198, 211, 213, 223
Battle of the Red Cliffs 81
Bayan 162, 163
Beijing 154, **(174)**
  British and French attack on 228–9, *229*
  Hanlin Academy 170, 200, 204
  Pavilion of the Star of Literature 162
  scholastic traditions 8
  Summer Palace (174), 215
  Temple of Heaven (174)
  Tiananmen Gate 6, (174), (176)
  see also Forbidden City
Beiping 166, 171
  renaming *see* Beijing
Bian River, boats on *94–5*
Bing Di, Southern Song emperor 151
Black Emperor 74
Black Feet People 15
boats, river boats *94–5*
bones, to make tools 12
book distribution (138)
books, burning of 214
Book of Songs, The 24
borrowing *see* lending and borrowing
Boxer movement (232), 237–8, *239*, **(239)**
Britain 223, 224–5
  immunity from Chinese laws 224–5, (227)
  Macartney mission 216, (217), 220, 223
  opening of ports to 224
  opium wars 223–4, *225*
bronze, state monopoly 55
bronze figures *35*, *54*, *70*, *91*
bronze working **(17)**, 165
  Auspicious Bronzes of the State (17)
  early 12, 16, (17)

bronze working (cont'd.)
  face masks *17*
  Shang period (17), 165
  Zhou period (17), 23–4
Buddhism 9, **(90–1)**
  imported from India 8
  monasteries and convents in Luoyang (85)
  plundering of monasteries 121
  revival 122
  in search of Buddhist truths *104*, **(104)**
  in south China 82
  v. Taoism 105
  White Lotus Buddhists 210–11
Burgevine, Henry (230)
Burma 210, 211, (219)

C

Cai Lun (71)
calendar, early Ming 168
calligraphy 6, 82
Cambodia, relations with (89)
canals 52, 72, 96, **(97)**, 100
  see also Grand Canal
cannibalism 190, (199)
Canton (199), 214, *223*
  opium trade 223–4
Cao Cao, General *79*, 80
Cao Pei 78–80
  as king *see* Wei Wendi
census, economic 168
Central Asia 102, (219)
  diplomatic relations 171
central states 25
ceramics, Jin dynasty jar *81*
ceremonies **(183)**
Ceylon, relations with (89)
Chang, Lady 180
Chang'an 46, *59*, **(59)**, 77, 96
  Early Tang capital 98, 100
  location (59)
  markets of *103*, **(103)**
  occupied by rebels 122–3
  sacking of *64*, 65
  Tibetan attacks on 119
  Xiongnu attack on 84
Chang Kuo-t'ao (Zhang Guotao) *243*
chariots, in burial pit 16, *19*

Chen dynasty 88, 94–5
Chengdi, Western Han emperor 57–8
Chengdu 66, *66*, 68
  printing in 130
Chenghua, Later Ming emperor 178–80
Chengzong (Temur Oljeitu), Yuan emperor 161
Chen Wudi 88
Chiang Kai-shek (Jiang Jieshi) 243
Chiang Pin 181
China
  pre-221 BC **12–29**
  221–207 BC **30–41**
  206 BC–AD 9 **42–59**
  AD 9–23 **62–5**
  AD 25–220 **66–77**
  AD 220–581 **78–91**
  AD 581–618 **92–6**
  AD 618–49 **98–107**
  AD 649–705 **108–13**
  AD 705–908 **114–25**
  AD 907–60 **126–31**
  AD 960–1126 **132–45**
  AD 1127–1279 **146–53**
  AD 1279–1368 **154–65**
  AD 1368–1464 **166–77**
  AD 1465–1644 **178–93**
  AD 1644–1799 **194–219**
  AD 1799–1874 **220–33**
  AD 1874–1912 **234–43**
  in the 21st century 243
  birth of **12–29**
  end of empire **234–43**
  First Emperor 15–16, 27, **30–41**, *31*
  first king 15
  Last Emperor **(241)**
  links with outside world **(89)**
  unified 33
  universalist tradition 20
  unreceptive to new ideas 220
'China's Sorrow' 16
  see also Yellow River
Chinese characters, Toba adoption of 86
Chongdi, Eastern Han emperor 74
Chongzhen, Later Ming emperor 189–90

Christianity
massacre of Christians 238
Nestorian 121, 157, (192)
Chu (kingdom) 25, (26), 27, 33, 42
prince of 130
Chudi, Later Jin dynasty emperor 129
civil service 168, 186
examination system 68, 72, 103, 118, (137), 139, 161, 162, 172, 238–40
Song dynasty 136, (137)
Cixi (176), 229–31, (232–3), 233, 235, 236, 237, 238, 240
clay figures 123
cloth, state trading in 62
Coiled-up Antiquity see Pan Ku
coinage see currency
commercial activities, Tang era (112)
communication, difficulties 9
comparadors (227)
compass, invention of 165
concubines (176)
Confucian Fascism 243
Confucianism 9, (28–9), 49
adopted by Qing dynasty 194
appeal of (29)
Early Tang revival 100
escape valve of (29)
Han Confucianism 44–5
promoted by Wudi 54
Sacred Edicts based on (203), 204
schools 168
v. Taoism (21)
teachings of Mencius 139
Confucius 27, (28–9), 29, 188
Analects (28)
superior man (28)
conscription 49, 96
convents in Luoyang (85)
copper, state monopoly 55
corruption 169, 180, 205, 207, 216, 222, 226
fighting against 200, 208, 213
cosmology 66–8
Coxinga 198, 199, (199)

creation, story of 12–14
crossbows 27, 27
currency 96, 171
coins 63, 100
paper money 130, 140, 149, 159, 161, 163
silk as (103)

D

Dadu 166
Yuan capital 154
dagger-axes 27
Dai 48, 49
Daizong, Later Tang emperor 119
Dali 226
Dalinghe 190
Daoguang, Qing emperor 222–3, 222, 226, 228
Daoism see Taoism
Dawlat Shah 161
defences, northern border 100
Dezong, Later Tang emperor 119–21
dialects 8
Diamond Sutra 131
disasters see drought; earthquakes; floods; natural disasters
Disunion, Period of 38–91
divination 16, (165)
Dodo, pacification campaign 198
Donglin Academy 186, 187, 189, 189–90
Dong Zhongshu (55)
Dorgon 197, 198
Dou, empress 49, 51–2
Dou Xian 72
Dou family 72, 73, 76
'Double Muddled' 145
dragons, sculpture 7
dragon symbolism 9, (9), 210
Dragon Throne (9)
dress, official, Qing dynasty 209, 210
drought 175, 187, 190
Duanwu celebration (183)
Duanzong, Southern Song emperor 151, (152)
Dunhuang 72, 73
cave paintings 119
Duzong, Southern Song emperor 151

dynasties, imperial 8
see also individual dynasty names

E

Earlier Qin dynasty 84
Earlier Zhou dynasty 84
Early Ming dynasty 166–77
emperors 172
life at court (176–7)
official and wife 177
Early Qing period 194–201
Early Tang dynasty 98–107
balance of government 102–3
emperors 100
earthenware 52, 89
earthquakes 74, 128, 189
Eastern Depot (176), 180
Eastern Han dynasty 66–77
Eastern Jin dynasty 82
influential military figures 83
Eastern Zhou dynasty 24
alliance with Jin 24
feudal states 24
Spring and Autumn Annals 24
Warring States period 24–7
East India Company 223
economic census 168
education institutes 69, 100–1
Elgin, Lord 228–9
Elliott, Charles 224
El Temur 162
emigration, to Southeast Asia 148
entertainment, Song era 135, (138)
equestrian displays (106)
Erhchu Jung (85)
Ershi Huangdi 38–9
Esen Khan 175
eunuchs
Eastern Han dynasty 73–4, 76
functions of (177)
Ming dynasty 169, 172, 175, (176–7), 180, 186, 190
Tang dynasty 118, 118–19, 119, 121, 128
Ever Victorious Army (227), 230, (230), 231

examination system see civil service
expenditure, cut back on 73
exports 214

F

face masks 17
famine 63, 122, 175, 234
Fan Wang (188)
farming
early spread of 12
under Qing dynasty 242, (242)
Fascism, Confucian 243
Feidi, Later Tang emperor 127, 128–9
Ferghana Valley 53, 54
festivals (183)
First Emperor 15–16, 27, 30–41, 31
Five Classics and Four Books 172
Five Dynasties 126–31, 128
Five Pecks of Rice sect 76, 83
five-toothed warships 94
floods 128, 187, 190
according to myths 14
Huai River 184
Yellow River 16, 58, 63, 96, 163, 175, 180, 189, 220
Foochow (Fuzhou) 146–8, 224
Food for the Afterlife (49)
Forbidden City 6, 7, (9), 174, (174), 196
Hall of Mental Cultivation (176)
imperial workshops 205
forced labour 49
foreign trade and contacts, Later Ming dynasty 186
Four Treasures 214
funerary figures 86–7, 106–7, 116
funerary pits 16, 19
funerary preparations (144)
furrier 149
Fu Su 37–8
Fuzhou (Foochow) 146–8, 224

G

Galdan (204), (218)
Gansu 53

Gaodi, Western Han
    emperor *43*, 44–7, *46*
    restoring order 47
    see also Liu Bang
Gaozong, Southern Song
    emperor 146, *147*
Gaozong, Wu Zetian era
    emperor 110, 112
Gaozu, Later Han emperor
    130
Gaozu, Later Jin emperor
    129
Gaozu (Wudi), Tang
    emperor 98–100, *99*
    see also Li Yuan
Genghis (Chinggis) Khan
    132, *151*, (160)
Gengshi, Xin emperor 65
gentry 222, 228–9, 231
geomancy 49
gifts and offerings to Tang
    court **(123)**
Gobi Desert (218)
Golden Stream people 210
Gong, Prince 229, (232), 236
Gongdi, Sui emperor 96
Gongsun Shu, king/emperor
    of Shu 66–8
    defeat of 68
Gongzong, Southern Song
    emperor 151
Gordon, Charles *230*, (230)
graduates, Qing dynasty 213
grain
    distribution 168, 173
    payment system 171
    shipments 162–3, *163*
    state trading in 62
    tax 171
    transport 52, 114, 118
granaries, establishment of
    117
Grand Canal (75), 96, *97*,
    (97), 117, 118, 158
    rebuilding 169, 171
*Grand Compendium for
    Ruling the World* 162
Grand Secretariat 158–9,
    169, 172, 173, 180, 185,
    186, 190
Great Wall of China 35,
    (60–1), *61*
    extension 53, 180
    rebuilding *77*, 96
    strengthening 48, *77*, 171,
    180

Green Standard troops (197),
    211, 223
Guan Daosheng 158
Guangtong Canal (97)
Guang Wudi, Eastern Han
    emperor 66–70
    see also Liu Xiu
Guangxu, Qing emperor
    236, 237
gunpowder **(142)**, (165)

H

Hall of Mental Cultivation
    (176)
Han (kingdom) 8, 25
    defeat by Qin 27, 33
    wealth disparities 212–13
Han Confucianism 44–5
Han dynasty 42
    geographical extent of *53*
    legacy of 77
    see also Eastern Han
        dynasty; Western
        Han dynasty
Hangzhou
    captured by Mongols 151,
        (152)
    markets and trade (152)
    printing in 130
    Southern Song capital
        146, 149, (152)
    West Lake (152)
Hanlin Academy, Beijing
    170, 200, 204
Hansen, Valerie 134
harmonious kinship (*heqin*)
    46–7
harmony (28)
Hart, Robert 238
harvest thanks festival (183)
heaven, supremacy of 23
Hedi, Eastern Han emperor
    72–3
Hedi, Qi emperor 83–4
Henan 122
heqin (harmonious kinship)
    46–7
Heshen 215–16, **(217)**, 220
High Qing period **201–19**
Homo erectus 12
Hong Kong 224
Hong merchants *221*
Hongwu, Early Ming
    emperor 166
    centralization of power
        169–70

Hongwu (cont'd.)
    Embroidered Guard 169
    power and paranoia
        168–9
    see also Zhu Yuanzhang
Hongxi, Early Ming emperor
    172
Hong Xiuquan 226, 228, 231
Hongzhi, Later Ming
    emperor 180
horses
    from Ferghana Valley 53,
        54
    symbol of wealth and
        military might **(106–7)**
    under the Tang dynasty
        (106), *107*, *119*
housing, pre-221 BC 12
Huaidi 81
Huainan 48, 49
Huai River, flooding 184
Huai River Valley 18
Huandi, Eastern Han
    emperor 74
Huang Chao revolt 122–3
Huangdi (Yellow Emperor)
    14
    memorial ceremony *15*
Huang He *see* Yellow River
Hu Hai 38
    as emperor *see* Ershi
        Huangdi
Huidi, Western Han
    emperor 47
Huidi, Western Jin ruler 81
Huizong, Northern Song
    emperor 145
Hu Jintao (29), 243
Hung Taiji 197
Huns 46
Huo Guang 56
Hu Weiyong 168
hydraulic engineering 23

I

immortality, search for 36,
    37
incense burner *140*
India 102
    relations with (89)
international influences
    (227), 234–6
inventions 135, **(165)**
Iquan, Nicholas *see* Zheng
    Zhilong
Iran, relations with (89)

Irinchibal, Yuan emperor
    162
iron, state monopoly 55, 57
iron production *140*, 143
irrigation (75), 78

J

jade burial suits 56, *56–7*
Japan
    diplomatic relations 171
    influence in 102
    invasions of Korea 187
    relations with (89)
    war with 236–7
Java, relations with (89)
Jehol 229
Jesuit Missionaries
    (192–3), *193*, 205, 214–15
jewellery *48*
Jiajing, Later Ming emperor
    182–4
Jiajing, Qing emperor 220–2
Jiang Jieshi (Chiang Kai-
    shek) 243
Jianwen, Early Ming
    emperor 170
Jin 145
    campaigns *134*
Jingdi, Western Han
    emperor 49, 51
Jing Ke 34, (34)
Jingtai, Early Ming emperor
    175
Jingzong, Later Tang
    emperor 121
Jin state, partition 25
Johnson, Reginald (241)
Julu 42
Jurchen, defeat by 145

K

Kaifeng
    Five Dynasties capital
        126, *127*, 129–30
    Qingming Festival *148–9*
    Song capital 136, (137),
        (138), 143, 145
Kaiyun era 117
Kangxi, High Qing emperor
    201–6, *202*, *205*
    control of information
        204–5
    economic depression
        205–6
    expansion of the empire
        (218–19)

Kangxi (cont'd.)
palace memorials 204
revolts against (218)
rise of 201–4
Sacred Edicts (**203**), 204
Kashgar 228
Ke, Madame 189
Khaishan (Wuzong), Yuan
emperor 161
Khitans 129–30, *139*, 140–2,
145
attacks by 139–40
Khoshila (Mingzong), Yuan
emperor 162
Kingdom of Pacified Souls
226
Korea 53, 58, 102, 210, (219)
attempts to conquer 96
defeat of 110
diplomatic relations 171
Japanese invasions 187,
236
relations with (89)
Kracke, E.A. 134
Kublai (Khubilai) Khan 132,
154, *155*, 156, 157–8
feasts 159
postal system 158
Kun, legend of 14–15

L
lacquer work, Zhou period
23, *23*
Lady Li, tomb inventory (49)
land
distribution 33, 62, 98,
100
ownership 86
reclamation 214
reform 96
*Landscape of the Four
Seasons 183*
landscape painting *82*, (138),
183
language
dialects 8
written *see* writing
Lao Ai 30–2
Laozi *21*, (21)
Last Emperor (**241**)
Later Han dynasty 130
emperors 129
Later Jin dynasty 129
emperors 129
Later Liang dynasty 126
emperors 129

Later Ming dynasty **178–93**
decline 187
disorder 189
emperors 185
rebellions against 180,
182, (185), 187, 189, 190
threats to 186–7
Later Tang dynasty
(**114–25**)
emperors 118, 129
rebellions against 118,
122–3, (124)
weakness and
decentralization 114
Later Zhou dynasty 130
emperors 129
law articles, codification 168
legal code 101, 117
legalism 33, (**37**), 49, (73),
80
lending and borrowing, Tang
era (**112**)
Liang dynasty 84
Buddhism under (91)
Liang Wudi 84
Liao dynasty 139, 145
Li Bo 117, *117*
Li Fuguo 118, 119
Li He 117
Li Hongzhang 231, 238
Li Jiancheng 101
Li Linfu 117, (124)
Li Ling, General (50), 54
Lingdi, Eastern Han
emperor 76
links with outside world
(**89**)
Lin Zexu 223–4, *224*
Li Shimin 101
as emperor *see* Taizong
Li Si 34, 36, 37–8
execution of 38–9
literature 117
Liu, Han emperor 56
Liu, T.C. 149
Liu Bang 42
as emperor *see* Gaodi
as king of Han 44
Liu Bei 78, 81
Liu Che, as emperor *see*
Wudi
Liu Heng, as emperor *see*
Wendi
Liu Jing 47
Liu Qin 181
Liu Shan 81

Liu Song dynasty 83
Liu Xiu 65
as emperor *see* Guang
Wudi
Liu Xuan 63
Liu Yuan 84
Li Wa (116)
Li Yuan 96, 98–100, *99*
declared emperor 96
as emperor, *see* Gaozu
(Wudi), Tang emperor
Li Zhi 105
Lizong, Southern Song
emperor 151
Loewe, Michael (73)
Longqing, Later Ming
emperor 184–5
Lord Shang's legalism 33,
(**37**)
Loti, Pierre (174)
Lü, Empress (Lü Huo) 47–8
Lü Buwei 30–2
quest for the Son of
Heaven (**38**)
lunar New Year (183)
Luo Binwang 108
Luoyang 24, 66, 81
Buddhist centre (90–1)
capture by Xiongnu 84
Early Tang capital 100
glory of (**85**)
Northern Wei capital 86
occupied by rebels 122–3,
(124)
Sui second capital 96
Xiongnu attack on 84
Lüshi Chunqiu (38)

M
Ma, Empress 70
Ma, General (Ma Yuan) 68,
69–70
Macartney mission 216,
(217), 220, 223
magicians 55
magistrates, reporting to
throne 36
Manchukuo, emperor of
(241), 243
Manchurians, settling in
China (89)
Manchus 196–7
bannermen *197*, (**197**),
198, 211, 213, 223
campaigns against urban
centres *196*

Manchus (cont'd.)
founding Qing dynasty
194
raids by 187, 189, 189–90,
190
wealth disparities 212–13
mandarin officials 10
Mandate of Heaven 9–10,
20–2, (29), 77
Manichaeanism 121
manuscripts, Zhou period 23
Manzhou shilu 187
Mao Zedong (Mao Tse-tung)
(26), 35, (73), 117, (174),
243, *243*
Mao Zedong (Mao Tse-tung),
Madame 113
Marco Polo 149, (**152–3**),
153, 157
maritime links 132, 148–9,
(152)
markets of Chang'an *103*,
(**103**)
'Marquis of Muddled Virtue'
145
martial emperor 52
Master Kung *see* Confucius
Master Meng (Mencius)
(21), (29)
Master Sun (Sun Tzu) (26),
27
mathematics 135
Ma Yuan (General Ma) 68,
69–70
medicine (165)
Mekong Delta, relations
with (89)
Mencius (Master Meng)
(21), (29)
teachings of 139
Meng Tian, General 36, 38,
(60)
Middle Kingdom 6, 25
military tactics (26), 27
Mindi 81
Mingdi, Eastern Han
emperor 70–2, (90)
Ming dynasty *see* Early Ming
dynasty; Later Ming
dynasty
Ming empire, map *168*
Ming Tombs *166*, *191*, (**191**)
Mingzong, Later Tang
emperor 127, 128
Mingzong (Khoshila), Yuan
emperor 162

missionaries (239)
British 225
Buddhist (90)
Catholic (192)
Jesuit **(192–3)**, *193*
modernizers, *v.* reformers **(73)**
Modi, Later Liang dynasty emperor 127
monasteries
in Luoyang (85)
plundering of 121
Wan'an 154
money *see* currency
Mongolia 102, 212
Mongolians, settling in China (89)
Mongols
campaigns of 13th century *156–7*
capture of Hangzhou 151, (152)
cavalry *159*
and Chinese traditions 157–8
classes of society 159
feasts 159, (160)
raids *182*
threat from 150
Yuan Mongols **(160)**
Zhengtong's offensive against/capture by 175
see also Yuan dynasty
monopolies *see* state monopolies
Mo Tzu (28)
Mukden (Shenyang) (218)
Muli 180
multi-ethnic emphasis 194, 208–9, 212
Museum of Chinese History and Culture, Shanghai (17)
Muslim revolts 211
Muzong, Later Tang emperor 121

N
Na-Cha 154
Naked People 15
Nanjing 24, 82
capture by Taiping 228
Early Ming capital 168, 171
Palace of Honouring the Ancestors 168

Nanjing (cont'd.)
recaptured by imperial forces 231
siege of 84
surrender to Manchus 198
Treaty of 224, (227), 228
Nanyue 36, 48
National Academy 168
natural disasters **(65)**
Eastern Han dynasty 74, 76
Five Dynasties 129
Ming dynasty 175, 180, 187, 190
Qing dynasty 222
Yuan dynasty 161, 163–4
see also drought; earthquakes; floods
navies
British 224
Chinese 148
Mongol 151, 156–7, *156*
Qing dynasty (199)
neo-Confucianism 134, 139, 182, 186
Neolithic cultures 12
Nepal 210, (219)
Nestorian Christianity 121, 157, (192)
New Territories 210, (219)
Nien 228, 231
Ningpo (Ninbo) 224
Ningzong, Southern Song emperor 151
nomads 8, 18, 24, (60)
Eastern Han dynasty 69–70
Five Kingdoms *80*
Northern Song dynasty 132, 139
Western Han dynasty 46, 49, 54
Western Jin dynasty 81
see also Xiongnu
Northern Song dynasty **132–45**
advances under 132–5
emperors 145
period of civility 132–5
printing (131)
Northern Wei dynasty (85), 86–8
warrior figurines *86–7*
Northern Zhou dynasty 92
nourishment of virtue payments 208, 213

Nurhaci 187, *187*, 197
nutritional care (165)

O
Oboi 202, 203, 204
officials, mandarin 10
'Old Buddha, the' (91)
Old Man of the Ten Completed Great Campaigns 215, 216
opium imports 214, 223
opium wars 223–4, *225*
oracle bones 16, 16–17, *16*
Ouyang Xiu 126, 128

P
pagodas, Qiyun pagoda *85*
painting 117, 135, *138*, *139*
landscape painting *82*, (138)
Palace of Heavenly Purity (176)
Palace of Honouring the Ancestors, Nanjing 168
palaces 214
Pan Ku 12–14
paper
invention of (71), (165)
power of *71*, **(71)**
paper money 130, 140, 149, 159, 161, 163
Partheon shot *25*
Pavilion of the Star of Literature, Beijing 162
peasant farmers *242*, (242)
peasant revolts 122
Peking Man 12
Pengcheng 44
Penglai 37, *39*
Period of Disunion **38–91**
personalities of China 10–11
Philippines 210, (219)
philosophies
Confucianism *see* Confucianism
neo-Confucianism 134, 182, 186
Taoism *see* Taoism
see also religions
Pingcheng 86
Pingdi, Western Han emperor 58
piracy 184, *184*, (185), 189, 190, 220
plague 163
talisman to ward off *163*

poetry 117
polo 102
population 6–8
Eastern Han dynasty 68
Mongol era 164
Qing dynasty 196, 214
porcelain 98, 130, 172, **(173)**
exports (173)
Portuguese, trade with *215*
postal system 158
pottery
early 12
figures *36*, *69*, *115*, *137*
printing 130, 132
development of 130, **(131)**, (138), (165)
prisoners *45*
provincial assemblies 240
punishment systems (37), 49
Puyi, Qing emperor (174), 240, *241*, **(241)**
as emperor of Manchukuo (241), 243

Q
Qi (kingdom) 27, 33
Qianlong, High Qing emperor 209–16, *211*
campaigns (219)
control of information 214
expansion of the empire **(219)**
mass appeal 212
population increase 214
revolts 222
tensions 212–13
territorial expansion 210
trade boom 214
wars *212*
Qian Yuan 154
Qi dynasty 83
Qin (kingdom) 25
Qin dynasty **30–41**
attacks on 42–4
colonization 27
fall of 39
geographical territories *31*
military machine 27
rise of 27
Qing dynasty
decline **220–33**
Early Qing period **194–201**

Qing dynasty (cont'd.)
élite 207–8, *207*
emperors 206, 231, 236
farming and rural life
242, **(242)**
foundation of 190
gentry 222, 228–9, 231
High Qing period **201–19**
life of the emperors *195*
official dress *209*, *210*
origins 8
power struggle 229
rebellions against 98, 196,
210–11, 226–8, 231
rejection of the West by 19
southern resistance
(199)
Three Emperors period
201
trade *198*, 214
Qing empire, map *219*
Qingming Festival *148–9*
Qinzong, Northern Song
emperor 145
Qiyun Pagoda *85*
Quanzhong *see* Taizu, Later
Liang emperor

R
racial equality 208–9, 212
radical idealism **(188)**
rebellions/revolts
Later Ming dynasty 180,
182, (185), 187, 189, 190
Later Tang dynasty 118,
122–3, (124)
Qing dynasty 98, 196,
210–11, 226–8, 231
by the Taiping 226–8, 231
Yuan dynasty 163–4
Red Eyebrows 63, *64*, 65, 66
storming of Imperial
Palace, Chang'an *64*
Red River Delta 68, (89)
Red Turbans 166
reformers, *v.* modernizers
(73)
religions
Buddhism *see* Buddhism
campaign against 121
Manichaeanism 121
Nestorian Christianity
121, 157, (192)
Zoroastrianism 121
see also missionaries;
philosophies

Ren Wei 72
Renzong, Northern Song
emperor 140
reforms 140–1
Renzong (Ayurbarwada),
Yuan emperor 161
revolts *see* rebellions/revolts
revolution 240–1
Ricci, Matteo *192*, (192)
rice production (75), *208*
rituals at court (176)
river boats *94–5*
roads 9, 35, 72, 158
see also transport
*Romance of the Three
Kingdoms, The* 78
Ruizong, emperor 112, 116
Russia, treaties with **(204)**,
(218)
Ruyi 47
Ruzi, Western Han emperor
58

S
Sacred Edicts **(203)**, 204
Sacred Way *166*, *191*, **(191)**
Sage Kings of Antiquity (38)
Sage Mother of Mankind
110, 113
salt
smuggling (120), 122
state monopoly 55, 57,
118, **(120)**, (242)
taxation on (120)
Sanskrit manuscripts *see*
sutras
Schafer, Edward (123)
Schall von Bell, Johann
Adam (192–3), 200, *200*,
202
scholars 134, *135*, (137)
scholastic traditions 8
under High Qing 204, 206
schools 101
Confucian 168
Yuan dynasty 158
sculpture 117
civil official *68*
Shaanxi Provincial Museum,
Xi'an *64*
Shandong 8, 122, 228
famine 63
risings in 66, 210
Shangdi, Eastern Han
emperor 73
Shangdu, Yuan capital 154

Shangdu War 162
Shang dynasty 15–20
burial pits 16, *19*
defeat of 20
foreign contacts 18–20
foreign trade 19
geographical extent 22
oracle bones 16, 16–17, *16*
power struggles 16
wars 18
written characters (18)
Shanghai 148, 224, *227*,
(227), 228
Ever Victorious Army
(227), *230*, **(230)**, 231
Chinese History and
Culture Museum (17)
refugees in (227)
Shang, Lord 33
Lord Shang's legalism 33,
(37)
Shaodi Hong 48
Shaodi Kong 47
Shaoxing, Treaty of 146
Shen Shichong (183)
Shenzong, Northern Song
emperor (141), 143
shi (28)
Shidebala (Yingzong), Yuan
emperor 161
Shi Huangdi, Qin emperor
30–41, *31*
death of 37, (40–1)
see also Zheng
shipbuilding 130
Shizong, Later Zhou
emperor 130
Shizu, Yuan emperor *see*
Kublai
Short Sword Society 228
Shu 66
Shu Han (kingdom) 78, *80*
Shundi, Eastern Han
emperor 74
Shunzhi, Early Qing
emperor 197, 200–1
will of 201
Shunzong, Later Tang
emperor 121
Sichuan 27, 81
campaign against 68
monarch 130
paper currency 130
risings in 66
silk
as currency (103)

silk (cont'd.)
state trading in 62
weaving (165)
silk badge, Ming dynasty *178*
Silk Road(s) **(52)**, (103)
cutting of 118
re-occupation of oasis
towns 72
re-opening 157
Sima Guang **(141)**
Sima Qian 30, (40), 45, *50*,
(50), 54, (60)
single cosmic system **(55)**
Sino-Japanese war 236–7
slash-and-burn agricultural
technique (75)
slaves 62, 148, 197
smuggling, salt (120), 122
Sogdiana 53
Solobun 210
Song dynasty 130
end of dynasty 151
entertainment 135, **(138)**
see also Northern Song
dynasty; Southern
Song dynasty
Song empire, map *134*
Songhwan, assault on *237*
Song renaissance 140
Song Yi 42
Son of Heaven, Lü Buwei's
quest for **(38)**
Southern Song dynasty
146–53
commerce and culture
149
emperors 151
growth of urban centres
146–8
maritime links 148–9
Mongol threat 150
Spring and Autumn Annals,
Eastern Zhou period 24
Ssu-ma Kung 77
state monopolies 55, 57, 62
salt 55, 57, 118, **(120)**,
(242)
tea (120)
statuettes, warrior *95*
stone carvings *25*
story telling **(116)**, 117
Sui dynasty **(92–6)**
Summer Palace, Beijing
(174), 215
Sun En 83
Sun Quan 78

Sun Tzu (Master Sun) **(26)**, 27
Sun Yat-sen (227), 241
superior man (28–9)
supremacy of heaven 23
surgery (165)
Su Shi 143
sutras **(104)**, 113
Suzhou 97
Suzong, Later Tang emperor 118–19, (124)
'swelling mould' 14

T

Taichang, Later Ming emperor 188
Taiding (Yesun Temur), Yuan emperor 161–2
Taiping 228
    rebellion by 226–8, 231
Taiping, Princess 114–16
Taiwan 198, (199), 211, (218)
Taizong, Early Tang emperor 101, *102*, 105, 110
    expansion of empire under 102
Taizong, Northern Song emperor 136
Taizu, Later Liang emperor 126
Taizu, Later Zhou emperor 130
Taizu, Northern Song emperor *133*, 135–6
Tamerlane (Timur the Lame) 171
Tang dynasty **98–124**
    gifts and offerings to **(123)**
    see also Early Tang dynasty; Later Tang dynasty
Tang empire, map *100–1*
Tang era, commercial activities **(112)**
Taoism 9
    v. Buddhism 105
    v. Confucianism **(21)**
    geomancy 49, 52
    promotion over Buddhism in Early Tang dynasty 101
    Sage Mother of Mankind 110, 113
    subversive aspect (21)
    warlike deities *164*

taxation
    Eastern Han dynasty 68
    Ming dynasty 168, 169, 173, 181, 185
    Qing dynasty 197, 200, 208
    on salt (120)
    Sui dynasty 96
    Tang dynasty 100, 101, 114, 117, 118, 127, 129
    Wang Mang 62
    Western Jin dynasty 81
    Yuan dynasty 162, 163
tax collection 54, 121
tea 130, 132, (165), (173)
    state monopoly (120)
Temple of Chief Minister, Kaifeng *127*
Temple of Heaven, Beijing (174)
temples, Buddhist (90)
Temur Oljeitu (Chengzong), Yuan emperor 161
Ten Kingdoms **126–30**, *128*
terracotta army 38, *40–1*, **(40–1)**
territorial expansion 210
Thailand 210, (219)
Three Emperors period 201
Tiananmen Gate 6, (174), (176)
Tianqi, Later Ming emperor 189
Tianshun *see* Zhengtong
Tibet 205, 210, 212, 219
    attacks on Chang'an 119
Tibetans
    invasion by 84
    settling in China (89)
Timur the Lame (Tamerlane) 171
Toba 84–6, 88
    adoption of Chinese characters 86
Toghto 163
Toghun Temur (Shundi), Yuan emperor 162, 163
tombs of the emperors (191)
Tongzhi, Qing emperor 236
tools, early 12
tortoise shells 16
tournaments, Zhou period 24
Tou Wan, Han princess, burial suit *56–7*

towns, Zhou period 23
Toyotomi Hideyoshi, Japanese emperor 187
trade, Silk Roads **(52)**
transport 68–9, 72
    of grain 52, 114, 118
    see also roads
Treaty of Nanjing 224, (227), 228
Treaty of Shaoxing 146
Triad secret societies 211
Triad self-help movement 226
tribute states 210
Tugh Temur (Wenzong), Yuan emperor 162
Turfan (112)
Tu Sung 187

U

urbanization 132, 146–8
Uyghur empire 121–2
    horse trade (106)

V

Victories at War of the Chinese Emperor Qianlong 212
Vietnam 68, (89), 210, 211, (219)
    relations with 102
    see also Annam

W

Wan, Lady 178–80
Wan'an Monastery 154
Wang Anshi, reforms 140, **(141)**, 143
Wang brothers, Fujian rulers 130
Wang Mang, Xin emperor 58, (59), **62–4**
    coinage 63
    natural disasters **(65)**
Wang Yangming **(188)**
Wang Zhen 175, (177)
Wang Zhi 178, 184
Wanli, Later Ming emperor 184–7
Ward, Frederick Townsend (230)
warlords 118, 119
Warring States period 24–7
warships, five-toothed 94
Wei, Empress 55, 55–6, 114

Wei (kingdom) 25, 27, 33, 78–80, *80*
Wei Ao 66
weights and measures standardization 35
Wei Wendi 80
    see also Cao Pei
Wei Zhongxian 188, 189
Wendi, Liu Song ruler 83
Wendi, Sui emperor 92–6, *93*
Wendi (Liu Heng), Western Han emperor 49
Wenxinn, Duke 30
Wenzong, Later Tang emperor 121
Wenzong (Tugh Temur), Yuan emperor 162
Western Depot 178, 180
Western Han dynasty **42–59**
    bad omens 58
    capital city **(59)**
Western Jin dynasty 81
Western Zhou period 22–3
    kinship and marriages 23
    land ownership 23
wheat (75)
White Horse temple (90)
White Lotus groups 210–11, 220, 226, 228
wine, state monopoly 55
Winged People 15
witchcraft 55
Wolf's Tail Rapid 94
women, dress *201*
women's liberation 108, 112
workshops, imperial 205
writing 6, 17, **(18)**, (160)
    development from symbol to script *18*
    Great Seal style (18)
    Small Seal script (18)
    standardization and simplification 35
    Toba adoption of Chinese characters 86
Wu, Northern Zhou emperor 92
Wu (kingdom) 51, 78, *80*
Wuchang, revolution originating in 240
Wudi, Liu Song ruler 83
Wudi (Gaozu), Tang emperor 100
Wudi (Liu Che), Western Han emperor 51–6
    superstitions 55

Wudi, Western Jin ruler 81
Wuhan, capture by Taiping 228
Wu Peifu 243
Wu-Yueh, king of 130
Wu Zetian, Empress 10, 98, *109*, (176)
    era of **108–13**
    reputation 110–11
    tomb of *113*
Wuzong, Later Tang emperor 121
Wuzong (Khaishan), Yuan emperor 161

X

Xanadu *see* Shangdu
Xia, treaty and trade with 142–3
Xia dynasty 15
Xiamen *see* Amoy
Xian 56
Xi'an 25, 96, 198
    scholastic traditions 8
    Shaanxi Provincial Museum *64*
    see also Xianyang
Xiandi, Eastern Han emperor 76–7
Xianfeng, Qing emperor 228, 229
Xiang Yu (40), 42, 44
Xianjiang, rising in 228
Xianyang 35
Xianzong, Later Tang emperor 121
Xiaozong, Southern Song emperor 148
Xin dynasty 58
Xinjiang 210, (219)
Xiongnu 46, 48, 53, 54, 84
    attacks on Chang'an and Luoyang 84
    pact with 69
    see also nomads
Xizong, Later Tang emperor 122–3
Xuande, Early Ming emperor 172
Xuandi, Western Han emperor 56
Xuan Zhang (104), 105
Xuanzong, Later Tang emperor (AD 712–56) 116–18, (124), *125*
    military defeats 118

Xuanzong, Later Tang emperor (AD 846–59) 121–2
    residence of *122*
Xu Hai 184
Xun Zi (29)
Xu Pingchun 56
Xu Shi 37

Y

Yakub Beg 228
Yan (kingdom) 33, 170
yang (9), 23
Yangdi, Sui emperor 96
Yang Guifei 117, 118, (124)
Yang Guozhong (124)
Yang Jian, Duke, as emperor *see* Wendi, Sui emperor
Yang Yinglung 187
Yangzhou, captured by Manchus 198
Yangzi River 81–2
    warships on 94–5
Yao Chong 117
Yellow Emperor *see* Huangdi
Yellow River (Huang He) *13*
    diversion 163, 180
    dykes 52, 58, 70
    flooding 16, 58, 63, 96, 163, 175, 180, 189, 220
    linking fortified cities (60)
    shifting of course of 63
Yellow River (Huang He) Valley, relics found in 19
Yellow Turbans 76, 83
Yesun Temur (Taiding), Yuan emperor 161–2
yin 23
Yin Anyang (Yin) *19*, 20
Yindi, Later Han emperor 130
Yingzong, Northern Song emperor 143
Yingzong (Shidebala), Yuan emperor 161
Yinreng 205–6
Yin Zhong 58
Yizong, Later Tang emperor 122
Yongle, Early Ming emperor 170–1, *170*, (176)
    scholar and warrior 172
Yongle Dadian, The 172
Yongzheng, High Qing emperor 206–9

Yongzheng (cont'd.)
    expansion and wars 208–9
    private memorials 209
Yoshitoshi *79*
Yu 14–15
Yuan An 72
Yuan Chonghuan 189, 190
Yuande (116)
Yuandi, Chen ruler 88
Yuandi, Wei ruler 81
Yuandi, Western Han emperor 57
Yuan dynasty 60, **154–65**
    arts 158
    decline 164, 166
    emperors 158
    natural disasters 161, 163–4
    origins 8
    porcelain exports (173)
    rebellions against 163–4
    roads 158
    schools 158
    secretariats 158–9
    spending 161
    see also Mongols
Yuan Mongols **(160)**
Yuan Shikai *236*, 237, 240, 241, 243
Yue Fei 146
Yuenzhi 53
Yung T'ai, Princess *111*
Yuwen Pin 92

Z

Zeng Guofan 231
Zhangdi, Eastern Han emperor 72
Zhang Guotao (Chang Kuo-t'ao) *243*
Zhang Jiuling 117
Zhang Juzheng 185
Zhao, funerary preparations (144)
Zhao (kingdom) 25, 33
Zhaodi, Western Han emperor 56
Zhao Gao 37–8, 39
Zhao Mengfu 158
Zhao Tuo 48
Zhaozong, Later Tang emperor 123
Zheng 30–3, 34, (34)
    assassination attempts 34, **(34)**

Zheng (cont'd.)
    as emperor *see* Shi Huangdi
    proclaimed emperor 34
Zheng, Lady 188
Zhengde, Later Ming emperor 180, 181–2
Zheng He (176)
    sea voyages 171, *171*, 172
Zhengtong (Tianshun)
    Early Ming emperor 175
    offensive against/capture by Mongols 175
Zheng Zhilong (Nicolas Iquan) (199)
Zhenzong, Northern Song emperor *136*
Zhezong, Northern Song emperor 143
Zhidi, Eastern Han Emperor 74
Zhongdu 150
Zhongli Yi 70
Zhongzong, emperor 111–12, 114
Zhou Chongxi (112)
Zhou dynasty
    agriculture 23, 24
    bronze working (17), 23–4
    Chinese writing **(18)**
    courtly warfare 24
    geographical extent 22
    tournaments 24
    towns 23
Zhou people 19–20
Zhuangxiang, King of Qin 30
Zhuangzi (21)
Zhuangzong, Later Tang emperor 127, 128
Zhuge Liang 81
Zhu Qianshen, as emperor *see* Chenghua
Zhu Wen 123, 126
    as emperor *see* Taizu, Later Liang emperor
Zhu Xi (131)
Zhu Yijun, as emperor *see* Wanli
Zhu Yuanzhang 164, 166
    as emperor *see* Hongwu
Zi Chu, Prince 30
Zi Cong 154
Zong Zizhen 222
Zoroastrianism 121
Zuo Zongtang 231

FURTHER REFERENCES

The multi-volume *Cambridge History of China* (Cambridge University Press) is an unrivalled source for each of the dynasties and the whole course of Chinese history. Valerie Hansen, *The Open Empire* (W.W. Norton, 2000) and F.W. Mote, *Imperial China 900–1800* (Harvard University Press, 1999) are both excellent studies full of original observations and telling detail. *A History of Chinese Civilisation* by Jacques Gernet (Cambridge University Press, 1996) contains a wealth of material.

For the Qin and Han empires, Mark Edward Lewis, *The Early Chinese Empires* (Harvard University Press, 2007) is the latest word. Frances Wood's *The First Emperor of China* (Profile, 2007) is an excellent study, while in *The First Emperor* (Sutton Publishing, 2006) Jonathan Clements has written one of a series of highly readable accounts of major Chinese figures. James Watt's *China: Dawn of a Golden Age, 200–750 AD* (Yale University Press, 2004) provides a fine account of how art and culture survived in the turmoil after the Han. *The Romance of the Three Kingdoms* can be read in the version by Lo Kuan-Chung and C.H. Brewitt-Taylor (University of California Press, 2003).

Excellent studies of the Sui include Arthur Wright's *The Sui Dynasty* (Alfred A. Knopf, 1978) and Victor Cunrui Xiong's *Emperor Yang of the Sui Dynasty* (SUNY Press, 2006). The *Judge Dee* mystery books by Robert van Gulik (Dover Publications) are set in the Tang era and contain much realistic detail. Charles Benn, *China's Golden Age* (Oxford University Press, 2004) describes life in high imperial China. *The Dragon King's Daughter*, translated by Gladys Yang and Xianyi Yang (Silk Pagoda Press online), presents ten Tang-era tales, while the legendary poet Li Po is vividly described in Simon Elegant's *A Floating Life* (Ecco Press, 1997). Empress/emperor Wu is the subject of Jonathan Clements's *Wu* (Sutton, 2007).

For the Song, Jacques Gernet describes *Daily Life in China on the Eve of the Mongol Invasion* (Stanford University Press, 1962). The richness of the Song's cultural achievement is shown in *Renaissance in China: The Culture and Art of the Song Dynasty* by Yuheng Bao, Ben Liao and Letitia Lane (Edwin Mellen Press, 2006).

John Man's *Kublai Khan* (Bantam Press, 2007) is an excellent biography, while Stephen Haw describes Marco Polo in China in his book of that name (Routledge, 2005). In her stimulating *Did Marco Polo Go to China?* (Secker & Warburg, 1995), Frances Wood inclines to the view that he never got further than the Black Sea. *The Mongol Warlords* by David Nicolle and Richard Hook (Headline, 2001) puts the Yuan in the wider context.

The peak and decline of the Ming are described in *Glory and Fall of the Ming* by Albert Chan (University of Oklahoma Press, 1982). Ray Huang's *1587, A Year of No Significance: Ming Dynasty in Decline* (Yale University Press, 1982) gives a penetrating portrait of the times through the lives of officials, while Jonathan Spence deals with the outstanding Jesuit missionary in *The Memory Palace of Matteo Ricci* (Penguin, 1984). Eunuchs in the Ming dynasty are the subject of the book of that name by Shih-Shan Henry Tsai (SUNY Press, 1995). Jonathan Clements's *Coxinga* (Sutton Press, 2005) tells the dramatic story of the Ming resistance to the Qing.

Jonathan Spence deals with the Qing in his *Search for Modern China* (W.W. Norton, 1999) as does Immanuel Hsü in *The Rise of Modern China* (Oxford University Press, 2004). The Qing conquest of the west is expertly covered in Peter Perdue's *China Marches West* (Harvard University Press, 2005). Evelyn Rawski has written several authoritative works on the Qing, showing the true dimensions of the last dynasty – *The Last Emperors* (University of California Press, 2001) and *Chinese Society in the Eighteenth Century*, with Susan Naquin (Yale University Press, 1989). The catalogue of the major exhibition of the Three Qing Emperors at the Royal Academy in London in 2006 is a treasure trove of scholarship and art (London, 2006).

Cixi has attracted many biographers, among them Marina Warner in *The Dragon Empress* (Prentice Hall, 1986) and In *Dragon Lady* (Random House, 1993) by Sterling Seagrave. Luke Kwong presents a convincing new version of the late-19th-century reform period in *A Mosaic of the Hundred Days*, (Harvard University Press, 1984). The Taiping rebellion is the subject of Jonathan Spence's sweeping *God's Chinese Son*, (W.W. Norton, 1997). Frances Wood's *No Dogs and Not Many Chinese* (John Murray, 2000) is the best general survey of the foreign treaty ports. Among the many books on the Boxers, Diana Preston's *The Boxer Rebellion* (Berkeley Books, 2000) is a fine publication, while Joseph Esherick presents a scholarly and fascinating account in *The Origins of the Boxer Uprising* (University of California Press, 1988). Marie-Claire Bergère has written the standard biography of the revolutionary leader Sun Yat-sen (Stanford University Press, 1998). The Last Emperor's autobiography, written under evident heavy ideological direction, is in *Pu Yi, Aisin-Gioro, From Emperor to Citizen* (Beijing, 1989), while Edward Behr has written a highly readable account in *The Last Emperor* (Macdonald, 1987).

Jonathan Fenby

PICTURE ACKNOWLEDGEMENTS

British Library Images © All rights reserved. The British Library Board. Licence Number: BCSPUB01 43; 50; 71; 93; 99; 102; 109; 117; 136; 142; 147; 164; 170; 171; 187; 198; 208;

Corbis
15 Corbis/© STF/epa/Corbis; 16 Corbis/© Royal Ontario Museum/Corbis; 17 Corbis/© Asian Art & Archaeology, Inc./Corbis; 19 Corbis/© China Newsphoto/Reuters/ Corbis; 21 Corbis/© Burstein Collection/Corbis; 23 Corbis/© Seattle Art Museum/Corbis; 31 © Charles & Josette Lenars/Corbis; 35 Corbis/© Viktor Korotayex/ Reuters/Corbis; 36 Corbis/©Christie's Images/Corbis; 39 Corbis/© Demetrio Carrasco/JAI/Corbis; 45 Corbis/ © Burstein Collection/Corbis; 46 Corbis/© Burstein Collection/Corbis; 48 Corbis/© Asian Art & Archaeology, Inc./Corbis; 56–57 Corbis © Asian Art & Archaeology, Inc./Corbis; 62 Corbis/© Charles & Josette Lenars/ Corbis; 63 Corbis/© Alfred Ko/Corbis; 64 Corbis/© Carl & Ann Purcell/Corbis; 68 Corbis/© Royal Ontario Museum/Corbis; 69 Corbis/© Asian Art & Archaeology, Inc./Corbis; 72–73 Corbis/© Jose Fuste Raga/Corbis; 77 Corbis/© Liang Zhuoming/Corbis; 79 Corbis/© Asian Art & Archaeology, Inc./Corbis; 81 Corbis/© Bowers Museum of Cultural Art/Corbis; 82 Corbis/© Burstein Collection/Corbis; 85 Corbis/© Werner Forman/Corbis; 86–87 Corbis/© Royal Ontario Museum/Corbis; 89 Corbis/© Royal Ontario Museum/Corbis; 95 (bottom) Corbis/© Royal Ontario Museum/Corbis; 97 Corbis/ © Ursula Gahwiler/Robert Harding World Imagery/ Corbis; 104 Corbis/© Burstein Collection/Corbis; 111 Corbis/© Archivo Iconografico, S.A./Corbis; 113 Corbis/© Lowell Georgia/Corbis; 116 Corbis/© Royal Ontario Museum/ Corbis; 122 Corbis/Werner Forman/ Corbis; 127 Corbis/© Demetrio Carrasco/JAI/Corbis; 129 Corbis/© Archivo Iconografico, S.A./Corbis; 133 Corbis/ © Charles & Josette Lenars/Corbis; 135 Corbis/ © Burstein Collection /Corbis; 138 Corbis/© Burstein Collection/Corbis; 140 Corbis/© Werner Forman/Corbis; 144 Corbis/© Lowell Georgia/Corbis; 149 Corbis/Hulton-Deutsch Collection/ Corbis; 151 Corbis/© Stapleton Collection/Corbis; 153 Corbis/© Bettmann/Corbis; 156 Corbis/© Bettman/ Corbis; 159 Corbis/ © Archivo Iconografico, S.A./Corbis; 160 Corbis/© Sakamoto Photo Research Laboratory/ Corbis; 165 Corbis/© Liu Liqun/ Corbis; 167 Corbis/© Todd Gipstein/Corbis; 169 Corbis/ Leonard de Selva/Corbis; 173 Corbis/© Royal Ontario Museum/ Corbis; 183 Corbis/© Burstein Collection/ Corbis; 184 Corbis/© Corbis; 188 Corbis/© Bettmann/ Corbis; 191 Corbis/© Marc Garanger/Corbis; 192 Corbis/ © Archivo Iconografico, S.A./Corbis; 193 Corbis/ © Bettmann/ Corbis; 195 Corbis/© Archivo Iconografico, S.A./Corbis; 197 Corbis/© Dave Bartruff/Corbis; 199 Corbis/© Asian Art and Archaeology, Inc./Corbis; 200 Corbis/© Bettmann/Corbis; 201 Corbis/© Archivo Iconografico, S.A./Corbis; 202 Corbis/© Pierre Colombel/ Corbis; 205 Corbis/© Arte & Immagini srl/Corbis; 207 Corbis/© Royal Ontario Museum/Corbis; 210 Corbis/ © Christie's Images/Corbis; 212 Corbis/© Corbis; 221 Corbis/© Christie's Images/Corbis; 223 Corbis/ © Historical Picture Archive/Corbis; 224 Corbis/© Keren Su/Corbis; 225 Corbis/© Hulton-Deutsch Collection/ Corbis; 227 Corbis/© Bettmann/Corbis; 229 Corbis/ © Historical Picture Archive/Corbis; 230 Corbis/ © Bettmann/Corbis; 233 Corbis/© Bettmann/Corbis; 236 Corbis/© Bettmann/ Corbis; 237 Corbis/© Philadelphia Museum of Art; 239 Corbis© Stefano Bianchetti/Corbis; 241 Corbis/© Corbis; 242 Corbis/ ©Bettmann/Corbis; 243 Corbis/ ©Bettmann/Corbis

Inner Mongolian Museum, Hohhot
139

Shutterstock
4 Yang Heng Wong; 5 (top) Paul Clarke; 5 (bottom) Michel Stevelmans; 7 Michel Stevelmans; 9 Rémi Cauzid; 13 Taolmor; 18 szefei; 22 Tamir Niv; 40–41 Ke Wang; 61 Ke Wang; 91 Paul Klisiewicz; 174 Volker Hopf;

TopFoto.co.uk
27 The Museum of East Asian Art/HIP/TopFoto; 54 AAAC/TopFoto; 70 Topham Picturepoint/TopFoto; 137 TopFoto/HIP; 155 AAAC/TopFoto; 177 AAAC/TopFoto; 182 AAAC/TopFoto; 209 TopFoto/HIP; 211 TopFoto; 222 Roger-Viollet/TopFoto

Wellcome Library, London
163

Werner Forman Archive
2; 25; 52; 59; 75; 94–5; 103; 106–7; 115; 120; 123; 125; 131; 148–9; 179; 181; 215; 217; 235

The author would like to thank Alexander Monro and Luke Hambledon for their assistance in the research and writing of this book.

Text © 2007 Jonathan Fenby

This 2008 edition published by Metro Books, by arrangement with
Quercus Publishing Plc

Metro Books
122 Fifth Avenue
New York, NY 10011

ISBN-13: 978-0-7607-9461-6
ISBN-10: 0-7607-9461-8

Printed and bound in China

1 3 5 7 9 10 8 6 4 2